This is a hugely welcome addi  :ion
Service, offering some critical in: hal-
lenges of probation, but also sel ;ing
context of criminal justice delive ling
it how it is' in real life. This is al , the
ways in which probation remair vide
readership.

Loraine Gelsthorpe, *President of the British Society of Criminology and Professor of Criminology & Criminal Justice, University of Cambridge, UK.*

Prison officer and police culture have been relatively well researched, but Worrall and Mawby's book begins to make good our limited understanding of the practice cultures of probation. This is not only a major study of probation, but stands as a significant contribution to organisational theory as an illuminating case study of the evolution and development of an occupational culture. It is also a refreshingly optimistic account of the resilience of probation practice to set against the discourse of decline that characterises many recent writings.

Professor Rob Canton, *Head of Research in Community and Criminal Justice at De Montfort University, UK.*

This book offers a highly original, empirical study of a subject that has been neglected for far too long. Mawby and Worrall are to be congratulated for beginning to open up the world of probation officers' occupational culture, showing their working lives and the meanings they attach to what they do.

George Mair, *Professor of Criminal Justice and Head of Research in the Law School, Liverpool John Moores University, UK.*

Whether a lifer, second careerist or offender manager, probation staff will recognise themselves in this superb piece of inquiry into probation's occupational cultures. The quality of the writing reflects the skill of the researchers, their sympathy for the subject matter and their ability to hold the balance between theorising, observing and reflecting the real world of probation. It is published just at the time that political decisions may do irreparable damage to the meaning and efficacy of probation.

Stephen Collett, *former Chief Officer of Cheshire Probation Area, UK.*

Doing Probation Work

A great deal has been written about the political, policy and practice changes that have shaped probation work, but little has been written on the changes to occupational cultures and the ways in which probation workers themselves view their role. This book fills that gap by exploring the meaning of 'doing probation work' from the perspective of probation workers themselves.

Based on 60 extensive interviews with probation workers who joined the probation service from the 1960s to the present day, this book reaches beyond criminological and policy analysis to an application of sociological and organizational theory to rich qualitative data. It explores the backgrounds and motivations of probation workers, their changing relationships with other criminal justice agencies, and the complex public perceptions and media representations of probation work. The book considers the relative influences of religion, the union, diversity and feminization and, while it acknowledges that probation work is stressful, it draws innovatively on sociological and organizational concepts to categorize how workers respond to turbulent times.

This book challenges the dominant narrative of probation's decline in recent literature and constructs three 'ideal types' of probation worker – 'lifers', 'second careerists' and 'offender managers'. Each makes an essential contribution to probation cultures, which collectively contribute to, rather than undermine, the effectiveness of offender management and the future of probation work. This book will be important reading for researchers in the disciplines of criminology, criminal justice, sociology and management as well as probation workers of all grades and those in training.

Rob C. Mawby has been undertaking criminal justice research for 20 years and his publications have focused principally on policing. With Anne Worrall he has also pursued his interests in the supervision of offenders and the development of organizational cultures. He currently works in the Department of Criminology at the University of Leicester.

Anne Worrall is Professor of Criminology at Keele University and Honorary Professorial Fellow at the University of Western Australia. A former probation officer, she has written extensively about her two overlapping research interests, namely, women offenders and the probation service.

Routledge frontiers of criminal justice

Doing Probation Work

Identity in a criminal justice occupation

Rob C. Mawby and Anne Worrall

LONDON AND NEW YORK

First published 2013
by Routledge
2 Park Square, Milton Park, Abingdon, Oxon OX14 4RN

Simultaneously published in the USA and Canada
by Routledge
711 Third Avenue, New York, NY 10017

Routledge is an imprint of the Taylor & Francis Group, an informa business

British Library Cataloguing in Publication Data
A catalogue record for this book is available from the British Library

Library of Congress Cataloging-in-Publication Data
Mawby, Rob C.
Doing probation work: identity in a criminal justice occupation/Rob C.
Mawby and Anne Worrall.
    p. cm.
    Includes bibliographical references.
    1. Probation officers–Great Britain. I. Worrall, Anne. II. Title.
    HV9345.A5M387 2013
    364.6'302341–dc23   2012033400

ISBN: 978-0-415-54028-5 (hbk)
ISBN: 978-0-415-81527-7 (pbk)
ISBN: 978-0-203-10740-9 (ebk)

Typeset in Times New Roman
by Wearset Ltd, Boldon, Tyne and Wear

To Ange and Andrew, for your patience and support.

Contents

Acknowledgements

Research depends on the support of many people, and we have accumulated a number of debts over the last few years during the planning and implementation of this project on probation cultures. We would like to record our thanks to the Economic and Social Research Council, who funded the research (ESRC grant reference: RES-000–22–3979), and we are grateful to the Economic and Social Data Service for accepting the generated data set for their national archive. We also thank the Probation Chiefs Association who facilitated access and co-operation in different probation trusts.

We have also been assisted by the insights and encouragement of the following people: Steve Collett, Mary Corcoran, Keith Davies, David Gadd, James Hardie-Bick, Mike Nellis, Graham Nicholls, our colleagues who hosted seminars to discuss the research at the Universities of Keele, Leicester, Manchester and Cambridge, and all the delegates who attended the presentation of initial findings in September 2011 and provided valuable and challenging feedback.

We are also indebted to Jo Kelly who transcribed all the interviews accurately and efficiently, and to Tom Sutton and Nicola Hartley at Routledge who, respectively, encouraged our original proposal and helped us through to publication. The generosity of our anonymous proposal reviewers reassured us that the enterprise was timely and worthwhile.

Material in Chapter 4 previously appeared in ' "They were very threatening about do-gooding bastards": probation's changing relationships with the police and prison services in England and Wales', *European Journal of Probation*, 3, 3: 78–94 and we are grateful to the guest editors, Lol Burke and Keith Davies, who invited us to contribute to the special issue on occupational cultures and skills in probation practice.

We would like to record our thanks to Bloodaxe Books for permission to reproduce Simon Armitage's poem 'Social Inquiry Report'.

Our greatest debt is to the 60 unnamed participants who shared with us their experiences of doing probation work. Thank you – it was a privilege to be allowed an insight into your working lives.

Abbreviations

ABPO	Association of Black Probation Officers
ACO	Assistant Chief Officer
ACPO	Association of Chief Police Officers
ADP	Anti-discriminatory Practice
BME	Black Minority Ethnic
CAFCASS	Children and Family Court Advisory Support Service
CO	Chief Officer
CQSW	Certificate of Qualification in Social Work
CRB	Criminal Records Bureau
DipPS	Diploma in Probation Studies
FPW	Former Probation Worker
IOM	Integrated Offender Management
KPI	Key Performance Indicator
LAGIP	Lesbian and Gay Men in Probation Group
MAPPA	Multi-Agency Public Protection Arrangements
MoJ	Ministry of Justice
NADPAS	The National Association of Discharged Prisoners Aid Societies
NAPO	National Association of Probation Officers
NOMS	National Offender Management Service
NPS	National Probation Service for England and Wales
OASys	Offender Assessment System
OMM	Offender Management Model
OMU	Offender Management Unit
PCA	Probation Chiefs Association
PDA	Practice Development Assessor
PO	Probation Officer
POA	Prison Officers Association
PPO	Prolific and other Priority Offender
PSA	Police Superintendents' Association
PSO	Probation Service Officer
PSR	Pre-Sentence Report
PW	Probation Worker
PWO	Prison Welfare Officer

SFO	Serious Further Offence
SOVA	Society of Voluntary Associates
SPO	Senior Probation Officer
TPO	Trainee Probation Officer
TSP	Thinking Skills Programme
UNISON	Trade union for public sector workers

1 Probation – a tainted but resilient concept

Despite governmental attempts to eradicate it from criminal justice vocabulary (Worrall 2008a), the concept of 'probation' has proved remarkably resilient and has, in recent years, come to signify resistance to and subversion of the dominant penal discourse of 'offender management'. It has become an 'imaginary penality' (Carlen 2008) – an area of work where it is necessary for practitioners to act *as if* they believe in the rules about the effectiveness of 'risk-crazed governance' while knowingly using those rules in ways that will also achieve meaning.

This is not a book about the history of probation, though we set the historic scene briefly below. Those who wish to read more about the history of probation are directed to Mair and Burke's (2012) excellent and challenging work, *Redemption, Rehabilitation and Risk Management*. Nor is it a book that describes or evaluates the work of the probation service with offenders in the community. Others (Raynor and Robinson 2009; Canton 2011; Robinson 2011) have recently completed that task. This is a book about probation workers and their occupational cultures. We intend it to fit as much into the literature on the sociology of organizations as it does into criminal justice literature. It is about what motivates people to become probation workers, how they make sense of their work, how they respond to turbulent political times and media criticism, and what stories they tell about the value of their contribution to society.

While a great deal has been written about the historical, political, policy and practice changes that have shaped the role of the probation officer, very little has been written on the changes to occupational cultures and the ways in which probation workers themselves view the impact of changes to their role and very little about the relationships between probation workers and other criminal justice agencies engaged in offender management. This book aims to fill that gap by exploring the meaning of 'doing probation work' from the perspective of probation workers themselves. Based on 60 extensive interviews with a range of probation workers, the book will reach beyond criminological and policy analysis to an application of sociological and organizational theory to rich qualitative data.

The probation service reached its centenary in 2007 but the response of workers to this was muted and more akin to a wake than a celebration, despite the imaginative efforts of both NAPO, the National Association of Probation

Officers (NAPO 2007) and Senior (2008) to compile books of recollections. Mair and Burke suggest that 'a more considered response would have been to ask how it had come to this' and they liken the service to a Cinderella who 'never actually arrived at the ball' (2012: 1). They also come to the pessimistic conclusion that while community sentences probably have some sort of future in criminal justice policy, this may well not be the case for the probation service. That it still exists after 100 years is something for which we should be grateful, they say, but 'it has lost its roots, its traditions, its culture, its professionalism' (2012: 192). It is the aim of this book to challenge this view and its narrative of decline. Our research suggests that, while working in a much changed world, probation workers retain a strong sense of all these things – possibly too strong for their own good. What Mair and Burke fail to give sufficient credit for is that modern probation workers can handle the 'imaginary'. They can do what is required of them – they can be competent offender managers – while constructing identities that allow them to believe that they are still part of an 'honourable profession' (Probation Worker 3[1]).

Setting the scene

The probation service has its roots in the work of the nineteenth-century police court missionaries, first employed by the Church of England Temperance Society in 1876 to 'reclaim' offenders charged with drunkenness or drink-related offences. The Probation of Offenders Act 1907 gave magistrates' courts the right to appoint probation officers, whose job it was to 'advise, assist and befriend' offenders placed under their supervision. The Criminal Justice Act 1925 made it obligatory for every court to appoint a probation officer, and during the first half of the twentieth century the work of the service expanded to include work with juveniles and families, as well as adult offenders. Part of that work included dealing with matrimonial problems and it was through this aspect of the work that the role of Divorce Court Welfare Officer developed. By the mid-1960s, where our research starts, the service had also taken responsibility for the welfare of prisoners, both inside prison and on release. In addition to the strong interpersonal skills required for supervising offenders in the community, the distinctive professional skill that probation officers developed was that of Social Inquiry (or Enquiry) – a social work assessment of an offender in their social environment, with the specific purpose of assisting courts to make sentencing decisions (Worrall and Hoy 2005: 78).

Although there had always been a degree of tension in the role of the probation officer between caring for offenders and controlling their criminal behaviour, these two aspects of the work were viewed as part and parcel of both the psychoanalytic casework and the paternalistic common-sense advice that combined to characterize the typical probation officer of the early and mid-twentieth century. By the end of the 1960s the probation service had grown from the status of a localized mission to that of a nationwide, secular, social work service to the courts. From the 1970s onwards a number of developments had paradoxical consequences for the service and resulted in a loss of identity or, to use Harris's (1980) term, 'dissonance'. Harris argued that probation officers were experiencing three kinds of dissonance. Moral dissonance resulted from conflicting ideologies about the purpose of probation; technical dissonance resulted from discouraging empirical evidence about the effectiveness of probation in reducing criminal behaviour; and operational dissonance resulted from the tension inherent in managing the 'care and control' aspects of the daily probation task (Worrall and Hoy 2005: 79).

By the mid-1980s the service was experiencing the rise of managerialism along with many other public sector organizations (Clarke *et al.* 1994; May 1994; Mayo *et al.* 2007). The most visible effect on probation officers was their perceived loss of professional autonomy and a greater emphasis on accountability through the devising of local and area objectives and, by the end of the decade, National Standards that directed practice in all aspects of report-writing and supervision. Few disputed the need to standardize some very variable and inconsistent practice across the country and between individual officers. Professional autonomy had undoubtedly been used in the past as an excuse for poor practice, but the overriding point about National Standards was that they limited the discretion of the individual probation officer and focused on the management of supervision rather than its content. In addition to making the individual officer more accountable to management, it also made the service more accountable to government (Worrall and Hoy 2005: 84).

Despite its acceptance that probation 'is a long-established concept, well understood internationally' (Home Office 1998: para. 2.13) the new Labour government elected in 1997 expressed its determination to abolish any terminology that might be 'misunderstood' or 'associated with tolerance of crime' (para. 2.12) by seeking to rename the service and to explore the possibility of merging it with the prison service (both attempts failing but only temporarily). The compromise reached was the creation of the National Probation Service in 2001[2] and the removal of the word 'probation' from court orders.

This compromise was short-lived, however, and there were further radical changes in the governance of probation. In 2003, the Carter Review (Carter 2003) and subsequent government response (Home Office 2004a) proposed a new National Offender Management Service (NOMS) which would finally bring together the prison and probation services (from June 2004) to provide 'end-to-end management of all offenders, whether they are serving sentences in prison, the community or both' (Home Office 2004b). Carter had envisaged that the services of probation might be provided by others – independent, voluntary organizations and even by the private and commercial sector. It was argued that competition between providers would raise standards generally. The Offender Management Act 2007 therefore empowered the Secretary of State (the Minister for Justice) to commission services directly, with the clear implication that they may be commissioned from providers other than the probation service. In 2010, the Probation Areas of England and Wales were reconstituted as 35 Probation Trusts, that would both provide probation services and also themselves commission services from others. In 2011 a 'procurement competition' to run community payback included potential providers from the commercial sector as well as from Probation Trusts (Worrall and Canton 2013). The first of these contracts was awarded jointly to Serco and the London Probation Trust in July 2012 (BBC News 2012).

These changes both reflected and confirmed a major change of ethos for the probation service, which now affirmed its objectives as 'enforcement, rehabilitation and public protection' (National Probation Service 2001). This has had considerable implications for work with offenders. *Enforcement* meant ensuring that offenders met the requirements of their orders. Returning an offender to court for non-compliance with an order (known as 'breaching'), which had been seen in the past as an admission of failure by the probation officer, was now viewed as essential to the credibility of orders and an act of strength (Hedderman 2003; Hedderman and Hough 2004). *Rehabilitation* was to focus no longer on the welfare of the offender (with some ill-defined hope that this will lead in some way to reform), but on the clear objective of measurably reduced reconviction. *Public protection* was to be achieved through the sound assessment and management of risk. The level of risk became the single most important criterion in determining the amount and type of subsequent intervention. Every offender who goes to prison or is placed on a community order is subject to an assessment of their risk of reoffending and of causing serious harm. There are various methods of calculating risk but the most widely used is a computerized system called the Offender Assessment System, or OASys (Burnett, Baker and Roberts 2007; Kemshall and Wood 2007). Under the National Offender Management Model, work with offenders is now divided into four 'tiers', depending on levels of risk and dangerousness. Tier 1 offenders are to be punished; tier 2 offenders are to be punished and helped; tier 3 offenders punished, helped and changed; tier 4 offenders punished, helped, changed and controlled (NOMS 2006; Worrall and Canton 2013).

Running in parallel to the changes in practice and management were debates about the need to change training to better equip new officers to meet the requirements of the modernized service. In 1995, the government repealed the legal requirement (that had existed for approximately 25 years) for all new probation officers to hold a social work qualification. The aim was to end the control by higher education over probation training but a compromise was reached that lasted until 2010, whereby trainee probation officers were required to study for a university degree at the same time as an NVQ Level 4 award. The programme was employment-led and run by consortia of probation services and higher education. While there was little doubt that this Diploma in Probation Studies was extremely demanding there was widespread disquiet that the specificity of the roles and tasks for which trainees were equipped did not produce the flexible, reflexive and creative employees that are needed to work imaginatively with offenders (Knight 2002). Some suggested the new training contributed to the de-professionalization of the service (Aldridge 1999a). In 2011 the introduction of the new Qualifications Framework moved even further towards a model of internal workplace training, resulting in a qualification that is intended to be available to any employer (including voluntary and private sector organizations) (Ministry of Justice 2012).

Occupational cultures

Our interest in occupational cultures was sparked during our evaluation of a number of projects involving the multi-agency supervision of prolific and priority offenders. Observation of the joint working and personal interactions between probation workers and police officers, and latterly prison officers, revealed some of the tensions and dynamics of culture clashes and crossovers between criminal justice practitioners which we have written about elsewhere (Worrall *et al.* 2003; Mawby and Worrall 2004; Mawby *et al.* 2007). During our discussions and subsequent writing about aspects of these cultural dynamics, we became convinced that the occupational cultures of probation workers was a topic worthy of further research in its own right.

At its broadest, the culture of an occupation or an organization can be described as the values shared by individuals that manifest themselves in the practices of members of that occupation or organization. Mullins (2010: 739) describes occupational culture as 'how things are done around here' and Liebling *et al.* (2011: 153) refer to common ways of thinking that affect approaches to work.

In the management and organizational behaviour literature, distinctions are made and contested between organizational, occupational and professional cultures. Schein (2010: 1–2), refers to organizational culture as applying to all kinds of government, public, private and voluntary organizations. Within these, occupational groups form subcultures, and cutting across the occupational groups there may be smaller teams that develop micro-cultures. Johnson *et al.* (2009: 320) describe occupational culture as a broader construct than professional culture, developing through 'social interaction, shared experience, common training and affiliation, mutual support, associated values and norms, and similar personal characteristics of members of a particular occupational group'. The development of cultures provides a resource which allows groups and organizations to function internally, to react and adapt to the external environment and to integrate new members into ways of working. According to Morgan (2006: 126–38) organizational culture includes: operating norms, symbols and rituals of daily routine; language used within the group; stories, legends and myths about individuals, the group, and the organization which sustain cultural values; the work atmosphere/context, including the physical environment; and shared systems of meaning that are accepted, internalized and acted upon.

Utilizing similar themes, Schein argues (2010: 23) that culture can be analysed at three different levels. The first is that of *artefacts*, and this is the level of the tangible, the visible and the obvious. The second is that of *espoused values and beliefs*, and the third level is that of *underlying assumptions*, the taken-for-granted beliefs that influence behaviours and characterize an organization.

Drawing on these concepts, our intention is to identify and explore the characteristics of the occupational cultures of probation workers where the culture of a group can be defined as:

> a pattern of shared basic assumptions learned by a group as it solved its problems of external adaptation and internal integration, which has worked well enough to be considered valid and, therefore, to be taught to new members as the correct way to perceive, think, and feel in relation to those problems.
>
> (Schein 2010: 18)

No comprehensive body of research and literature exists on the occupational cultures of criminal justice practitioners. Perhaps one of the most enduring attempts to find the common ground is Rutherford's (1993) conceptualization of the 'working credos' that underpin the daily work of criminal justice personnel. Based on interviews with senior practitioners, he developed a typology of three 'credos' – Credo One (associated with punishment and degradation), Credo Two (associated with efficiency and the smooth running of the system) and Credo Three (associated with caring and rehabilitation). He concluded that the system in the early 1990s favoured the Credo Two practitioner over the Credo Three practitioner, whose position was ambiguous and precarious. He speculated about the increasing influence of Credo One practitioners but considered that they remained more a feature of the US than the UK criminal justice system.

Despite recent re-emergent interest in the cultures of prison officers (Crewe *et al.* 2010; Tait 2011), probation officers (Burke and Davies 2011), police auxiliaries (Dolman 2008) and private security workers (Button 2007; Hucklesby 2011), only police culture has been subjected to in-depth study (for recent examples, see Skolnick 2008 and Loftus 2009, 2010). Some of the early classic studies of policing examined police culture, even if they did not explicitly seek to do so. For example, Banton (1964) and Cain (1973) explored how officers made sense of their work and Skolnick (1966: 42) developed the idea of the 'working personality' of the police officer, arguing that there existed 'distinctive cognitive tendencies in police as an occupational grouping'. Other studies have revealed racist tendencies (Holdaway 1983) and debated the difficulty of changing police culture (Chan 1997). Robert Reiner (2010) has summarized this literature and categorized the core characteristics of 'cop culture' as: mission-action-cynicism-pessimism; suspicion; isolation/solidarity; conservatism; machismo; racial prejudice and pragmatism. It is widely accepted that all organizations have cultures and that these can be resistant to change and an obstacle to progress or alternatively a source of stability and a force for good. As Reiner's core characteristics suggest, 'cop culture' has been more often regarded as a problem than an asset, evidenced through the damaging and lingering condemnation of the police investigation into Stephen Lawrence's murder in 1993 (Rowe 2007). Despite this, Foster (2003: 222) has commented on positive police culture characteristics, namely 'the sense of mission, the desire to rid the streets of "the bad guys", the dedication and long hours, the willingness, on one level, to do society's dirty work'.

It is also significant to note that researchers now recognize that police culture is not monolithic, something which carries across to the literature on prison officer culture. This literature is not large, but existing studies suggest that there are multiple cultures, yet consistent characteristics that include discretion, cynicism, suspicion, nostalgia, physical and emotional strength, male-domination, authority and solidarity (see, for example, Crawley 2005; Arnold *et al.* 2007; Liebling *et al.* 2011). As Liebling *et al.* (2011: 154–5) point out, in contrast to studies of police culture, there have been comparatively few examinations of the 'working personalities' of prison officers, possibly due to the lack of glamour in their role and their ambivalent, often stereotypically negative, media representations.

The literature on probation cultures, like that on prison officer cultures, is similarly limited in size. It is a 'largely neglected and under-researched area of academic enquiry' according to Burke and Davies (2011: 2) perhaps because, as Mair and Burke (2012) point out, probation workers have never sought the symbolic status of other criminal justice practitioners. Nevertheless, in recent years a number of welcome studies have emerged that indicate a growing interest in this area of probation research. These, together with others that inform on probation cultures without explicitly investigating them, include Nash (1999, 2004, 2008); McNeill (2001); Vanstone (2004); Treadwell (2006); Gelsthorpe (2007); Nellis (2007); Robinson and Burnett (2007); Annison *et al.* (2008); Forbes (2010); Gregory (2010); Burke and Davies (2011); Deering (2011) and Phillips (2010, 2011). Some of the themes that are prominent in these works are: the early religious and philanthropic influences, an emphasis on the individuality and creativity of probation officers and the significance of professional autonomy, 'humanistic sensibility' (Nellis 2007), and the influence of social casework and discretion. It is to this previously neglected but increasingly significant area of research that this book seeks to contribute.

Having discussed the concept of occupational cultures and referred to some of the influential literature, it is worth summarizing why occupational cultures are deserving of study. We would argue that:

- They indicate 'what really matters' and 'how things are done around here'
- They provide insight into how practitioners perceive their occupation
- They influence how work is done and how effective it will be
- They influence how new members are introduced into ways of working
- They are a resource for adapting to change and the external context
- They can be a stabilizing force for good
- They can be an obstacle to reform, change and progress
- They come to the fore during turbulent times

Probation as a tainted occupation

In seeking to characterize the occupational cultures of probation work, our starting point is the work of Ashforth and Kreiner (1999) and Ashforth *et al.* (2007)

on the concept of 'dirty work'. One of the dilemmas that emerged during our interviews was the extent to which workers felt that the social status of the probation officer had changed from that of being 'an authoritative person' (CO14) 'almost priest-like' (FPW7) to being 'a waste of time' (PW9). The cosy image of the probation officer as 'ever such a nice lady' (Todd 1964) has been transformed to someone who is doing society's dirty work and should probably be ashamed, rather than proud, of themselves, for working with the 'undeserving':

> Can't we just actually say 'well done' [to ourselves]? Is it because you're worried that a member of the press or member of parliament will walk into an office and see self-congratulation, accuse us of being complacent? Must you take away any bit of joy, just to demonstrate this public penance or incompetence?
>
> (TPO2)

Drawing on much earlier work by Hughes (1951) and Goffman (1963), Ashforth and Kreiner (1999), Kreiner *et al.* (2006) and Ashforth *et al.* (2007) have developed the concept of 'dirty work' to describe those occupations that society regards as 'necessary evils' – jobs that someone has to do but which are considered to be unpleasant, disgusting and/or morally questionable. People who undertake such work are attributed with a stigma or negative identity as 'dirty workers', who may be physically, socially or morally tainted. Workers who are physically tainted undertake work that is intrinsically dirty, such as rubbish collectors or embalmers, or they have to do their work in 'noxious' conditions, such as miners. Workers who are socially tainted have regular contact with stigmatized groups, for example prison guards and social workers, or are in a servile relationship with their employer or clients, for example domestic servants. Finally, workers who are morally tainted do work that is morally dubious, for example exotic dancers, or utilize unethical methods, for example debt collectors. While it might be argued that many occupations contain some elements of stigma, Kreiner *et al.* (2006: 622) distinguish between those where stigma is idiosyncratic (neither routine nor strong), those where stigma is compartmentalized (affecting limited aspects of the job), those where it is diluted (widespread but mild) and those where it is pervasive (where stigma is both strong and widespread). The final dimension in this schema is that of relative prestige. Using (arguably outdated) USA occupational prestige rankings, Ashforth and Kreiner (1999) and Ashforth *et al.* (2007) distinguish between high-prestige dirty work (which is perceived as requiring skill and/or specialist knowledge to a professional or semi-professional level) and low-prestige dirty work (which is not).

Within this model, it is not too difficult to identify probation workers as being socially tainted. On behalf of society, they engage regularly with stigmatized people and run the risk of being stigmatized themselves. Alongside the work of other criminal justice occupations such as police, prison guards and criminal lawyers, society reluctantly accepts the necessity for probation work:

> People just want that reassurance that there's somebody doing it.
>
> (CO4)

> Most of the public don't give a toss about us, but they're quite glad to know we're around.
>
> (CO15)

Time and again in our research, however, people told us that the public really did not know what the work was about or what it entails so the taint was, in their view, based on both limited knowledge or experience and in many cases, after initial curiosity, a reluctance to find out more:

> People either don't want to have a conversation about it, they just don't wanna go there, or they say 'oh that must be depressing work – that's kind of dirty, depressing'. They don't wanna know about that, 'Let's talk about something happy'.
>
> (CO5)

> A lot of people are like 'oh what do they do?' I've found that quite a bit, that nobody really understands what probation does or … so they start … they're quite inquisitive about what you do and who you work with. And some people say 'oh I couldn't do that, I couldn't work with those kind of people'.
>
> (PW14)

Some interviewees avoided saying much about their work in social situations with unfamiliar people:

> I often don't say I'm a [laugh] … I try to avoid saying I'm a probation officer … well I remember once saying I was a plumber and then someone tried to … then they started talking to me about fitting a [laugh] … fitting you know, like … I thought no, you know, so [laugh].
>
> (PW12)

One (male) interviewee was at a party with his male partner and seemed more uncomfortable about disclosing his occupation than his sexual orientation, as his turn of phrase indicates:

> There was an awkward moment … Do I *come out* as a probation officer?
>
> (TPO4)

One reason for the low public profile of the probation service has been its marginal media profile in the past; it has been 'a bit of a secret service' (CO12) and this has offered protection from the worst excesses of media criticism. But high-profile cases such as those of Hanson and White, Rice, and Sonnex[3] (Fitzgibbon

2011, to be discussed more fully in Chapter 5) – cases where people under probation supervision have committed murder – have changed public attitudes from benign indifference to marked negativity, as this interviewee explains with great clarity:

> I think prior to those cases, probation had a fairly good reputation amongst the public, amongst courts, amongst judges and magistrates, as an organization that was doing a good job, that was actually, you know, working positively with offenders, was very much focused about change, wasn't just about risk management, but was also about addressing needs and social work in individuals in the community. Whereas I think, you know, as the service has changed structurally and strategically, its image has shifted and it's much more of a negative perception now, I think, by the public.
>
> (FPW4)

Our argument here is that there have been significant changes in both the relative prestige and the depth of stigma dimensions within the occupation. According to the model of socially tainted 'dirty work', social workers, counsellors and police officers are considered to be relatively high in prestige, while prison guards and welfare (care) assistants are considered to be relatively low in prestige. We suggest that recent changes in their training and their organizational position (within NOMS) have caused probation workers to slip from 'high' to 'low' prestige. Additionally, while probation workers traditionally identified themselves as 'courtroom officers' (or 'servants of the court') whose experience of stigma was widespread but mild (diluted), their more recent association with prison officers has resulted in a strong and widespread (pervasive) experience of stigma.

There is nothing new about arguing that personal or occupational stigma has negative consequences, resulting in a spoiled identity (Goffman 1963). For Ashforth and Kreiner (1999), however, the research conundrum is that stigma can result in a positive identity among dirty workers:

> [T]he real issue for dirty workers, then, is not so much 'How can they do the work?' but 'How do they retain a positive self-definition in the face of social assaults on the work they do?'
>
> (Ashforth and Kreiner 1999: 418)

Ashforth et al.'s (2007) model of dirty work gives rise to a number of processes whereby dirty workers construct positive work identities. First, they develop ideologies that reframe, recalibrate and refocus the purpose and value of their work. They reframe by foregrounding the virtues and benefits of the work (for example, 'advise, assist and befriend' becomes 'enforcement, rehabilitation and public protection'), recalibrate by adjusting the standards that evaluate the extent of 'dirt' (for example, massaging the statistics to demonstrate reductions in reoffending) and refocusing by emphasizing the rewarding aspects of the work over the dirty ones (for example, concentrating on 'good news' stories about the offenders who have been successfully rehabilitated rather than the 'bad stories' of those who commit serious further offences). Second, dirty workers engage in social weighting tactics – not unlike Sykes and Matza's (1957) 'techniques of neutralization' – condemning those who condemn them, supporting those who support them (if any) and making selective social comparisons 'to draw more flattering inferences about themselves' (Ashforth *et al*. 2007: 150).

We use the model of 'dirty work' throughout this book to gain insight into the ways in which probation workers routinely construct and maintain a positive work identity for themselves. However, the model does not entirely capture or explain all our data. In particular, the concept of dirty work, as presented by Ashforth, Kreiner and their colleagues assumes a stable, or relatively stable, external environment and a consistent public attitude towards the work. As indicated above, our interviewees believe that public perceptions of probation work have changed. Whether this is a symptom or a cause of the turbulent political, social and economic changes in the external context of probation work is a matter of serious debate. The concept of dirty work provides us with a meso-level tool with which to analyse group attitudes and behaviour, but it does not fully account for either macro-level societal changes or micro-level individual responses. It is to these aspects of our theoretical framework that we now turn.

Turbulent times and worker responses

We have already alluded to some of the challenges faced by probation workers since the 1970s, including the onslaught of managerialism, changes in training frameworks, roles and organizational structures including a 'forced marriage' with the prison service, all contributing to a potential loss of identity and certainly an element of dissonance. The fieldwork for this research was conducted in 2010–11 and at that time a number of factors contributed to the turbulent operating conditions for probation workers.

First, following the general election of May 2010, the Conservative–Liberal Coalition Government promised (HM Government 2010: 23) to overhaul 'the system of rehabilitation to reduce reoffending and provide greater support and protection for the victims of crime'. They would do this, they claimed, through a 'rehabilitation revolution' involving paying 'independent providers to reduce reoffending'. The implied threat to the domain[4] of the probation service was reinforced in the subsequent Spending Review of October 2010 which projected budget cuts of 23 per cent for criminal justice agencies (HM Treasury 2010). On the ground, the practical consequences of this meant that as we visited probation areas to conduct our interviews, probation workers were not only unclear about the continuing place of the probation service within the criminal justice landscape, but were also awaiting announcements concerning redundancies within their offices.

Second, the training framework was changing again, with the new vocational 'Probation Qualifications Framework' replacing the Diploma in Probation Studies. The TPOs whom we interviewed in 2010 were part of the last cohort and were well aware that if they failed there was no follow-up cohorts that they could join. Third, overlaying this climate of uncertainty was a challenging political and media context in which the dominant discourses foregrounded concerns over rising prison populations, 'weak' community punishments and popular anxieties around crime and victimization (House of Commons Justice Committee 2011; Ministry of Justice 2012). These were also characterized by media interest in criminal justice failures, some of which implicated the probation service, including the previously mentioned cases of Hanson and White, Rice, and Sonnex. Such cases were constant touchstones in our interviews and during the course of the fieldwork, a fresh case emerged to question the efficacy of probation supervision, that of Jon Venables, though a case review subsequently confirmed that the level of probation supervision was appropriate.[5] In addition to negative media coverage of these cases, midway through our fieldwork, fresh media criticism of the probation service emerged after 2 September 2010, when ITV1's *Tonight* programme screened undercover footage of community punishments in three probation areas. The headlines that resulted were in the vein of 'holiday camp for offenders'.

Turbulent times have profound effects on organizations and their employees. Both, in their own ways, need to engineer responses in order that the organization meets its objectives and the employees feel that their work has a purpose and is meaningful or is at least tolerable and manageable. The specific question that arises for us from these conditions is 'How do probation workers respond and manage their identities while negotiating routine work within a difficult operating climate?' To answer this, we will draw on, and further develop, a theoretical model put forward by Hirschman.

Hirschman's (1970) 'exit, voice, and loyalty' (EVL) model has been used widely to analyse and compare employees' responses to adverse workplace conditions. As an economist Hirschman's original work examined customer and employee responses to lapses in an organization's behaviour. He posited the responses of 'exit' 'voice' and 'loyalty'. Exit includes not only employees leaving the organization (1970: 4), but also the state of thinking about leaving, that is, making a psychological exit. Voice is a response whereby employees speak up, expressing their concerns and dissatisfaction to management and others. This is not necessarily a negative response; it can be a positive attempt to improve the situation, namely a 'pro-social voice' (Van Dyne *et al.* 2003, quoted in Naus *et al.* 2007). Loyalty characterizes the employee who feels an attachment to the organization such that there is a psychological barrier to exiting and describes those employees who passively and loyally wait for better times, supporting the organization publicly and privately. A fourth component of 'neglect' has subsequently been added to applications of Hirschman's model (EVLN), evidenced through lax behaviour such as persistent lateness, absenteeism and poor performance (Farrell 1983).

More recently, the EVLN model has been further extended. Naus *et al.* (2007) added a fifth dimension of 'organizational cynicism', a response which arises in situations where employees feel that the organization has broken a psychological contract, disappointing their expectations and generating disillusionment. Employees come to believe that the organization lacks integrity and they respond in two ways. They either adopt a negative attitude toward the organization and tend to disparage it (2007: 689), affecting apathetic and alienated behaviour, or alternatively they become a more positive influence, responding as a critical but caring voice of conscience.

A sixth response of 'organizational expedience' (McLean Parks *et al.* 2010) moves us more clearly into the arena of rule-breaking, describing 'workers' behaviours that (1) are intended to fulfil organizationally prescribed or sanctioned objectives but that (2) knowingly involve breaking, bending or stretching organizational rules, directives, or organizationally sanctioned norms' (2010: 703). Arising from the subjective experiences of role overload, emotional exhaustion, tension and/or task conflict, expedient behaviour can result in increased organizational effectiveness but may also result in 'workers attempting to "make it by faking it" – acting out their roles as if they understand expectations and doing whatever it takes to look successful, while hoping results will follow' (2010: 714).

These six responses come together in a theoretical model which helps us to make sense of the data collected through our interviews with probation workers, yet they do not fully explain some aspects of the data. While the concept of 'organizational expedience' comes closest to providing an explanation of contemporary probation work, we suggest that there are some elements of the work that can only be explained in terms of 'voluntary risk-taking'. In an organization obsessed with risk assessment and risk management, we will argue that it is not inappropriate to draw upon the sociological concept of 'edgework' (in particular 'workplace edgework') to extend our understanding.

Edgework refers to activities that involve voluntary risk-taking, where there is a 'clearly observable threat to one's physical or mental well-being or one's sense of an ordered existence' (Lyng 1990: 857). It is most easily illustrated in dangerous pastimes such as sky-diving (Hardie-Bick 2011), solo rock climbing (Fawcett 2010: chapter 7) or even criminal behaviour (Ferrell *et al.* 2001), but the 'edge' can be any boundary, such as that between life and death, consciousness and unconsciousness, sanity and insanity, where the actor, potentially, can lose control. Controlling the boundary involves the deployment of a specific skill 'to maintain control over a situation that verges on complete chaos, a situation most people would regard as entirely uncontrollable' (Lyng 1990: 859). Edgework tests this skill by getting as close as possible to the edge without crossing it. It is not, therefore, gambling, recklessness or the result of a psychological predisposition to take risks (Lyng 2009: 120), and edgeworkers are unlikely to place themselves in threatening circumstances beyond *their* control.

In the analysis of our data, we have chosen to imagine that (some) probation workers engage in edgework. This is partly because 'to a considerable degree, we all engage in edgework at some time. What varies is the intensity, duration, manner and form' (Milovanovic 2005: 51–2), but more significantly because edgework is 'increasingly what institutions expect of many people' (Simon

2005: 206). By *imagining*, we are choosing to enter the world of 'imaginary penalities' where ossified official justifications continue to struggle to exclude alternative or imaginative discourses of justice (Carlen 2008: xiv). We have data that can only be made sense of in relation to a desire for autonomy and 'action'. While we might draw on Goffman's concept of action as 'knowingly taking consequential chances perceived as avoidable' (1969: 145) or Csikszentmihályi's (1975: 182) state of 'flow'[6] where enjoyment is derived from the uninterrupted internal logic of a challenging activity, neither of these concepts takes full account of the 'highly unstructured, chaotic conditions that often must be negotiated' (Lyng 2009: 111). Nor should this desire be dismissed as harking back to a 'golden age' of social work professionalism, because many probation workers have no investment in that history of probation. They are products of a service that is saturated with the concept of risk and everything they do – including their own responses to their work environment – is defined by risk assessment and risk management. If we accept Milovanovic's (2005) typologies as locating edgeworkers along an 'in-control/out-of-control' spectrum, we imagine that this data can be best understood as constituting 'workplace edgework' – firmly towards the in-control end of the spectrum but nevertheless challenging the boundaries between acceptable and unacceptable behaviour in heavily rule-governed environments (Milovanovic 2005: 57–8).

There is a structural context to edgework, which is both a form of escape from (or resistance to) the rules and routines of contemporary life (Ferrell 2005; Katz 1988) and an implicit requirement imposed by organizations that displace their collective responsibility for risk management on to individual employees through a mechanism of responsibilization (Lyng 2009: 106). Edgework is the great 'unspoken'. Paradoxically, therefore, workers are both freeing themselves from, and better integrating themselves into, modern working conditions when they pursue edgework (Lyng 2005).

Edgework is also a gendered concept. Just as Goffman concedes that 'action … seems to belong to the cult of masculinity' (1969: 156), so, traditionally, edgework relates to male-dominated activities and assumes the subjective sensations of the masculine mind and body. Increasingly women are engaging in the same activities, although their experience of the risk-taking is different, involving different emotional management (Lois 2001, 2005). Perhaps more significantly, as the definition of edgework has developed, it has increasingly embraced the experiences of women's routine lives, both at home (see Rajah, 2007 on edgework in violent intimate relationships) and, as we argue here, in the workplace. For this reason, the feminization of probation work (which we discuss in Chapter 7) does not preclude engagement with edgework.

Many probation workers spend the majority of their time in front of computers in open-plan offices, undertaking important but routine risk assessment and risk management. The rest of their time is spent interviewing offenders in the security-conscious environment of anonymous public sector offices frequently located on industrial estates or technology parks and away from the places where offenders live. The work is demanding and the consequences of making mistakes could be serious, but opportunities for action are very few. Yet probation work is as much about controlling the boundaries between order and chaos as is police work, albeit on a smaller and more specific scale, as we will seek to establish in the chapters that follow.

Methods and participants

Many of the existing criminological studies of occupational cultures have used observational methods (e.g. Skolnick 1966; Cain 1973; Punch 1979; Holdaway 1983; Young 1991; Loftus 2009). These researchers, following anthropological traditions, would no doubt argue that the most valid way to understand and interpret cultures is to observe them over a period of time. In contrast, at the outset we decided to use an interview-based design for this study. While aware of the standard criticisms of interviews as a reliable method, it was not our purpose to compare policy with practice in action or to observe the minutiae of probation work; rather we wished to examine how probation workers themselves construct, and tell the stories of, their occupational identities, values and cultures. Our aim was to investigate the stories that probation workers tell about the job they do, rather than to uncover 'truths' about how they actually behave. To achieve this, we needed to talk to current and former personnel about their working lives rather than observing them at work.

The research design was based on 60 face-to-face semi-structured interviews with current and former probation workers (Appendix A). The interview sample was constructed through our own network of contacts and, importantly, the cooperation of the Probation Chiefs Association (PCA). The former enabled the recruitment of eight former probation workers and ten trainee probation officers (through emails approved by their university lecturer). The latter endorsed our research and encouraged chief officers/CEOs to facilitate access, without at any stage trying to influence the direction or outcomes of our research. As a result 16 staff of chief officer grade agreed to be interviewed, and in two probation areas we arranged for emails to be sent to the whole workforce requesting volunteers in the sample categories to contact us direct. From these responses we undertook 26 interviews.

Geographically, we interviewed COs from across England, with the other samples taken from the south-east of England (including London) and two areas in the north of England. The sample included former and current probation workers who had: trained under different training regimes; had long and short experience of being a probation worker (from two years to over forty); had experience of different probation roles; had worked in different geographical locations, including urban and rural settings; and had worked at probation service officer, probation officer, senior probation officer or chief officer grades. The purpose of identifying a varied sample of probation workers was to examine the extent to which a range of probation workers perceived themselves to be making a unique contribution to the criminal justice system.

In terms of gender and ethnic origins, 33 (55 per cent) of our 60 interviewees were female and eight (13 per cent) identified themselves as being Indian, Black African, Black Caribbean, Irish or mixed other. Regarding age, 26 (47 per cent) were under 50 years and 34 (53 per cent) were over 50 years. Our age profile was distorted by the unexpectedly high number of COs who volunteered to be interviewed (enabling us to increase our overall sample from an original target of 50 interviews to 60). COs represent 27 per cent of our sample. We analysed their responses separately from other grades, but found no major differences to support the existence of distinct 'management' and 'operational' cultures. Indeed the similarities were marked, possibly because all the interviewed COs were career probation workers with a wealth of experience in different grades.[7] The sample's demographic profile is not greatly out of line with that of the service at the time of the fieldwork, which was approximately 68 per cent female (45 per cent of COs), 14 per cent black minority ethnic (BME) (26 per cent of support staff), and 34 per cent over 50 years (90 per cent of COs).[8]

The interviews were divided between Rob Mawby (28) and Anne Worrall (32) and all but two (due to prison rules) were recorded and transcribed. Prior to each interview, an information sheet and list of themes covered by 25 questions was sent to each participant for them to reflect on (Appendix B). During the interviews each participant talked about their working lives based on these questions. They talked about their original motivations and aspirations on joining the probation service, their knowledge of the service at the time of joining, their training experiences and career development, their views on public and media perceptions of probation work, their daily routines and relations with probationers, courts and other criminal justice practitioners, and they described crises and typical working days.

All the interviewees signed participant consent forms and we discussed carefully with them how the interview transcripts would be anonymized for archiving purposes. We then analysed the transcripts to produce thematic summaries for selected categories of probation worker. These provide the data on which we draw in the chapters that follow. We draw heavily on direct quotations throughout the book in order to convey the richness and complexity of probation work and also to evidence the arguments that we develop. We found on completing the first draft of the book that we had, without specific intent, used quotations from 59 of our 60 interviewees. We could then not resist seeking out an appropriate quotation from the final participant! Consequently, we are proud to say that everyone we interviewed has contributed to this book, not only indirectly by providing a transcript that is now archived[9] for use by future researchers, but directly by providing a range of views and illustrations, without which the book would be much the poorer.

Outline of book

In this introductory chapter the reader has been reminded briefly of the history of the probation service and the key developments that have shaped the service as it now is. This was followed by a discussion of the term 'occupational cultures' as it pertains to the criminal justice system and an introduction to the literature on police and prison officer cultures. The book's theoretical framework was then set out, focusing on the concepts of probation as a 'tainted' occupation in a context of 'turbulent times'. It has been hypothesized that probation workers respond to adverse working conditions in a number of ways, including engaging in edge-work, expedience and organizational cynicism. A description of the research on which the book is based followed and the chapter will conclude with an outline of the remainder of the book.

In Chapter 2 we explore the backgrounds and motivations alongside the signifi-cance of the changing training regimes that have taken the role of probation worker increasingly away from its religious and social work roots. Our research has estab-lished that probation workers come from a variety of backgrounds, although there are identifiable groupings that we have called 'lifers', 'second careerists' and 'offender managers'. We find many common motivations between these groups but also some important differences that both reflect and reinforce the changes within the service. In this chapter we introduce the reader to many of our interviewees and conclude by presenting pen portraits of three participants whose characteristics might be regarded as representative of the three groupings we have identified.

In Chapter 3 we attempt to answer the question, 'What do probation workers actually *do*?', by utilizing the concepts of 'time' and 'place' to structure an examination of the daily routines of probation workers and the variety of physi-cal environments in which they work. We follow probation workers through typical and non-typical days from the past and in the present and ask how they have been transformed – for better or worse – from largely autonomous community-based workers to highly accountable desk-bound operatives.

In recent decades the probation service has been encouraged to work closely with a range of public and voluntary sector agencies. Chapter 4 examines proba-tion's changing relationships with the courts, police and prison services. Drawing on Davidson's (1976) typology of inter-organizational relationships, we argue that, despite both structural and cultural transformations, there remain cultural continuities in each organization that create tensions, the significance of which should not be underestimated.

Our research established that probation workers feel misunderstood by family and friends, the wider public and the media. Family members are generally sup-portive but bemused, friends admiring or incredulous and the public contemptu-ous. Public perceptions and misconceptions about the work are discussed in Chapter 5 together with media representations of the work in film, fiction and television. The near-universal failure of the probation service to manage its media image, particularly in comparison with the police and especially at national level, is analysed.

Probation work is stressful, but it also offers many opportunities to work in a variety of settings that require a range of skills and provide different experiences of job satisfaction. In Chapter 6 we consider the ways in which probation workers manage – or 'craft' – their careers and the extent to which they can exercise control over their work. We examine their collective and individual coping mechanisms and the ways in which they manage their self-presentation. The perceived erosion of professional autonomy and probation workers' responses to working in turbulent times will be discussed, including organiza-tional cynicism, expedience and workplace edgework.

Chapter 7 examines four dimensions of the cultures – or 'voices' – that have influenced the construction of the identities of probation workers over five decades. We consider the tenacity of religious influence, the declining influence of the trade union (NAPO), the service's commitment to diversity, and the 'feminization' of an organization that (unusually for a social work-based agency) was male-dominated until the early 1990s. It will be argued that this latter does not herald a return to traditional social work values but rather the emergence of a new breed of female offender manager whose influence on the organization is profound.

In our concluding chapter, we identify the characteristics of contemporary probation cultures and, using theoretically informed typologies, discuss how probation workers construct their occupational identities, values and cultures. We examine the role of nostalgia in probation cultures and we challenge the narrative of decline that pervades much writing about the probation service. We ask how such cultures contribute to, or undermine, the effectiveness of offender management and the future of probation work. We conclude that criminal justice will be much the poorer if probation work becomes fragmented and the cultures that underpin it become diluted.

Summary: the square of probation work

In this book we argue that understanding the occupational cultures of probation workers is an essential component of understanding the workings of criminal justice, specifically in England and Wales, but more generally in all those jurisdictions that take the concept of 'alternatives to custody' seriously. To assist the reader in navigating what we hope will be some complex conceptualizations, we are introducing the idea of a 'square' of probation work (Figure 1.1). This is a

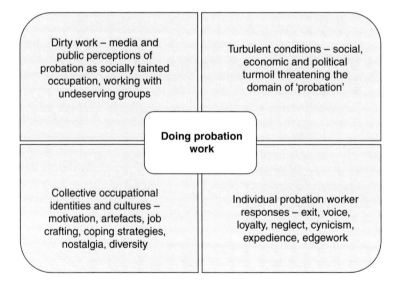

Figure 1.1 The square of probation work.

device for showing the relationships between the four key elements of our data analysis. First, we propose that probation work now ranks among the 'tainted' or 'dirty' occupations that at best attract ambivalent feelings, and at worst, public opprobrium. Second, we reiterate and restructure the well-known turbulence of the social, economic and political environment in which probation is required to function. Third, we suggest that it is possible to identify a number of characteristics that comprise collective probation cultures. Finally, we argue that, faced with these three components, individual probation workers will choose to respond in one or more ways at any given time, depending on their personal motivations and experiences.

2 Lifers, second careerists and offender managers

> I applied for a temporary probation officer job in late 1972. And yeah, I knew nothing about probation.
>
> (CO1)

In this chapter we examine who probation workers are. We look into their backgrounds and explore what motivated them to consider the probation service as a career choice. We track their routes into the service and their progress through different training frameworks. The probation workers we interviewed come from a variety of backgrounds, although there are identifiable groupings, that we have called: 'lifers' (a term first coined by CO8 and comprising predominantly baby boomers,[1] first-generation university-educated, idealistic people, who joined the service at a young age); 'second careerists' (often having had previous careers in teaching, the armed forces, the police, health and social work); and 'offender managers'[2] (more recent recruits with varied backgrounds, for whom probation is one of a number of jobs they expect to have throughout their working lives). To illustrate this embryonic typology, we present three individual pen portraits.

Beginnings and routes into probation

Our interviewees came from backgrounds ranging from economically deprived and tainted with criminality at one extreme to comfortable and privileged at the other. At one end of the spectrum, a female probation worker who joined in 2001 had experienced extreme poverty as a child, together with a period in foster care. Her father was at one point in custody for domestic violence and her mother had been on probation. Although only young, she remembered well her mother's probation officer: 'Mr B. I was only six or seven but I used to have long talks with him about politics; I would test out my world view, even at that age' (PW3). Obviously bright, PW3 claimed to have been 'saved by education'. This background contrasted sharply with another female interviewee, PW8, whose father was a diplomat and with a chief officer who recalled:

My father was a consultant psychiatrist, … my mum a nurse and grandfather a doctor, and a lot of clerics [in the family]. And I declared at the age of four I was going to be Archbishop of Canterbury.

(CO15)

Between these extremes, it was notable that many of our interviewees came from professional middle-class or aspiring working-class backgrounds with encouraging parents. Among the middle-class group, the medical and legal professions were prominent. One interviewee (PW17) with five years experience, and whose mother is a psychotherapist, only realized his relative privilege after joining the probation service and working with offenders, but more typical was a chief officer, now in his fifties who joined the probation service in the 1970s. He recognized his advantaged background at an early age:

I went to school in Surrey, leafy Surrey, but it was next to a kind of an approved school. I think that's what they were called in those days. Anyway, they were naughty boys and they were there as residential and it was literally the next building, and we used to play football with them. And I was aware of these kids, these boys coming from a completely different world and they were in this institution. And that I suppose was my first awareness … I thought I was going to go into medicine and do that kind of thing … my dad was a doctor, and my mum was a nurse, so I came from that sort of background; sort of public service and, you know, all that kind of stuff. So that's what I grew up with.

(CO5)

Among the interviewees from working-class backgrounds, a number of patterns were discernible in their narratives. Some grew up in areas where crime was a significant problem. Some remembered the hardships of their parents and, in contrast, the life-chances that were opening up for their own generation. The following two extracts are from interviewees, one male and one female, who both joined the probation service in the 1970s:

When I think back, my parents both left school when they were 14, they had no choice, they went to work, went through the war, had very little money. And both my brother and I went to Cambridge, which was extraordinary. Both of us got virtually full grants. They thought … I mean education to them was absolutely the be all and end all of, I mean they were very intelligent people, who had had no opportunities. And I thought I'd been incredibly privileged to have that kind of … you know, not financially, but to have that kind of support and background, and all the rest of it. And when I went to university, I found there were people who were very [laugh] privileged, in a way that I had never realized existed, I suppose. But I think that stuck with me. I thought well I've done really well out of this system, and I wanted … I think felt quite strongly I wanted to put something back into people who hadn't had those opportunities.

(CO13)

My family were probably upper working class, lower middle class, with aspirations for their children. I mean my dad left school during the Depression and got a job in Sheffield, in the steel industry. He was a blue-collar worker, so it was [working in] the offices really. But they'd always supported education ... they just wanted to support their children, and that's it. But we didn't have any ... there was no connection with crime or problems; it was a very secure, reasonably frugal upbringing, but there was no issues. In fact, I often look back and I think that what I got from my upbringing was just stability, just support. I can't really recall having a major problem until way after university you know, having to confront anything that was difficult in life.

(FPW6)

Lifers

While these interviewees come from different backgrounds, they form part of a distinct group within our sample whom we have called 'lifers'. For them probation was often regarded as being a vocation, a lifelong commitment and their one main career. Members of this group often discovered an interest in probation work at a young age, one interviewee deciding she wanted to be a probation officer after reading Brendan Behan's book *Borstal Boy* at the age of 13 (CO14).[3] She mentioned this to a teacher, who arranged for a relative who was a probation officer to come and talk to the class. She never looked back. Another lifer (CO4) came from a 'long line of teachers' and recalled as a sixth-form student picking up a brochure on the probation service and thinking that it promised a meaningful career with a purpose. PW9, a practising Catholic while at school, remembered being interested in Catholic social policy on imprisonment and enjoyed studying penal affairs in class, although he trained for the priesthood before joining the probation service.

Other lifers were influenced after leaving school. One male chief officer who joined in the 1970s took a gap year before university and worked as a volunteer in an inner city Simon Community hostel. While doing this he was inspired by a probation officer who used to visit the hostel to check on a schizophrenic alcoholic man. The probation officer made an impression as 'a servant of the state, a street-level bureaucrat [Lipsky 1980], if you like, who was demonstrating a warmth and a humanity to this individual' (CO2). This theme of volunteering is common among the lifers. Although a few were volunteering before leaving school, the majority engaged in some form of volunteering while at university. For example, a female lifer who joined the probation service in 1982 studied English at university and undertook unpaid work with homeless people. In her final year, she contacted different agencies about careers and was invited to spend time in a probation office. She liked the people she met and their values:

> I decided that probation, both in terms of what it did, but also … I think this is really quite pertinent [laugh] … I actually liked the people I met. More than liked, I found I could quite admire the values they stood for and what they talked about.
>
> (CO3)

The volunteering was not always with the probation service, and while CO14 worked in probation offices close to her university, CO15 volunteered in an assessment centre for adolescents while studying theology and became interested in offenders, and FPW1 volunteered for prison visiting and working with young offenders while studying for a degree in classics, self-deprecatingly claiming to have left university 'fit for nothing'.

While volunteering was important to a number of lifers and formed part of their university days, to others the experience they gained and their personal growth and development while studying for a degree proved a critical point in their career decisions. Following a degree in history and education and while studying as a postgraduate to be a teacher, FPW6 became radicalized through his studies and decided to join the most radical profession of the time (the late 1970s), which he judged was social work (Bailey and Brake 1975; Statham 1978; Brake and Bailey 1980; Walker and Beaumont 1981); a change of direction in his training ensued. For PW23, studying for a criminal justice degree in 1990, combined with what he saw around him as a student in Liverpool, set him on a path towards probation work:

> I lived in Toxteth, and there were a lot of stuff going on there. You could see people walking around like I thought 'God there's a lot of people need some help here'. Then I noticed an advert for Victim Support up in the university refectory and I gave them a call, did some training, and then started working for them … [The degree course] it were just fantastic stuff, really were, made you look at things in a different light.
>
> (PW23)

These formative experiences encouraged PW23, after graduation, to start work in a hostel for young people at risk of offending. He encountered probation officers in the course of this work and went on to train as one himself, having decided that he wanted to work with offenders.

While some lifers recognized their vocation at university and applied to train as probation officers following graduation, others applied for ancillary jobs to gain experience before applying for training places. A number of chief officers began their careers as assistants. CO4 left university and secured a job as an assistant warden in a hostel:

The stint I did at the bail hostel really just confirmed this is what I want to do. And actually, I've never gone back into residential work, but I loved that 18 months in that hostel; I learnt so much. Every single new person that walked through the door just stretched my imagination.

(CO4)

Similarly, CO3 began her probation career as a hostel assistant in London. After leaving university, she decided to seek an assistant's job to 'check out' the work before applying for a Home Office-sponsored training place. Willing to move anywhere, she turned down a post in Manchester 'basically driving people around or bagging up people's property when they went to prison' because she was seeking more meaningful work; she duly found it in the hostel, working there until she obtained Home Office funding to study for the Certificate of Qualification in Social Work (CQSW). PW9, who had worked as a prison volunteer while at university, failed with his application in 1979 to the security services, and applied for a job he saw advertised as an assistant warden in a probation hostel. He was successful and stayed in the hostel for five years until he was seconded to do his CQSW. CO16 travelled abroad for a year after graduating and returned home in 1986 looking for a career:

I was interested in the probation service because I was interested in the criminal justice system but I was also interested in people and people's stories, if you like, and why they got themselves in situations that actually most of us could get ourselves into, if we went down a certain path. Human behaviour fascinated me, but also the criminal justice system did. And so I was thinking what would combine the two? Because obviously, there's other areas of criminal justice that didn't appeal, and this did, because the focus was on people and building working relationships with people.

(CO16)

She phoned her local probation office and began working there the following week as a volunteer helping offenders with literacy and numeracy skills. After applying for and securing a job as an assistant probation officer, she moved into hostels as a residential worker before going off for CQSW training.

Like CO16, CO9 found her way into the probation service after a brief post-university sojourn, though working in a museum rather than travelling. Although the museum job was a logical progression from her archaeology degree, she had wanted to work with people and subsequently started voluntary work with the probation service, which led to an ancillary post, from where she applied to be a probation officer. While claiming to have 'wandered into' probation, her motivation to join had been 'to make a contribution and feeling that I had something to offer, in terms of changing individuals' lives' (CO9).

Another lifer, CO8, had seemed destined for a legal career after completing his Law Society finals in 1974. However, he decided to apply for and take a job as an ancillary worker, before going on to take his MA in Social Work. The social justice element of probation work interested him in a way that a law career couldn't satisfy:

> It was an ideological time. Most people that I knew, who came to probation at that point, had a very strong political and structural understanding. Which kind of led people, I think, to say well, let's go and work in the bits where you can actually change things, and actually redress some of the social injustice and social imbalance around … that level of structural understanding of how society works as a day-to-day kind of part of your job, you know, you absorbed it, you understood that, that was part of what was making the world tick.
>
> (CO8)

CO8 clearly had a political awareness and social conscience; he thought deeply about the structure of society and its inequalities. This belief in social justice and a commitment to 'doing something' was evident in other lifers. As discussed above, PW23 in 1990 was influenced by the conditions he saw around him in Toxteth, coupled with his university education and, in the late 1970s, CO1 described himself as:

> A young, left-leaning person, that was absolutely committed to helping people who, at that point in time, I would have said were oppressed and who were suffering all the consequences of poverty. And my God, did I see that in the late '70s, in Middlesbrough. You know, that was the highest unemployment rate in mainland UK at that point in time.
>
> (CO1)

These lifers, therefore, found their worldviews developing during their university courses and saw a career in probation as a means to confront inequality. As we will see, some of these same attitudes and values existed among the second careerists, though commonly they were more latent as they pursued other careers, but not always finding them sufficiently fulfilling.

Our lifers group then comprises approximately 25 people who felt the pull of probation work early in life, at school or university, shortly after graduating, during post-university gap years, postgraduate training, during false starts in unsuitable jobs or while drifting and 'looking for something'. Some had clear vocations, some had a sense of public service, many felt a sense of relative privilege. Some, too, were influenced by faith. Probation in its origins had strong religious connections, and we found a strong sense of duty and service running through our interview sample that contributed to interviewees' motivations to join the probation service. Although the service ethos was not always religious, in some cases it was. Two retired probation workers had been directly influenced in their career choice by their religious convictions:

> I think my decision to become a probation officer goes right back to late adolescence. And I think I can identify a number of facets which influenced

my decision. It was partly the developing religious sense that you get in adolescence, you know, wondering what life's all about and what you ought to be doing and I think I was brought up with an ethos of service, so there was that there.

(FPW7)

Both my wife and I were very active members of different Baptist churches and there was, if you like, a sort of a Christian vocation. We met a lot of people whose lives were devoted to service. A lot of them were missionaries. I didn't think that was for us, but the idea of service was very strong. And I was involved in working with young people in an open church youth club, which was quite tricky, quite demanding, sometimes quite dangerous. But that was a lot more appealing and attractive to me, than the day job I did with IBM, where I was doing quite well, and making more money than I subsequently did as a member of the probation service. But the appeal of probation was strong.

(FPW5)

CO15 remembered being a serious, pious young boy with clerics in his family; he studied theology at university and described himself as an atheist, though one with faith. He felt he was 'stuck' with faith in the sense of believing there is a purpose to life and he had always felt a responsibility to 'making the world a better place and giving this person the best opportunity to change'. In a similar way, PW9 had grown up as a 'keen practising Catholic' and spent three years in a seminary training to be a priest. However, this had not worked out and he went off to university before finding work in a probation hostel.

Rather to our surprise, we found that some more recent recruits were also motivated by their faiths, and we explore the changing nature of the tenacious 'voice' of religion in probation work further in Chapter 7.

Second careerists

Our second group, the second careerists, form a distinct group by virtue of having already forged a career seemingly unrelated to probation or by spending a considerable number of years in several jobs before joining the probation service. At least 24 of our 60 interviewees fell into this group. Of these, nine had been employed in health and social service-related work, six had armed forces or police backgrounds and four had been teachers. Some had joined the forces and/ or the police and worked in other disparate occupations before finding their niche in probation work.

Three interviewees (PW5, PW19, PW20) had formerly served as police officers. PW20, a PSO in his fifties, had been a police officer 'way back when, a lifetime ago'. He had also worked as a miner, builder and plumber before joining probation in 1996:

Essentially I kind of wandered in by mistake, if you like. I've always wanted to get involved with people and I were volunteering at the time, SOVA (Society of Voluntary Associates). I were volunteering with those and then I kind of moved into probation, basically as an assistant to the accommodation officer. That were a role that somebody had got within the organization and I became their assistant, if you like. At that time, nobody wanted the job [laugh] … there was quite a lot of jobs about, nobody wanted it. It were really poorly paid. But I thought it were an opportunity to get involved and help people make that change, you know, so that's what I did.

(PW20)

His motivation for joining the probation service partly reflected a sensibility, like the lifers, to help less fortunate people but, in addition, his comments reflected his other careers that required practical and problem-solving skills:

I almost wanted, when I started, to get inside people's heads and say right, let's have a look at what's going on here, let's put it back together. Because, you know, even if you can't change 'em, you can contain the risk until they're ready to change themselves. Surely we can do that.

(PW20)

While PW20 dwelled lightly on his police service experience, PW5 (a male senior probation officer (SPO) in his fifties with 25 years' probation experience) found it a formative experience. He joined the merchant navy from school aged 17 and left in the late 1970s to join the police. He found that he had walked into something like *Life on Mars* only worse.[4] Disturbed by the levels of violence towards offenders and the routine fabrication of evidence, he complained and found that he was ostracized by other officers, leading to his resignation after less than two years:

The levels of violence and criminal activity in the police was just totally unacceptable. It didn't fit my value system or my beliefs, I just decided to leave. But one of the things that I found when I was in the police is, you were quite often dealing with either people who were bad or people that were mad. It's probably not a nice way to put it, but at one extreme, you had criminals who needed to be arrested. And other times, we were dealing with people who had a whole range of mental health problems. And we weren't, as an agency, going in, in those days, and saying how can we try and solve this issue? So when I resigned from the police, I thought well I don't quite know what it is I want to do. So I went to a careers office and they said well you can do one of our computer tests and see what it comes out as. And it came out, the first choice going away to sea as a deck officer, second choice came out being a police officer. And the third choice was social work/probation. So I thought well I've tried the first two, I'll give the third one a shot. So I became a probation volunteer.

(PW5)

The police culture also troubled PW19, a female probation officer in her thirties with ten years' probation experience. She joined the police after leaving university with a law degree, but left after 18 months:

> I knew that culturally, being a police officer wasn't for me. The culture of the police, it didn't fit with my view of criminal justice, I guess. I just didn't feel comfortable. On one level, some of the negativity about me being a graduate; negativity about me being female. And I just realized quite quickly that I didn't wanna just lock people up and move onto the next prisoner; I wanted to find out a bit more about people. So I realized I couldn't hack it in the police, decided to leave, and thought well, what am I gonna do? And I actually went to a careers office and did one of those computer program things. And that [probation officer] was one of the jobs that came up, and it was just luck really that they were just recruiting the second lot of TPOs. I managed to get the application form in literally on the last day of the closing date. And that was it.
>
> (PW19)

The transition from the forces to probation was not always a direct one. PW5 went from the merchant navy to the police before finding probation. PW13 also experienced a transitional period between the navy and the probation service. Now a probation officer in her late forties with 20 years' probation experience, she spent 14 years in the navy and during her last two years as a chief WREN, she was responsible for family welfare matters. When she left the navy, she took a job doing telephone sales. Finding this unfulfilling she called into the probation office she walked past daily and volunteered her services. Finding an aptitude for the work, she applied for, and obtained, a temporary job in a probation hostel:

> And I have to say, my old boss, who was a lieutenant commander, because I asked him to do a reference, he said to me, 'do you know what you're doing?' I said I haven't got a clue but, you know, it's a job [laugh]. But I then worked in this hostel for 18 months, because it was only a temporary contract and I found that there were certain similarities, there were certain things that crossed over about separation, about family abuse, what happens, alcoholism; because there is quite a drink problem, in my opinion, in the navy, and that kind of culture, and that is often common with families that are linked to offending. I thought really, you know, I might do the CQSW then. And I applied and got it.
>
> (PW13)

It has only been in recent years that the problems of resettling ex-forces personnel and their possible high risk of offending has been the subject of professional and academic debate (NAPO 2008, 2009; Treadwell 2010; McGarry and Walklate 2011). However, the existence of empathy and transferable skills among those second careerists who have worked in the forces has been taken for granted and rarely acknowledged in probation work. In fact, PW13 claimed to have experienced discrimination on her training course, based on stereotyped judgements, because she was a member of 'Patten's Army' (named after John Patten, a Home Office Minister between 1987 and 1992, who encouraged ex-forces personnel into probation).

Two interviewees who had served in the army followed considerably more circuitous routes into the probation service than the naval cases just referred to. PW12, a probation officer in his forties with ten years' probation experience, left school at 16 and joined the army without any qualifications. He left five-and-a-half years later:

> I'd had enough by the time I was 21, so I had no sort of direction, if you like. By the time I was 21, I'd done so many things with the army. So I sort of flitted through different jobs, different careers. I worked for the security industry, security supervisor; I worked for Butlins for a few years, on and off working as, again, a security supervisor; worked as a postman, driver. And then I worked as a manager, running bars and restaurants for ten years on and off. The salary was okay but I just felt a bit burnt out and I just wanted a change. So I didn't really know where I was going. I resigned and I started studying with the Open University social sciences, just to see if it gave me some direction where to go. In the interim, I was just sort of [laugh] packing sausage rolls or whatever, just to keep the mortgage payments, etc. Worked for the post again, a courier driver. And then I identified the sort of work … I looked at what transferable skills I had, you know, life skills, working with people, and I sort of identified the probation service as somewhere where I might be able to bring some of my life skills, if you like. And I applied for a post as a relief supervisor in the hostels.
>
> (PW12)

PW10, a probation officer in her forties with 18 years' probation experience, came from a services family background, joined the army herself, but had to leave when she married a serviceman. She was accustomed to discipline and structure, adapting to living abroad and meeting different kinds of people. However, in the early 1980s she divorced and became homeless with a young son:

> Then I was housed by the local authority. And I suppose my value system changed, because I'd got a job as a community worker. I did all sorts of things really. I was a community worker, I was an auxiliary nurse, I was a care assistant, I washed dishes. My whole value system changed and I think what came out in me was probably a caring side. Then I was a home help with social services, and I decided that, I was getting older and I thought I'm enjoying this caring role, but I need to study, I need to gain qualifications because I need to improve my income. So that's when I applied to do social work.
>
> (PW10)

She went to university to study social work and while there discovered the probation service:

> They gave me a placement with probation. And because prior to that, I didn't know anything about probation, I didn't know anything about probation officers, and I did a six-month placement with probation, and just thought I like this; I like the structure, I like the people, I enjoyed the placement. At that time, they had day centres and things that you worked in. I liked working with primarily men. I liked … I was comfortable with the court arena. And again, I suppose, it probably made me feel quite comfortable because it reflected, for me, things that felt comfortable from my own childhood. So that was it then, I decided that, that's what I wanted to do.
>
> (PW10)

In addition to careers in the forces, health and social work were strong themes that ran through the working lives of our second careerists. On the health side, no fewer than seven interviewees had at some stage trained and/or worked in a health-related occupation. One had been a hospital administrator, others had experience closer to the frontline of healthcare, either supporting people with mental health issues, undertaking nurse training or working as psychiatric nurses or nursing assistants.

The social work thread in second careerists' backgrounds is not surprising: between the early 1970s and the mid-1990s probation workers were required to train as social workers. Of the social workers that crossed over, their motivations varied. PW11, a probation officer in his fifties with over 20 years' experience, initially worked as a mental health nurse before training to be a social worker. He left after eight years having been refused an extended leave period for his honeymoon and then worked in computing for a short period. Deciding that this was not for him, he fell back on his qualification, phoned his local probation service, was interviewed and offered a job. In contrast PW8, a probation officer in her fifties with over 20 years' probation experience, knew at age 17 that she wanted to be a probation officer but did not realize this ambition for many years. She did voluntary work while at school and left after her GCEs to take a job in residential childcare. From this she went on to work for the charity Toc H before moving on to co-ordinate the setting-up of victim support schemes. At the same time she worked as a probation volunteer before making the decision to study to qualify as a probation worker: 22 years after deciding she would be a probation officer, she realized her ambition.

In addition to the clusters of second careerists with forces/police and health/social care backgrounds, the third distinct cluster comprised those who had formerly been teachers (FPW2, FPW3, PW1, PW26). The length of time they had been teaching varied. PW26, in his twenties, qualified as a probation officer in 2010, but had formerly trained to be a teacher and worked for several years for a charity teaching numeracy and literacy. He came to the decision that he had taken this job as far as he could and decided to move into probation work, where he could continue working with disadvantaged people but in a more structured organization which offered him the scope to move around and progress. In contrast FPW2, a former assistant chief officer in her fifties, had taught biology for 15 years and was head of department when she made the move because she reached a point 'where I thought now, am I gonna continue doing this same thing for the rest of my life, or am I going to have a different experience and do something else?' While still teaching, she worked as a probation volunteer for two years, the experience of which confirmed to her that she should make the leap. Subsequently she enrolled to take an MSc in Applied Social Studies with the CQSW.

In these clusters of occupations, the second careerists had developed transferable skills suitable, they believed, for employment in the probation service. However, deployment of these skills was not the only factor in applying to the probation service. Former social workers were looking for a more structured and focused outlet for their skills, while those with experience of 'command and control' occupations were looking for more autonomy and humanity.

Not every second careerist fitted neatly into these clusters. FPW8, a retired probation officer in her sixties, left school at 16 to work in a public library and pursued a career as a librarian until her marriage broke up. She then went to university as an undergraduate, subsequently took a research job but left it to work in a probation hostel, having developed an interest in criminal justice through a family incident. Hostel work surprised her:

> It was a total culture shock and I thought I'm not gonna stick this for long, this is not really what I imagined it would be. But within weeks, I was totally hooked; I absolutely loved the work. I didn't particularly like the hours because it was really tiring doing 24 hours, but I did really enjoy the work. So I suppose that's how I got into probation. So by the time I decided to do my professional qualification, I really knew what it was all about.
>
> (FPW8)

PW2, a probation officer in her thirties with six years' probation experience, had:

> [H]ad hundreds of jobs before. I was in sales, had a company car and I thought 'What's the point of this?' I had a friend in nursing so I became a nursing assistant, I loved it. But then I deviated into probation.
>
> (PW2)

Similarly PW7, a probation officer in her fifties with over 20 years probation experience, had worked in numerous jobs including journalist, jewellery shop manager, Lake District tour guide, pub worker and receptionist. While the interviewees with these zig-zag careers may have appeared to have stumbled into probation, they were clearly seeking meaningful work; as PW7 reflected, 'the pieces of the jigsaw were already there, but I didn't have the picture on the box'.

Discovering 'the picture on the box' meant that this group in particular had the expectation of being able to 'make a difference' through building relationships with offenders, and some had become disillusioned as the job became increasingly desk-bound (see Chapters 3 and 6).

The role of serendipity

As we have discussed thus far, our interviewees came to probation through a number of routes, with a few noticeable trends that we have highlighted. One other trend was the serendipitous route. While some probation workers decided early in life that they would pursue a career with the probation service and others found a way in through the voluntary work they had undertaken, others drifted into the service. A number of these people were uncertain about their career direction and the catalyst for at least four proved to be encountering publicity material and job advertisements. Two of these discovered the probation service when they were looking for something more in their lives. One, PW25, was working in a supermarket in 1985, aged 25, having left teacher training college after becoming pregnant:

> I used to read the *Sunday Times*, before it was a Wapping rag [laugh] and every Sunday, there'd be a big half page or a page, saying 'why don't you become a probation officer?' And I thought yeah, that's what I want to do, without knowing what they did, or how they did it. And I was working at Makro [the supermarket chain] at that time, with a woman who became a big friend, and she said do you know what, I keep reading things in the *Sunday Times* about 'why don't you become a probation officer?' It must have said 'Why don't you become a probation officer, you can help people to blah blah blah blah'. And both of us had thought hey, that advert sounds like it, and then she said I'm going. So she trained a couple of years before me, and she retired last year. I think, it was about working with people, that's what I wanted to do.
>
> (PW25)

The other, CO12, was a university fresher who was questioning her future direction following a family bereavement:

> I was in my first year at university, studying politics, with no real sense of where that was leading, what I wanted to do … And crazy as it sounds, I got onto a bus one day, I was in Newcastle at the time, studying, and sat down, and there on the seat next to me was a leaflet all about the probation service. I'd never heard of the probation service, didn't know anything about it. Read the leaflet, and I knew instantly that, that was what I wanted to do. And from that day on, because I'd only just finished my first year at university, my career, if you like, was mapped out.
>
> (CO12)

The two others were different in their motivations. The first, CO13, was drifting slightly, having decided that teaching was not for her despite completing a PGCE:

> I graduated, I did a year's PGCE teacher training and didn't really like it. Applied for a couple of jobs in schools and didn't get them, probably because I was pretty half-hearted. Really didn't know what to do. So I was doing some temporary jobs in London, just, you know, paying the rent really. And I literally, I was leafing through the *Guardian*, or whatever the equivalent of the Wednesday section then was, in about 1973 it would have been. And I saw one of these Home Office adverts for, you know, graduates to train to be probation officers. And I thought well that sounds a bit interesting. So I went along to my local probation office, chatted to somebody there. And I thought this sounds alright, another couple of years at university paid for, I'll apply for that. I'll do it for a few years and then I'll decide what I really want to do.
>
> (CO13)

The second, CO6, was in his first social care job following university and questioning its morality and worth:

> I became a probation officer by answering an advertisement in the *Sunday Times* in about 1980. Graduated from college/university and I was working in social care locally; worked in residential social work. Very quickly twigged that, that institution was run for the benefit of the staff, not for the youngsters who were actually remanded there, and that any changes you wanted to make, you know, the longevity of well-established staff would mitigate [sic] any kind of initiative, or anything like that. So I answered an advert from the *Sunday Times* and just went through a recruitment process.
>
> (CO6)

Offender managers

We have called our third distinctive group 'offender managers' and these tend to be more recent recruits, principally those who joined the probation service after 1997 and who experienced the TPO training framework that ran until 2010 (the Diploma in Probation Studies). To some of this group, the term offender manager will be as familiar as probation officer. They will have joined the service after it had been confirmed by Paul Boateng in August 2000 to be an enforcement agency and may not have experienced probation work without the Offender Management Model (OMM) introduced in 2005. Many of this group shared much of the motivation of lifers and second careerists, with common values and a capacity for critical thinking and reflection, but interviewees in this group saw their daily job differently in at least three ways: it was dominated by computer-based risk assessment rather than engaging in face-to-face work with offenders (explored in Chapter 3); it did not involve any significant time visiting offenders at home or in the community (explored in Chapter 3); and inter-agency collaboration was regarded as essential and uncontentious, at least in principle (explored in Chapter 4). We also found an additional dimension among the offender managers. On the surface we saw a pragmatism, a sense that working for a public sector organization offered job status, security and promotion, though one interviewee commented that her parents would have preferred her to go into medicine or business. Beneath the surface, however, was a principled rehabilitative approach to working with offenders and a readiness to move on to other jobs if they were not allowed to work in the way that they wanted. This group contained some people who felt they had been 'mis-sold' the job. As one interviewee said, 'I should have really looked at the application form when it kept talking about compliance and enforcement' (TPO9).

The veneer of pragmatism is illustrated by TPO7 who, now in his thirties, had worked as a legal executive before joining the service as a probation service officer and then moving on to train as a probation officer. He explained that his reasons for changing career and choosing probation, were:

> More accident than design … it was interesting but I wouldn't say it was kind of a mission, if you see what I mean … I was working as a legal executive, and it was shorter hours for more money, and I'd always worked in criminal law firms, and there isn't really any money in that at all. That sounded terribly mercenary but I don't mean it quite like that. But I couldn't really afford to progress. So this seemed really interesting in terms of just who you're working with … and it turned out to be much more broad-ranging about what you do with people and how you deal with people, and things you know and learn. … And I thought that sounds nice, they'll pay us reasonable money to do that and huge public service holidays, just to be nice to people. Hey that's a great job [laugh]. So that's kind of why I went for it really [laugh].
>
> (TPO7)

Moving from the private to the public sector TPO7 was surprised by the levels of anxiety that colleagues were experiencing over computerization and changing job roles, and after four years of working for the service he admitted that he understood but did not share their anxiety. While TPO7 was committed to his work and was keen to progress his career, he wore his occupation lightly and, figuratively, didn't take his work home to reflect and dwell upon, unlike many interviewees in the other two groups.

Though less flippant, TPO10 was also pragmatic in her work. In her twenties and on the verge of qualifying as a probation officer, she had studied sociology and psychology at university and had worked in the courts for 12 months' experience before joining the probation service. She had found probation training to be a steep learning curve, but was able to reconcile public protection, risk management and rehabilitation:

I think that people that have been in the service longer, that come from a social work background, they're resistant on a personal level to the changes, you know, and they take it as a personal affront.... And although people take their jobs very seriously, the ultimate goal should be to protect the public as best as they can, and to help this person. And I think the new breed, perhaps, of people coming from my cohort, certainly perhaps in the last five/six/seven years, I think we're very much more adaptable ... I think now, we can sometimes feel swamped but it's part of the job. I always think just like, you know, you're not gonna die, get on with it [laugh].

(TPO10)

She was looking forward to building a career following her qualification. Despite the turbulent context of probation work, she refused to be dragged into the pessimistic mindset of some of her colleagues and was optimistic about contributing to the specialist ongoing work that the service was doing to manage risk. Arguably, she could be described as being one of a 'new breed' of effective young female probation workers who are also good pragmatic managerialists, contributing to the feminization of probation work, which we discuss further in Chapter 7.

While pragmatic, our offender managers were committed to their work and many had been pulled towards probation work through their commitment to helping people less fortunate than themselves. Unlike the lifers, who frequently studied unrelated degrees, they tended to have studied social science degrees at university but, like the lifers, they expressed interest in criminal justice and working with people at a relatively young age. Echoing Deering's findings (2010), our probation workers tended to hold similar common values irrespective of when they joined the service and how they were trained. Nevertheless, the offender managers recognized their own difference from their longer-serving colleagues, highlighting a clash of cultures:

I have had a few run-ins with one of the officers here, who is very much the social work, 'befriend, advise, assist', and I think has a more relaxed view, and ... we're very much target-driven now and, you know, enforcement, that kind of thing. I kind of sit on the fence, I'm kind of in the middle, I would say. But he's very much sort of left wing, 'give 'em a chance, give 'em a chance'. And I think there's gotta be boundaries, and we have argued, or had some discussions. He would give me his view that I should do, and I would give him my view, and we wouldn't agree [laugh], we'd just agree to disagree.

(PW14)

This is two-sided. The lifers were all too aware of the way that probation had changed and while some had adapted, others had trouble accepting the rise of offender managers, the propensity of some for control rather than care and their adherence to process:

When I've worked with TPOs, this lot that have come through, you know, I've done home visits with people and they've said 'can you really say that', and 'can you really do that', and thinking, and panicking all the time about things. And it's just like yeah, of course you can, yeah as long as you've logged these things and you can justify what you've done, of course you can. And the whole panicking factor, shall I breach them, shall I breach them? Well do you really think ... can we justify not breaching them, can we work our way through this? They're just like so hell bent on this breaching.[5]

(PW23)

The pragmatism of the offender managers extended to an expectation that they may leave if the probation service failed to provide opportunities for career progression or failed to promote ways of working with offenders that accommodated their personal beliefs. Drawing on Hirschman's model introduced in Chapter 1, our offender managers would be more likely than lifers or second careerists to 'exit' as a means of satisfying their occupational needs.

Training

The Home Office introduced the first probation officer training course in 1930 and in 1946 the Rainer House training centre was established in London (Vanstone 2004: 98). FPW5, now in his seventies, joined the probation service in 1965 at the age of 27 and remembered undertaking the Rainer House one-year certificate of probation course that combined practical experience with theoretical input taught by Home Office Inspectors and by criminologists invited in from universities. After two months gaining experience in a family welfare agency followed by three months' intensive academic work, FPW5 had to prepare and pass several academic pieces of work before being sent out to spend five months' placement in a probation office, which he found 'absolutely outstanding'. Of a similar age, FPW7 also completed the Rainer House course and was similarly positive in that it 'just reinforced what I wanted to do and what I thought I was coming in to do'.

The training framework has moved on since the Rainer House days and the recent history of qualifying training for probation officers has been one of a steady move away from social work. Most of our interviewees could be divided into three groups in terms of their training. Many qualified as social workers under the CQSW regime, from 1970 to 1990, though even within this framework, they saw themselves as 'different'. This was generic social work training and probationers would always be in the minority – as a small group (and self-styled elite) specializing in work that was always on the periphery of social work. Most interviewees enjoyed their placements whether these were in a probation setting or not, but the value of the academic content was more contested. Attitudes towards training within this group ranged from 'transformative' to 'useless' depending, it seemed, on the extent to which courses were either inspirational or recognized the different skills required to work in probation. On the one hand, at its best, the training could create a hothouse, bringing bright people together who formed strong networks that would endure as each individual went off to build their career:

> I applied to Manchester, got in on the course, which was quite prestigious. I mean there were all sorts of people there, people who became big hitters really, and it was obviously then a combined social work and probation course, with a sort of specialist element. And on that course, there was five who became chiefs; one, who became one of the regional managers [laugh]. So it was quite a seminal [group]. I mean there were some extremely bright people on the social work course as well, some of them have gone on to quite influential careers in social work.
>
> (CO13)

On the other hand, some probation workers succeeded despite their training, which brought back uncomfortable memories. During the mid-1980s, CO16 experienced a worrying training exercise:

> It was at the height of all the diversity kind of stuff that was coming out of everywhere. And we had this cross-cultural studies set, and it was just awful. It was quite a big mixture in the group of white, Asian, black people. And initially, all got on really well until we started doing this cross cultural studies and the teacher seemed hell bent on turning us against each other somehow.... One of the things that she told us to do, she said I want to split all the white people off and the black people, I want you to go into separate rooms and I want you ... and our instructions were negative images, negative stereotypes of black people. And I want you to be honest, got to get it up there, put it on flipcharts ... so you're naive, I would never do anything like that now, but then, okay all of us thinking well, she's asked us to do it, it's about learning, we'll do it. Put all the stereotypes up there. Felt very uncomfortable, walking back in, but thinking well actually, they'll be told to do the same. [But] their brief was positive stereotypes of white people. So, of course, the disparity between the two sets of information was really startling and when it was up on the wall, it ... visually, you can imagine it, can't you? We looked like racist pigs, the whole lot of us.... And it really started off a problem between us all and it never mended. And it's stayed with me ever since.
>
> (CO16)

The probation specialism became more marked under the new regime of the Diploma in Social Work introduced in 1989 and the final break from social work came in 1997 with the Diploma in Probation Studies (DipPS) which lasted until 2010. The DipPS was regarded by those who experienced it as being extremely demanding and as generating a high level of anxiety, both in terms of the requirements of the work and the availability of jobs at the end of training. The TPOs we interviewed were acutely aware of the need to successfully complete the training as they were the final group, with no follow-up cohort below them to act as a safety net:

> Incredibly difficult. Very, very pressured. But I think I've had a good two years, I've been quite fortunate in terms of managers, good managers; I've had positive experiences; I haven't failed any modules, at the moment; and the pressure of failing ... especially it being the last course, there's limited opportunity for that kind of buffer of being held back a cohort. There isn't that any more. So if you fail, I mean, that's not gonna happen but ... because of my own anxieties, fail something and does it delay my qualification, it has implications ... there's a lot riding on it.
>
> (TPO4)

The training itself was a blend of practical on-the-job training and classroom-based academic input. The on-the-job training was described as haphazard, ad hoc and undertaken in pressured probation offices. One interviewee, TPO3, who had a supportive PDA (practice development assessor – formerly practice teacher) described the experience as 'fantastic', as it opened 'a whole world of experiences'. Another, TPO10, found it to be the steepest learning curve she had experienced, with 'no mollycoddling', as she found when put into an interview situation at short notice and without training:

> I think I was a bit shocked that, as someone who had only just come to the service, I know I passed CRB [criminal record] checks and gone through the interview process, but I think I was a bit shocked that I could step into it that quickly, you know, because I felt very green. I felt like, God, I was only in university a year ago, reading about things that you people do, and now I'm sat here, listening to it, realizing that it's very real.
>
> (TPO10)

The academic element, though difficult for some and too basic in parts for others, was generally regarded as a beneficial time for learning and reflection. For example, TPO6 felt the benefits thus:

> The university side of it has really helped. I think the theoretical underpinning and what we've been taught at university has been amazingly relevant, which has been a real shock to me, but having done a degree before, I know it can be quite vague and quite theoretical, and not really ... you know, I mean, you get out in the real world, it doesn't apply in the slightest. That is sometimes true with this university work but I think, on the whole, it's been very relevant; it's given you a much better understanding of why people behave like they do and the kind of underlying social developmental problems that make people like that. And also, you know, a lot of the

university training has been about the law side of things and also the development of kind of evidence-based practice, and why the probation service works like it does. Which also helps you really, I think, to deal with it; you can kind of see why the service has developed like it has, which I think helps you in your practice.

(TPO6)

It was notable, however, that few of the offender managers talked about the 'political and structural understanding' of society that CO8 (see earlier in this chapter) and others of that generation spoke about with such passion.

Several spoke of experiencing financial hardship in order to train. According to one TPO, it had been 'like an emotional roller-coaster [but] … parts have been joyful … and exciting' (TPO5). Others talked about splitting up with partners and friends, partly as a consequence of the pressure of training but partly as a result of being personally challenged to think about new ideas and reflect on their own lives. It was clear that both those delivering and those receiving the training viewed the job as requiring a high level of intelligence, skill and reflection.

Conclusion

Regardless of age or experience, our interviewees shared a belief in the worthwhileness of working with offenders in the community. This central tenet was expressed in a variety of ways but always included a belief in the capacity of the individual to change for the better under the right guidance, supervision and monitoring. For some this belief stemmed from a past or present religious conviction; for others it was rooted in personal experiences and humanitarian or political concerns. A sense of duty and a structural analysis of society were common in the lifers group. For those at the experiential rather than intellectual end of the spectrum, personal influence through relationship-building was key (in criminological terms, interactionist and differential association theories implicitly underpinned their view of the work). Everyone we interviewed recognized the importance of public protection, risk assessment and risk management and many expressed a 'left realist' position, recognizing the rights of victims and the law-abiding community.

In this chapter we have excavated the backgrounds of probation workers and have explored their motivations to join the probation service and their various routes into the service; we have considered the groupings that they fall into and discussed their training experiences. We are not arguing that every probation worker fits neatly into one of our categories, nor that it is possible to 'read off' a comprehensive set of characteristics and attitudes from them. Nevertheless, we found sufficient distinguishing features to suggest that these three categories are influencing probation cultures and identities in different ways. In this final section, we present three pen portraits to illustrate our three categories. We have chosen (and given fictitious names to) three interviewees whose stories seem to us to convey in human form the more abstract motivations and experiences that we have introduced in this chapter. They have also managed to retain a positive sense of identity, despite the turbulent and troubled conditions under which they are working. While we heard – and will later refer to – unhappy stories from our interviewees, we were nevertheless struck by the overwhelming determination of most of our participants to 'make probation work'. As the book progresses, we will refer back and add to these portraits, bringing them together with other data to construct a model of probation worker cultures and identities in Chapter 8.

The Lifer: Peter

Peter is a male chief officer in his late fifties, with more than 35 years' experience.

Peter has a privileged background, coming from a family of medics and clerics. He attended public school and studied theology at university but decided he didn't have a vocation for the priesthood. Now an atheist, he retains a faith in human nature and a duty to serve. He did voluntary work while at school and worked in an assessment centre for young adolescents after university ('I've locked nine-year-olds in cells'). He had a strong sense of social justice, social inclusion and 'giving people another chance'. He believed that, given the chance, everyone would choose to be a 'socialized insider' rather than a 'disturbed outsider'.

Peter applied for a postgraduate two-year CQSW course and recalls the mixture of psychodynamic and cognitive behavioural approaches that were taught. But he had a 'Damascene moment' during one lecture that convinced him he wanted to work in probation. He qualified in 1972 and worked in London with a generic caseload. Later, he moved to the training centre for two years, then became a senior, followed by two years in a day centre, developing programmes for women offenders and Black offenders ('I was seen as a bit of a Tigger – probably a bit overactive') and then managing a hostel. After this came promotion to assistant chief probation officer.

Peter was active in NAPO (see Chapter 7) at local level and stayed so until he was appointed chief. He recalls going on strike as well as telling a court that he couldn't write a report on a 'not guilty' plea because his union said he shouldn't and being disciplined by his manager.

Peter retains a belief in the importance of relationships with offenders, and the Christian value of hating the crime but not the criminal. He is optimistic for probation under the coalition government and thinks that it will possibly give discretion back to professionals. He is optimistic about new (predominantly work-based) training arrangements because he thinks the service will be able to carry more influence.

He believes that no other organization understands offenders like probation.

The second careerist: Bill

Bill is a male senior probation officer in his fifties, with over 25 years' experience.

Bill joined the merchant navy and went away to sea aged 17 as a deck officer cadet with an apprenticeship to become a navigating officer. After seven years in the navy, in the late 1970s he left to join the police and stayed less than two years, troubled by the corruption and violence of police culture. He then became a probation volunteer and enjoyed the work so much that he applied to his local polytechnic and did a BA in Applied Social Studies followed by the one year CQSW at a university, qualifying in 1986. He was the first member of his family to attend university and found it a struggle to cope financially as he had a mortgage; he sold some of his naval souvenirs to help his funds. As a mature student he treated university as a nine-to-five job and particularly enjoyed the placement element of his training. On qualification he started work in a town centre probation office and inherited a heavy caseload from the start due to the death in service of a colleague.

Bill spent his first 18 months doing general probation officer work, i.e. writing court reports, court duty, seeing both custody cases and those in the community. He then moved on to manage a day centre and ran programmes with colleagues most days of the week. This was before accredited programmes and they would design and deliver programmes themselves. After three years in the centre he needed a new challenge and moved to a prison secondment for 18 months. The prison officers were quite militant and resistant to changes he tried to introduce but he found they responded better to him in his role as a union (NAPO) representative. He had ambitions for progression and left the prison when he obtained a senior's post in a well-established office. It was hard initially because old practices needed updating and staff were resistant to the point of refusal. It felt like a 'baptism of fire'. He went on to manage community service teams, programme/intervention teams and a victims unit.

Although the pay is inadequate for the level of responsibility, Bill has always enjoyed working in probation and would recommend the job to anyone, 'I go home, you know, most days thinking I've done a good, worthwhile job that is making a difference.' He is 'an eternal optimist' and feels that whatever the government does, a probation service will remain.

The offender manager: Gemma

Gemma is a female probation officer in her twenties, with four years' experience.

Gemma's childhood ambition was to be a solicitor and she was interested in criminal justice from an early age. She studied law and criminology at university but found that she enjoyed criminology more than law and wanted to work more intensively with offenders. She applied to be a TPO in 2006 and was accepted for the DipPS. She found the training intensive but it equipped her with transferable skills which are potentially useful for other jobs.

Gemma carries a generic caseload but is specializing to a degree in work with prolific and priority offenders. She considers that she wears many different 'hats': the work involves a mothering role, an enforcer role and a supportive role. The work is never boring. She works long hours, sometimes until midnight and at weekends, but is happy to do so, even though it has caused problems at home and she is now separated from her partner, bringing up her small daughter on her own. She assesses that the ratio of computer work to working with offenders face-to-face is 70/30. She enjoys working in an open-plan office and finds her colleagues supportive. Most of her colleagues have a similar mindset to her, but she has debates with older officers who are more social-work oriented. 'We agree to disagree'. As a woman, she takes it for granted that 'the majority of us are women' and that she is always treated with respect (see Chapter 7 for further discussion about the feminization of probation).

Gemma is happy with the term 'offender' and is comfortable working with the police, prisons and social services. She believes that the public doesn't understand what probation do, but 'nobody else works with offenders like we do'. She has no wish to be promoted because this would take her away from direct work with offenders and because she thinks senior workers are 'run ragged'. She would love to work in the courts at some point but she does not necessarily see herself remaining in probation for ever. She is passionate about domestic violence work and, ideally, she wants to run a women's refuge in the future.

3 There's a time and place

What do probation workers actually *do*? In this chapter we examine in detail the daily routines of probation workers and the physical environments in which they work. We discuss the changing nature of the buildings in which probation offices are located and their greater focus on security. We analyse the benefits and frustrations of working predominantly at computers in open-plan offices or delivering classroom-based 'programmes' rather than making home visits and being a recognized part of a local community. We acknowledge the variety of different settings in which probation work is undertaken, including approved premises, prisons and unpaid work in the community.

Daily routines

The tyranny of the computer

> I've become de-skilled in human contact but highly skilled in IT. I'm a kid of the enforcement brigade. I've lost confidence.
>
> (PW2)

All our interviewees and the recent Justice Committee Report (House of Commons Justice Committee 2011) confirm that most qualified probation officers (as opposed to workers delivering programmes or working in specialisms) spend the majority of their time in their offices with their computers. One recent recruit anticipated the Justice Committee by guessing that 70 per cent of her time was spent at her computer (PW14); other workers suggested more:

> I mean the research has shown, what was it, 80 per cent of our time in front of a computer, which as far as I'm concerned, never changed anybody. Even I find myself at times thinking oh, so and so's coming in, they're getting in the way of what I've got to do. No, *they're* what I've got to do.
>
> (PW24)

OASys, or the Offender Assessment System is the latest in a series of computer-assisted risk assessment tools used by the probation service and was rolled out across the probation service in 2003. While probation workers were already well-socialized in the concept of risk assessment tools, Mair *et al.* (2006) point out that the introduction of OASys was closely associated with other major political changes in the service that made it less than welcome:

> OASys, then, is not just a neutral, systematic assessment instrument; it is burdened by links to the centralization of the probation service, the What Works initiative, the erosion of PO autonomy and clinical judgement, and integration with the Prison Service to form a National Offender Management Service (NOMS).
>
> (Mair *et al.* 2006: 11)

Despite this, Mair *et al.* found that workers were less opposed to OASys than might have been expected, given its time-consuming nature, with around half of respondents being at least reasonably positive about it. Significantly, in terms of the argument we promote in Chapter 7, they found that women were less opposed than men and younger workers less opposed than older workers. However, their survey was conducted in 2004 and views seem to have hardened since then, especially in relation to the amount of time spent at the computer:

> Computers supposedly came in to help me do my job. No, they run my job. And that's not the way it should be. And I would imagine, especially colleagues who have as many years in as I've got, would complain about I spend more time in front of that thing than I do with the offender. And that's not right; there is no way that that's right. Also, this bloody thing about OASys. People seem to forget … they keep saying this magic thing, like you can't do anything without OASys. I'm sorry, I'm the person who put it in. So … so actually, what comes out is what I put in it.
>
> (PW8)

Nevertheless, Bullock (2011) argues that practitioners have more room for manoeuvre in the use of OASys than they may imagine and, precisely because 'what comes out is what I put in', 'risk management practice continues to be moulded in terms of practitioner values and preferences' (2011: 133).

The typical day

Although a number of respondents made the point that every day was different, and that anticipating the unexpected added to the appeal of the job, one interviewee, PW13, provided us with 'a typical day' schedule (see Table 3.1) demonstrating the long hours and pressure of work she experienced routinely. When presenting our emerging findings at seminars, we were questioned about the typicality of this illustration. We revisited our data and found that this was not an isolated or unusual case among our sample. While future observational research might challenge our findings, there was no doubt in our sample that *this* was how probation workers perceive themselves, as the following quotations indicate:

> I'm not doing 9 'til 5.30, I'm working over that time. [Until] 6, 7. For the last four weeks, I've been going home at 8, 9 o'clock.
>
> (TPO2)

> I mean I've separated from my husband now, but we had … we had a few arguments about how late I was staying at work, you know, having to get more childcare, that kind of thing … yeah, there has been times when I've stayed 'til 12 o'clock at night.
>
> (PW14)

> [In order to see offenders properly] something has to give, and if that means coming in work at 7 and not going home 'til 7, it has to be worth it, you know [laugh]. I think at one point, we were … myself and my colleague who did my training with me were comparing hours, and we were talking about the fact that on the workload management tool, we would need an extra 21 days a month to manage the … caseload that we were managing.
>
> (PW21)

What was missing in these accounts of long hours and ever more frenetic activity was any sense that it was legitimate to spend time *thinking* or *reflecting* on what one was doing. Time was for *performance*, not *process* (Davies 2009). Workers had no time to think about *how* they might undertake a task – they just had to 'do it'. As we shall see in Chapter 6, those workers who constructed a positive identity were those who could resist or subvert the demands of the organization to work ever faster and more mindlessly.

How different is this from the past? The most obvious differences are the dominance of computers and the time pressures of a performance culture (discussed above), the changing physical environment and the decline of home visiting (discussed below). But among former probation workers and chief officers, predominantly lifers, there was also a very different tone. A minority view was that things had improved:

> I think [pause] collectively, we kidded ourselves before about 2001, how good we were at that core task. I think there were some very, very skilled and experienced practitioners, who did it very well, and would be perfectly at home actually in the modern probation service. Do I believe the vast majority of probation practice met those high standards? Do I hell. It was a million miles away. People kidded themselves. I remember having arguments in, you know, the early 2000s, with probation colleagues, who argued that actually seeing someone once a fortnight or once every three weeks, for half an hour, really had an impact on offending behaviour. It was nonsense. We were kidding ourselves.
>
> (CO1)

Table 3.1 A typical day?

A day in the life of a Probation Worker (PW13)	
05.45	Get up, dress, have breakfast
07.00	Leave for work
07.30	Arrive at work
07.40	Unlock – get files for day – log on – coffee
07.50	Start – reports/records
09.00	First appointment – either PSR (90 minutes) or supervision (30/40 minutes)
10.00	Appointment – supervision
11.00	Appointment for absent colleague – record contact and next appointment
12.00	Write up video link with prison from previous day – phone and email to prison
12.30	Appointment for absent colleague – record contact and next appointment
13.00	Second call to prison – liaison with hostel staff – deal with emails – case discussion with SPO
13.20	Telephone call from prisoner wanting information
13.30	Telephone call from neighbouring area – unhappy about OM response
14.00	Appointment – domestic violence work
15.00	Appointment – victim empathy work
15.40	Bowl of cereal/coffee – start PSR on OASys
16.00	Appointment – drug client attends (hooray!)
16.30	PSR on OASys
17.00	Appointment – poor response, difficult interview
17.40	Late for appointment due to overrun
18.00	Last appointment finishes – coffee/biscuit – PSR until 20.00
20.00	Leave for home
20.30	Arrive home – tea, soup, talk
22.00	Bed

But the majority view was that things really *were* better in the past – there *was* a golden age of autonomy and professionalism:

> The big difference is, we didn't have the computer and the pressure on recording, so we recorded a lot less. We used to have a dictaphone and just do Part Cs[1] as people came in, onto the dictaphone, and you used to have a secretary that would type them up for you.
>
> (CO2)
>
> My memory of it as a practitioner is that it was [pause] an immense privilege to sit down in a room with people and have them just talk about their lives. And that ... within that process, you can feel the change occurring in people's lives. You may not be able to measure it and map it, but you can feel it, you can feel the process of change.
>
> (FPW1)

Several chief officers recounted examples of innovative work that they had been allowed to do – though always in their own time – and for which the organization took credit. But the work depended entirely on the commitment of individuals, as the following story illustrates:

I ran a prisoners' partners programme, which was just something I came up with, because I had quite a few women whose partners were in prison, with young children. So we set it up and it really got off the ground. And they met … we met in each of their houses. They shared clothes, they swapped washing machines. I got a bit of money out of the magistrates and we took the kids off to the park in the summer and to the pantomime at Christmas. And I wouldn't be allowed to do any of that now. So that could have been something that I was doing that was a bit maverick really, but it was popular and I think it was effective, as far as keeping those families engaged and together, and supported through prison. It was a sort of the thing that got rolled out at magistrates liaison meetings as something exciting that we're getting up to in the office. It was actively promoted really. But you were doing it on the back of goodwill. You weren't being given any extra reduced caseload for it, or anything like that; you found the time and made it happen … [and] it wound up the minute I left that office.

(CO2)

Buildings – from swamps and crocodiles to barricades

Buildings stabilize social life. They give structure to social institutions, durability to social networks, persistence to behaviour patterns. What we build solidifies society against time and its incessant forces for change.

(Gieryn 2002: 35)

Historically, the buildings that housed probation workers were heterogeneous. Some were in court buildings, some were in town centres in the middle of shops, some were on 'dog shit parade' (PW5) in the windswept, run-down shopping centres on council estates. The point was, they didn't look like anything in particular and they didn't *represent* anything in particular. We heard stories of poorly maintained fabric that was the responsibility of the senior probation officer, reminiscent of the burst pipe in the opening scenes of the book and TV series *Hard Cases* (Harvey 1987) discussed in Chapter 5:

In those days, seniors were responsible for buildings. When it rained, the water poured in through the ceiling, down the electrics. We had dry rot.… The windows were always being smashed by the kids who lived near. One night, we had 40 windows put in. In those days, I was the key holder and lived, you know, like an hour away. I was getting called out at two o'clock in the morning, and there was just glass everywhere. So … as well as all the staffing difficulties, a whole range of building issues. In those days when you became a senior, you went on a new seniors course, that was two separate weeks. And on one of the weeks, you had to like give a case example of something challenging in terms of being a manager. And I talked about some of the changes I was trying to drive forward, whilst you've got a building that's being constantly vandalized. You know, and talked about there being a swamp and crocodiles, and how difficult it is to … the object of the exercise is to drain the swamp while you're up to your arse in alligators.

(PW5)

Experienced workers remembered working 'on their patch' in the 1970s and 1980s, with many offices located on or near housing estates, with little or no security:

Quite a rickety old building, staircases and nooks and crannies, and no concept of risk management, health and safety, any of that stuff. You'd take your offender off with you – very little security.

(CO12)

Although there was a general lack of security, several interviewees pointed out that probation officers could retreat to their individual offices, leaving vulnerable receptionists to deal with 'difficult' clients:

So we had … you came in off the street and there was a sort of general office here, with reception here and here [gestures], I think, if I remember. And then this long corridor, going down, round in a … in an 'L'. And absolutely what was typical at that time, not any longer, but all of us in our own individual offices. And because we made a fuss about the violent incidents, what happened one day was, somebody came along and they fitted a door at the end of this corridor, with a lock on. Which, of course, what that did was isolate the receptionists out on their own [laugh]. And you just think 'isn't that typical?'

(CO7)

Then things started to change in the 1980s when probation centres sprang up, 'providing programmes of normalizing instruction to compulsorily attending groups of offenders in increasingly lavish purpose-built buildings as the visible representation of "punishment in the community"' (Worrall 1997: 101).

Many offices are now open-plan and anonymous – 'like typing pools' (PW24) – often located on industrial estates away from where offenders live (though it was pointed out to us that many are on bus routes into city centres). Interview rooms sometimes have to be booked and this creates problems when too many offenders arrive at the same time or if an offender is late for an appointment. Reception areas are bleak with few movable objects and high levels of security:

Waiting rooms in probation are horrid [now]. Everything's nailed down and minimal. Oh no, we can't offer them a cup of tea, can't give them a biscuit in case they throw a hot drink over us.

(FPW1)

One office we visited ameliorated the atmosphere by playing local radio, which also helped to give a degree of confidentiality to conversations at the reception desk. Another office employed a probation service officer as a 'duty' officer to see offenders who turned up without appointments or whose probation officer was off sick:

> My task, as far as I'm concerned with duty, is to keep the reception, the waiting, the offender area empty because … the nature of our attendees, sometimes the dynamic's not really helpful [laugh]. So … I keep it empty, so that there's no flash points, there's no people bumping into each other who shouldn't be bumping into each other.
>
> (PW20)

By contrast, we saw several very pleasant and well-equipped kitchens and staff areas which were well-used and appeared to enhance staff morale. Given that some officers told us they worked very late (even until midnight) on occasions, such facilities were clearly important. In addition to very late nights, officers also frequently worked at weekends and, since they were not allowed to work from home, this meant spending a great deal of their lives at the office.

Inside the modern probation office, accommodation is open-plan, like many other public and private sector office buildings. Opinions on this arrangement differed sharply, largely by generation. Younger workers mostly found open-plan supportive and positive:

> In terms of open plan, when you've got other colleagues easily accessible, you know, you can share something with them, you know, if you're having difficulty with a case and the response you just get it straightaway, which is very good.
>
> (TPO2)

However, the view was not universal:

> I'm a very private person. I just wanna come in and get on with the work … and because of the time constraints, I don't like chitchat and noise … I just wanna get my head down.
>
> (TPO3)

Older workers found it more difficult to work in this way:

> I spent a lot of time today [laugh] and other days, with my iPod in, because there's so much distracting conversation going on about soap operas, about fashion and about all sorts of stuff, I'm not willing to listen to anyway [laugh]. And if I'm trying to write a report, I'm going to stick my iPod in. I can cope with the distraction of music in my ears more easily.
>
> (PW11)

The worker who told us earlier that she worked occasionally until midnight in the office (PW14) – a young single mother – responded thus when asked how comfortable she felt being in the building on her own at night:

> I mean it's good when it's quiet and there's nobody in, you can just get on with it. I mean programmes are here 'til nine anyway. So there's normally somebody in the building up 'til nine o'clock. But no, I didn't feel scared or anything. But the other problem we've got is the tinted windows. In the day, people can't see anything; at night, with the lights on, you can see everything.
>
> (PW14)

Gieryn (2002) examines the interplay of agency and structure in the use of buildings: 'we mould buildings, they mould us, we mould them anew' (2002: 65). He argues that 'interactive routines are built-in' to the floor plans, the walls and the doors 'concealing the possibilities that never happened (and why)' (2002: 65). Nowhere is this more true than in the changing structures of probation offices: industrial estates, sterile waiting rooms, universally locked doors, bookable interview rooms, open-plan offices and comfortable staff kitchens. There are no incentives for workers to move outside their safe cocoons and certainly no incentives to mix with offenders in anything other than a highly structured environment. As one CO regretfully pointed out:

> The whole service has withdrawn behind its barricades … the majority of what we do is in some big faceless modern office block, and the offender comes in.
>
> (CO11)

This marked difference in physical environment speaks to a deep cultural change in attitude towards offenders – or least a deep *official* change in attitude towards offenders. Instead of being regarded as fellow human beings who have made (sometimes very bad) mistakes, the probation office reinforced offenders as being 'different' and 'other':

> I think it [purpose-built premises] says to the people who are coming in immediately, you know, you're separate … you're different. I think it also kind of says we think you're dangerous, or we are slightly scared of you. And, that can be reinforcing. But I'm not saying that there are [not] people [laugh] who we need to be scared of. But you know … that can also reinforce that.
>
> (PW1)

Home visits – the fear factor

The 'home visit' has been an iconic symbol of traditional probation work for three broad reasons. First, it was considered an essential part of the preparation of any court report, as Le Mesurier (1935) explains:

It is in the home and its immediate associations that the most powerful environmental influences are found, and it is from the home, therefore, that the most important information will be obtained. ... The home visit might be made the central point in the investigation.

(Le Mesurier 1935: 91 and 96)

Although later radical writers criticised both the underlying condescension of this view and the reality of many home visits (Walker and Beaumont 1981), there was, until well into the 1990s, a culture that believed that a report written without a home visit was lacking in credibility:

> And in respect of assessing risk, your best risk informant is the person you're working with, and if they feel safe with you, they'll tell you. If they don't, they're not gonna tell you anything. And if you're not doing home visits and you're not out in the community and you're not engaging, well then how good's your information?
>
> (PW10)

Second, it was considered essential to the general work of the probation officer that they should be seen as being part of the community. In order to have credibility, they had to be seen 'out and about' on their 'patch', showing an interest in the locality, getting the 'low-down' on the neighbourhood:

> You know, because of the quite high levels of unemployment, I knew where half my caseload congregated of a lunchtime. So if they didn't come in of a morning, at lunchtime I'd go to the shopping centre, where I knew they used to hang around. And, you know, I don't think we had the Data Protection Act in those days. I'd go you, you, you and you, in my office this afternoon [laugh].
>
> (PW5)

> I went to visit a chap, who was a registered sex offender. And I went and did the home visit, looked around and thought, oh my God, and said 'P, go off to the Spar, get me some Jif', and I ended up cleaning his sink [laugh]. That was a probation officer. Now I don't know what that says about me. And in those days, I remember I went back to the office and I'd probably be open and honest about it. I mean I wouldn't do it now, I'd get into serious trouble for doing it now.
>
> (PW10)

Third, and possibly most open to abuse, it provided a legitimate means of getting away from the office. Although home visits for the purpose of writing reports were strictly accountable (that is, the quality of the report was testament to the quality of the visit – unless one was willing to lie outright, which was risky), the recording of other routine home visits was far more flexible, if not actually haphazard:

And then, probably after lunch, because I can remember the days when we used to have lunch [laugh] and we'd go and have a beer sometimes, I would set off to my patch. I'd have a few appointments, but I'd also just drive around and I'd see some of the lads on the street and stop and have a chat. And I'd spend most afternoons on my own, without complicated telephone systems, booking in to see if I was still alive and, you know, no one would know where I was really. I'd just go and have cups of tea and talk to people, and occasionally have some difficult times, do reports. I ran little groups at the school sometimes, and we had a report centre out there, so one afternoon a week, I would be there and people would come in.

(FPW6)

It was from home visits that many workers learned about the realities of the lives of offenders – the sheer poverty and drabness of council estate and private rental living – and at the same time they demonstrated a personal commitment to working with offenders as fellow human beings:

I do think the context, when you see the way that some people are living, if you've not actually experienced that ... and we get a lot of people who, you know, have done psychology degrees, come into training, and you know, who have come from a generally, you know, nice background, etc., and have no idea of the circumstances that some people are living in, or you know, dynamics, etc. And I don't see how you can understand, you know, their offending and then attempt to address that, if you don't have a picture of the context.

(PW1)

And it was the stories that workers brought back to the office (elaborated at will, since there were no witnesses to the truth or otherwise of the story) from which much of the humour derived that enabled probation workers to cope with the pressures of the job. The poet, Simon Armitage, who used to be a probation officer, captured the dark humour of making home visits:

You went to a block of flats to interview an old woman about something or other and her Alsatian dog followed you through the door and into the front-room. After about half an hour, the dog got up and crapped in the corner, then sat back down by the fire. At first you thought it was none of your business, but eventually you couldn't keep your mouth shut and asked her why she didn't make her dog go outside. 'It's not my dog', she said, 'I thought it was yours.' *Actually, that story isn't true but people told it so many times you started to believe it happened to you.*

(Armitage 1998/2009: 9 – emphasis added)

Then, somewhere along the line, home visits stopped, or, to be more precise, the *culture* of home visiting stopped. Offenders are still visited at home on occasions and for specific purposes, but such visits normally have to involve two workers and that, in itself, makes the exercise more costly in terms of time and the availability of colleagues. The trainees we interviewed were less than enthusiastic:

> It's got a bit of a stigma behind it, home visits, because they're kind of reserved for the more kind of really concerning, you know, cases, where there are social services involvement or whatever. I just wouldn't go to see an ordinary … an offender who I regard as a medium kind of risk and there's no other attached issues, at home. You literally don't have the time, number one, to go out of the office and come back. And number two, finding someone to come with you, because you have to go accompanied and there's just no support sometimes, you know.
>
> (TPO5)

Those most likely to visit more regularly are those working on prolific and priority offender projects who visit alongside police officers, though even here, there was a hint that the police did more visits because they were better resourced (PW16 and PW17). More significantly, offender managers generally no longer *see the point* of home visits, as the extract above illustrates. Community sentences and prison licences are about offenders *reporting* to offices and *attending* programmes. This way, it is easier for workers to see whether offenders are doing what they should be doing and for managers to see that workers are doing what they should be doing. That it is also *safer* is a bonus though, as one second careerist told us in exasperation, 'I made intelligent decisions about whether it was safe to make a home visit … now, if you don't follow the procedure and you get hurt, it's your fault' (PW8). But for most less experienced workers it was an irrelevant issue.

Given the clear change of policy and culture in respect of home visiting, we were perhaps surprised to find that most of the chief officers were, on the one hand, passionate about the importance of home visits – 'It's in my DNA, my probation DNA' (CO6) – but, on the other, pessimistic about the likelihood of their reinstatement:

> I think I spent ten years campaigning to, you know, restore home visits, in an assistant chief role, involved in the early drafting of national standards. I was responsible for keeping some reference to home visits in. But I gave up; I gave up at some point, after I was appointed as chief in '99 I decided it was a battle I could no longer win.
>
> (CO1)

> Oh, I do [encourage them], but [here], it's like an alien thing. You know, you'll have a health and safety thingy, you can't do that, you know. I've pushed for years about home visits because we found, about ten years ago, that one of the factors, other than age, that meant you were not gonna go into breach, was if you'd had a home visit. And that's because (1) you've

checked they're living where they say they're living, (2) you're showing some interest and you've gone to meet them. You also pick up a whole load of other information. You know, there's lots of reasons why.... And, of course, then this other idea about, you know, working more with the family, which I think is one of those negative swings we've had. You know, we're very focused on the offender and not the family.

(CO14)

Only one chief officer claimed to have successfully reinstated home visits:

We've done a big piece of work here on home visits. When I came, the director of operations took it on as a cause célèbre. There was virtually no home visits at all, even on high-risk offenders. It would be exceptional for there to be home visits. Now, we absolutely insist on home visits.

(CO11)

Clear (2005) argues that caseloads should be replaced by 'placeloads' and that probation workers should stop 'watching offenders', since this is something that the police are better equipped and skilled to do. There is no evidence, he argues, to support the view that probation workers earn their keep in crimes prevented by their surveillance and enforcement work. Instead, they should abandon attempts to work individually with impossibly high caseloads and return to geographical specialization and the concept of 'community probation'. This is an extreme view that we encountered no evidence of a move towards, but a desire to move away from the opposite extreme was universally evident among those who had experienced the culture of home visiting at any time in their career.

Alongside the decline in home visiting has been a decline in prison visiting (Williams 2008). This has always been a very expensive and time-consuming aspect of the work and there have been limitations on travel to prisons for many years. Increasingly, it has been viewed as unnecessary for community-based workers to travel scores of miles simply to keep in touch with prisoners. Teleconferences are widely used and, as in courts, the introduction of videolinks with prisons has supposedly made such journeys a thing of the past. But one respondent told a different story:

We've got crap equipment, it always ... every time we use it, at least once a week, it goes wrong. Last time, I actually had to hold a note up to the camera, saying I cannot hear you, please ring me again. It's just a joke. And quite often ... ours is the cheap version and we have to do it through a third party, who can only offer you maybe one slot a week. And, of course, the prison can never make that date.

(PW7)

Different times, different places

Prisons

Four of our interviewees were currently working in prisons and many others had worked in prisons in the past. We discuss the changing relationship between probation and the prison service in more detail in Chapter 4. Here we consider the daily routine experiences of workers in a custodial setting. A probation manager working in a prison described a typical day thus:

> My daily routine? If the weather's good, I'll cycle in. I'm in 8–8.30 and allocate work. I go to the prison morning briefing at 9 every day and sometimes I don't get back because I'm called in to all sorts of meetings around the prison. I do staff supervision. I'm responsible for OASys Q and A. I respond to requests. I still do face-to-face work with prisoners, either complaints or the Thinking Skills Programme (TSP), which I lead on.
>
> (PW3)

She went on to describe other activities that she participated in on a voluntary basis within the prison, such as taking part in the prisoners' Christmas play. She took the view that 'you have to give something to the prison' if you want to be respected and taken notice of. It might be argued that she was also responding to the 'domestic' nature of the prison environment in which much of the routine staff–inmate interaction is of an intimate 'family' kind (Crawley and Crawley 2008). But for others, working in prison was something of an escape from the pressures of community-based work:

> The good thing about working in prison is that you can leave on time. I arrive between 8.30 and 9 and I know I can leave between 4.30 and 5.
>
> (PW2)

This interviewee was disillusioned because she felt she had been seconded to the prison to do one job but had ended up with another:

> I've been here [in prison] for two years out of a four-year contract. I came to take the lead on public protection and I was told I wouldn't have a caseload [of prisoners] but I've had to acquire a caseload of life-sentence prisoners. I dealt with lifers in the community but that's very different. The ones in here are very demanding.
>
> (PW2)

Yet another probation worker in prison had been shocked by the extent to which her role in prison had been dictated by the prison governor rather than her probation line management. She had been heavily involved in delivering drug treatment programmes alongside colleagues in the prison psychology department (Towl and Crighton 2008), then a new prison governor arrived:

That was a big shock for me about prisons ... that the governor decides what goes on in that prison full stop. And when you get a new governor, every-thing changes, and no matter ... you know, if they decide they're gonna run it differently, it changes. So ... we wrote lots and lots of parole reports, sec-onded parole reports ... and we got quite a large probation department. We worked closely with the psychology department, in terms of running the programmes. We had the senior probation officer there, who was quite influ-ential in terms of management; attended all the management groups. Whereas now, they've pulled the senior out, so we don't have a senior in there, and the team is cut down to the bone. We don't deliver any of the pro-grammes, we're not involved in programme delivery at all any more ... [Then] all I was doing was chairing post-programme reviews. It was incred-ibly boring; it's like groundhog day ... and I was losing all my skills.

(PW1)

One of the myths about working in prisons is that one works more intensively with prisoners than in the community. Although this may be true in some prisons for uniformed staff (Crawley and Crawley 2008), it can be exactly the opposite for non-uniformed staff because, as this worker explains, the 'windows' avail-able for seeing prisoners within the prison's daily routine are very limited:

I suppose the biggest frustration for me, as I say, because I used to work ridiculous hours [in the community] but that meant, you know, from the time I got in ... from the time it was reasonable for an offender to turn up, so say about 9 o'clock [laugh] 'til 6 or 7, I could see offenders, and you'd be seeing them every hour, every half hour, whatever. In the prison, you've got such very small windows in which to see them ... I can get hold of them for about 8.00, so I'd have my first interview at 8.00. Well if it's for [a risk assessment] or something like that, then it's probably gonna be two hours. By the end of which, they're knackered, I'm losing the will to live slightly, and I'm thinking right, if I'm going to ... I've got one more prisoner I can probably see, unless it's just simple things. But obviously, you know, that whole thing about probation officers doing the welfare bit, we don't do that. So there aren't simple things very often, it is usually meaty things. So again, I do one-to-one work because I think that's right and proper. There are a few of my prisoners, for whom I'm an offender supervisor, who are not getting the best service off me, because of the amount of oral hearings, the amount of [risk assessments], and the one-to-one work that's part of their sentence plans, that I've got to do. And some kind of just drop off a bit, which is the saddest thing.

(PW8)

As we shall see in Chapter 4, workers tend to either love or hate working in prisons – they can't wait to get out or they have to be prised out with a crowbar. Much depends on the extent to which they can identify with the host institution and retain a sense of occupational identity. Since the creation of NOMS this is becoming increasingly difficult, even at a routine level. Both selected prison officers and probation workers are titled 'offender supervisor' and often share offices. PW3 illustrated the different cultures by explaining different policies towards smoking breaks. Prison officers considered that they were entitled to several smoking breaks each day, whereas probation workers would be expected to make up the time. In this, and other details of daily routines, it might be argued that probation workers viewed themselves as being more 'professional' than prison officers.

Approved premises

Only one of our interviewees was currently working in approved premises but many had done such work in the past, and we quickly became aware of a very different world and culture among those working intensively with offenders 24 hours a day, seven days a week, in the community. Historically, probation hostels (often run by voluntary organizations) existed to provide housing – and often a family environment – for homeless offenders. FPW8 remembered those days well:

> We used to take them out on trips, and [my husband] could get involved, and he'd help me. So we'd always take them to the Christmas market, and my biggest fear would be that they'd disappear into one of these antique shops and, you know, lift something. But they never did, we never … well, I always felt fairly confident. And they did always stick by you. Because again, they were out of their comfort zone. They came from all over the country, not just locally, the residents at the hostel. Some were on bail, some were sentenced on a probation order, with a condition of residence. They were all different statuses really and all types of offenders. We did Christ-mas … I did four Christmases, I did the Christmas dinner for four years, and my kids used to come as well. The assistant chief would bring us in a bottle of wine, or enough for everyone to have a glass of wine at Christmas. It was just so different then. It was more like having a big extended family … and it changed so rapidly, didn't it, I guess?
>
> (FPW8)

Being the only woman on the staff team and being alone on duty overnight was not considered problematic, despite concerns from the neighbours:

> Yeah, it was really interesting … there was a residents' committee, and the next door neighbour of the hostel, because it was in quite a nice residential area, he had a big house next door and he'd always opposed this hostel opening. It had been open not many years when I started working there. And he was always coming round and complaining and he thought it was abso-lutely … I think he used the word 'sick' that a woman would be left all

night on her own in charge of 16 male offenders. And I used to say well, that's more in your head than in mine, that's the way you're thinking about it, but it really isn't like that. I had my own separate room obviously [laugh], which was separated by a little corridor. So we had our own room and shower and toilet and everything, separate from all the other bedrooms. They were shared bedrooms. And you'd go in at 5 o'clock at night and you'd work 'til 5.30 the next day, the next night. So you'd do the whole 24 hours. So there were day staff there, like a secretary, a cook, the warden. I was an assistant warden. So we had a warden, a deputy warden and I think there were three male assistant wardens and me ... But you had so much freedom in those days. I mean this was in ... this was 1984.

(FPW8)

Nowadays, however, the role of approved premises is 'to protect the public from offenders or bailees who pose high or very high risk of harm' (Thurston 2002; Wincup 2002; Dunkley 2007; Reeves 2011) by providing enhanced supervision. Staffing levels are very different with double cover insisted on at night, though not necessarily for much longer:

I can remember when there was the warden, the deputy warden and a warden. And only 9 to 5 were there two of you on duty. At all other times, there was just one person. And you used to sleep at night as well between midnight and 6. So there was nobody awake. Now we have two people awake. That's gonna change, that's not affordable any more.

(PW9)

As indicated above, hostels have never been popular in residential areas, especially those that house sex offenders. But it is not only the residents who are subject to hostility from neighbours; staff also experience animosity. As Cherry and Cheston observe, 'staff – some of whom have been threatened – have anxieties about getting to work safely, about the hostel being attacked, and about being followed home' (2006: 261). And physical and verbal abuse from residents was also by no means uncommon. Despite this, there was clearly a level of job satisfaction experienced by staff in hostels that was different to that in a field office team. When asked why he had remained so long in this work, PW9 responded: 'It's very varied, isn't it? It's not quite such a treadmill, you know.' FPW 8 simply said 'I loved it, absolutely loved it.'

A typical day for an approved premises manager might now go something like this:

Come in, go through all the signing-in procedure. Usually I'd come in straight in here [my office]. I'll read the log [written by the night staff]. Usually have my computer on straightaway, to make sure all the tracking systems we have for referrals and who's in and who's out, who's going, who's coming, checking emails, dealing with on-call arrangements from the previous night. So we're also on call – the managers. So I'm on call at the moment 24 hours a day. Well, you're on call when you're not in the place, working. So you do your nine to five and then you're on call from five 'til nine. So there might have been things that needed ... that happened ... overnight, and then you have to deal with those the next morning. So that will be contacting ... well, I won't necessarily do all this, but I will need to identify what needs doing and make sure that people are onto it. So contacting case managers, your bloke was half an hour late for the curfew; or he didn't really come back at all; or he got very, very drunk and was very abusive to staff; or there was a fight between residents; or, you know, there was a fire or there was a flood, or you know, all those things. So you sort of try and get a grip of all of that within the first half hour or so, and see what needs ... action needs progressing on it. And I'd just carry on like that all [laugh] ... all day. Or I might have meetings to go to. So today, I've been to a MAPPA (Multi-Agency Public Protection Arrangements) meeting, where there's two cases that are relevant to the hostel. I might have other management meetings, or planning meetings. So tomorrow, I've got an all-day meeting, where we're doing this benchmarking exercise.

(PW9)

Hostel work has been described as the 'Cinderella' of the service (White 1984) but PW9 had no sympathy with this view:

I don't think there's been any justification for people in hostels to talk in terms of us being the Cinderella probably for about ten years at least, if not 15. I've often found, when I've been in teams where you ... there is this received wisdom about the isolation from the rest of the organization, and my response is, well why don't you do something about it; why don't you make sure you read all the emails; why don't you talk to your colleagues that are doing things in other places; why don't you read the research that says what's going on in other places? There's no need to stay isolated.

(PW9)

Unpaid work

None of our interviewees was working currently in unpaid work (formerly community service) but several had done such work in the past and, as with approved premises work, we noted a very different culture being recounted to us.

Unpaid work/community service is a relatively recent penal innovation, emerging as a result of increasing concern about the rising prison population in the 1960s, coupled with attacks on rehabilitative treatment. It was one of the recommendations of the Wootton Advisory Council on the Penal System in 1970 and 'its novelty and practicality' fitted well with the 'climate of penological optimism' of the time (Oakley 2011: 274). It was incorporated into legislation in 1972 and six experimental pilot schemes were set up in 1973. One of our interviewees was involved in community service from the outset and reflected on the very different kind of management style required by senior probation officers:

> It came as a culture change when I became a manager in a factory sense in community service. I mean, as you know, we took aboard a lot of people from the factory floor and, you know, as project officers and supervisors at weekends. And I remember walking past the project officer's door once and I just overheard this conversation, and this chap who'd spent his life in industry says we wouldn't have this problem if X would just issue a directive. And I mean that was so foreign to my career previously, you know, you weren't into this, giving directives. But I just said he's right, you know, it would make life so much easier if I just told them ... and they were happy with that. I mean that's just a little example of a process that went on when I started working with people who were not social work and probation trained.
>
> (FPW7)

In 1977 *Probation Journal* devoted a complete issue to reviewing the first five years of community service. The editorial asked the question 'What exactly is the purpose of a community service order? What has the probation service made of this new provision?' There followed several heart-searching articles, all of which, though cautiously optimistic about community service, were conscious of its contradictory underlying philosophy and its challenge to traditional perceptions of the probation officer's job. For the first time, offenders were to be formally supervised by 'unqualified' community service officers rather than by probation officers (Worrall and Hoy 2005). The ambivalence surrounding unpaid work and the probation service's role in it remain unresolved:

> Even to this day, community payback, as it's now called, is not truly integrated into the probation service. It's still a kind of bit of arm's-length intervention, and the language of offender management and intervention hasn't actually helped in relation to that.... Because there is still an elitism within those who have got a probation qualification, and those that haven't.
>
> (CO1)

In the 'What Works' era of evidence-based practice, community service came to be regarded as a vehicle for 'pro-social modelling', with 'supervisors acting as models and consciously implementing the principles of reward, encouragement and "pro-social expressions and actions"' (Canton 2011: 152) in an environment that was more 'real' than an office. But the 'reality' was sometimes rather different (though possibly more effective!):

> I can remember community service officers holding offenders by the throat against the wall and telling them that, you know, when they're told to come

in for their appointments, they will, and if they don't, they'll tell their dad or their uncle, who'll give them a hiding. Not the sort of thing I'd expect to hear a probation officer saying. I mean it had the desired effect, in that they were there every week, did their community service.

(PW5)

This interviewee talked in detail about the very different attitudes and values of those recruited to supervise offenders on unpaid work and the problems he experienced in trying to encourage and promote a prosocial attitude towards offenders among 'trade people' who have an 'industrial attitude' towards 'training apprentices':

I expect, encourage and promote supervisors to be far more prosocial. So I won't tolerate any bad language, any name calling, I want offenders treated with respect. I expect exactly the same thing out of supervisors in terms of how they relate to and treat offenders on community service, or community payback as it is now, as I would if I was managing a field team of probation officers, dealing with offenders on, you know, community orders.

(PW5)

In recent years, a major political issue has been the visibility of unpaid work (Johnson and Ingram 2007; Casey 2008). While the requirement for offenders on unpaid work to be visible to the public has been the subject of considerable debate both inside and outside the probation service, perversely the consequent increase in the visibility of supervisors has received scant attention. Nevertheless, with the increasing probability of community payback contracts going to private companies, it seems unlikely that there will be any further integration of supervisors into probation culture.

Conclusion

In this chapter we have considered the contribution of time and place to the cultures of probation work. We have examined the daily routines of probation workers in a variety of locations and roles and have explored how these routines have changed over time in the experiences of lifers, second careerists and offender managers. The growing influence of computerization, combined with a retreat from the community in the sense of places of work and time with offenders, is marked. In the process of constructing our argument that probation is socially tainted work, we reach two provisional conclusions at this point. First, probation work is tainted by the constraints of hours in the day and the struggle to find time to reflect on, as opposed to undertake, the work. But this constraint of hourly time is mitigated by the variety of work that is available to any one individual over a career lifetime and the opportunities to construct a multifaceted identity with a range of very different experiences. Second, probation work is tainted by buildings that mould and restrict the interplay of agency with structure. But this constraint of place is mitigated by the range of locations available to any one individual over their career lifetime and the opportunities they have to interact in very different physical environments. These themes are picked up again and explored in greater depth in Chapter 6, where we examine how probation workers shape their careers.

4 Probation's changing relationships with courts, police and prisons

The probation service has always been closely associated with the criminal courts, but in recent decades it has also been encouraged to work more closely with a range of public and voluntary sector agencies. This chapter examines probation's changing relationships with the courts, the police and the prison service. We begin by exploring the changing relationship with the courts, arguing that probation workers no longer view themselves as merely 'servants of the court'. We follow this with a discussion of the concept of 'partnership' and the ways in which criminal justice agencies' interactions have been conceptualized in policy and legislative changes. We then analyse probation–prison and probation–police relationships pre- and post-1998 and, drawing on Davidson's (1976) typology of inter-organizational relationships, argue that, despite both structural and cultural transformations, there remain cultural continuities in each organization that create tensions, the significance of which (both positive and negative) should not be underestimated. While recognizing that the probation service works with numerous other organizations in the community, our research found that it has been the changing nature of relationships with these three key agencies that has most greatly affected the occupational cultures of probation workers.

Still servants of the courts?

> There are so many vested interests in the court – police, probation officers, magistrates, solicitors, social workers. It's a matter of them all fighting over one carcase.
>
> (Probation officer cited in Carlen 1975: 347/2010: 11)

The historic relationship between the probation service and the magistrates' courts can be traced back at least to the latter part of the nineteenth century when the Church of England Temperance Society first employed police court missionaries to 'reclaim' offenders charged with drunkenness or drink-related offences. As noted in Chapter 1, the Probation of Offenders Act 1907 gave magistrates' courts the right to appoint probation officers, whose job it was to 'advise, assist and befriend' offenders placed under their supervision and, in 1925, the Criminal Justice Act required every court to appoint a probation officer. For decades, probation officers regarded themselves as 'servants of the court', seeing their main functions as those of advising magistrates on sentencing, through the preparation of social enquiry reports, and supervising those offenders the courts allowed to remain in the community (Worrall and Hoy 2005). Attending court was regarded by many as the highlight of the working week:

> Court duty was a big deal. And it's something that I think everybody looked forward to, because it got you at the cutting edge; it grounded you in terms of what sentencers were looking for and what it was about. But it was also a brilliant way of networking with your colleagues in a big urban court complex; you know, it was the place where you picked everything up.
>
> (CO2)

Nevertheless, the relationship was never an entirely comfortable one and required a mix of skill, assertiveness and diplomacy:

> You have to earn your position in the court, by becoming somebody known for doing a particular job, otherwise the magistrates and clerks just ride roughshod and even the ushers treat you with contempt until you get established.
>
> (FPW8)

Carlen (1975/2010) utilizes a games framework to analyse the interactions of courtroom personnel, their professional alliances and the tactics they use to maintain credibility with – and not antagonize – the magistrates. She found probation officers to be very protective of their expertise in writing social enquiry reports, resenting the extent to which defence solicitors appropriated (plagiarized) their reports and disparaging social workers for their lack of know-how in handling magistrates. Probation officers prided themselves on 'signalling' – 'the routine operation of a taken-for-granted and implicit network of signs, gestures and cues which routinely transmits messages between the performers in a complex information game' (Carlen 1975: 365/2010: 29):

> We're fairly careful how we put things – you know – 'he says', 'he claims', that kind of thing. I think there's a sort of understanding between the magistrates. If we say 'he says', 'he claims', we haven't checked. If we say 'We …' and then make a categoric statement, he generally assumes we've checked. Also there's a certain code, if you like, for recommendations – but 'a certain course of action' indicates probation. It's things like this, when you're working close to magistrates that they get to understand what you're getting at – you know – *why*.
>
> (Probation officer cited in Carlen 1975: 367/2010: 31)

Our participants recollected a personal, almost intimate relationship with courts in the 1970s, with magistrates and judges being possessive of *their* probation officers (PW24). The same worker recalled kindnesses during the 'winter of discontent':

> When there was the fuel strikes and things, the local magistrate who lived up the road would bring us down hot drinks and scones, if their electric was on or, you know, provided heaters and, you know, they'd call by and drop us off bottles of sherry at Christmas. That's one of the things I noted, very much more distance between us and the sentencers now.
>
> (PW24)

But the probation service has undergone many structural and cultural changes since then, and its relationship with magistrates' courts has inevitably changed (McWilliams 1981). A key turning point in the relationship between probation and the courts came in 1999 with the introduction of Specific Sentence Reports, later to become 'fast delivery' reports (Haines and Morgan 2007). In line with the principle of speeding up justice, reports delivered 'on the spot' are regarded as being advantageous for the court, the probation service and the offender (Worrall and Hoy 2005:113). The disadvantage is the perceived threat to professional judgement, since fast delivery reports are inevitably based on limited information and do not have to be prepared by qualified probation officers. As we see below, probation officers are now routinely replaced by lesser qualified probation service officers in courts.

Consequently, we heard mixed views about magistrates but, by and large, we found that probation workers still enjoy working in magistrates' courts and want to be involved as much as possible. They believe that they are the *experts* in risk assessment and in working directly with offenders, rather than mere *servants*, and that this is a complex task. As one respondent put it, 'it *is* rocket science' (FPW3). Some expressed the view that they had lost their former authority in the courtroom and that magistrates appear not to understand the complexity and time-consuming nature of getting to know an offender sufficiently well to make an accurate assessment of their risk of harm and reoffending:

> [The probation officer] used to be an authoritative person and had a very key role in the court … we sort of moved down to … almost the bottom of the pecking order.
>
> (CO14)

While recognizing the constraints under which magistrates work, there was a feeling that they were sometimes unrealistically demanding in their expectations:

> There were two different sorts of attitudes … magistrates being extremely supportive of the service … but also extremely demanding at the same time.
>
> (FPW2)

Some commented on the inconsistency of their relationships with different benches in different areas, suggesting that much still depends on the individual personalities of magistrates and the mini-cultures of different benches. Despite these tensions, our research suggests that magistrates and probation workers are getting a better understanding of each other all the time and we heard a number of examples of excellent communication and partnership. For example, one court-based probation officer was actively promoting better working relationships and mutual understanding:

> I think that magistrates' attitudes to probation officers have changed and I think it's because they have a better understanding of what we do ... I produced a newsletter for the magistrates, which just promotes who we are, what we do, and I'll often put a quiz on the end because they like stuff like that.
>
> (PW21)

Thus the court might be regarded as a 'shop window' for the probation service 'where it can advertise the range of services and interventions that it offers and ensure that it gains an appropriate "market share" of sentencing disposals' (Robinson 2011: 154). And for many newer recruits, court can be an exacting proving ground and an exciting place in which to work. As one trainee said, 'I really enjoy courts because it's theatre and you're playing a part in this massive drama, *although it's real*' (TPO4 – emphasis added).

Two of our interviewees were currently working regularly in the crown court and one of these had some interesting views on the status of probation there. He expressed concerns that the probation presence had been quietly 'downgraded' from that of probation officer to probation service officer, without the judges noticing:

> Now yes, they can do the job at the functional level very well, but I get concerned because they haven't got the experience of having supervised anybody, or the qualification that ... they haven't got the probation officer qualification. And I'm not sure that you shouldn't have a more forceful voice in court from a qualified position.... But no, I don't think the judges, barristers and others generally will know. And they have muddied the waters by calling everybody offender managers. And 'probation service officer' and 'probation officer', to the lay public, wouldn't mean a lot of difference either, to be honest.
>
> (PW11)

He felt that probation management had been 'taking the carpet away from us' by removing qualified probation officers from the daily crown court presence and, furthermore, implying that this was liberating probation officers to make better use of their skills in report-writing and direct work with offenders. For this particular participant, removal from daily interaction with judges, barristers, court clerks, ushers and security was demoralizing rather than liberating. His work identity was dependent on the 'time and place' (see Chapter 3) of mixing with particular criminal justice personnel (some, though not all, of high status) in the dramatic physical environment of a higher court.

Below we discuss Davidson's (1976) typology of inter-organizational relationships. At this point we can provisionally conclude that probation's relationship with the courts has moved from a very close one historically (in Davidson's terms 'federation') to one of clearly separate organizations with elements of 'coordination' (legally defined roles in the courtroom) but predominantly a relationship of 'co-operation' where close working only occurs if and when mutual benefit is identifiable.

The concept of partnership

Relationships between the probation service and other criminal justice agencies in England and Wales have changed considerably in recent decades and there have been a number of catalysts encouraging agencies to work more closely together for the greater goods of crime prevention, community safety and, more latterly, risk management and public protection. These catalysts have included official reviews (Morgan 1991), policy initiatives, changes in recruitment and training regimes for criminal justice practitioners, and legislation. Examples include the Crime and Disorder Act 1998, which put partnership working on a statutory basis, the Multi-Agency Public Protection Arrangements (MAPPAs), established by the Criminal Justice and Court Services Act 2000, the development of the Prolific and other Priority Offender (PPO) schemes and, most recently, the establishment of Integrated Offender Management (IOM) units. In addition, the relationship between the probation and prison services was formalized in 2004 when the two agencies were brought together to form NOMS, providing, on paper at least, a seamless system for the efficient management of offenders.

These ever-closer formal relationships between agencies have not always been comfortable, raising issues of information sharing, conflicting objectives, different ways of working, contrasting attitudes towards offenders and, not least, cultural tensions.

The practical and conceptual consequences of closer working relationships are reflected in the scholarly and policy-oriented literature. On the one hand, at a conceptual level, writers have theorized the implications of greater collaborative working for role boundaries and the blurring of agency roles. In this regard Kemshall and Maguire (2001) wrote about the 'polification' of probation and Nash (1999, 2004, 2008) has made incisive contributions on the entry and possible exit of a generic criminal justice practitioner, the 'polibation' officer, the notion of which has been revisited (Mawby and Worrall 2004) and stretched to 'prisi-polibation' (Mawby *et al.* 2007). At the heart of these works has been a debate concerning the loss of distinct roles and cultures that have provided valued checks and balances in the practice of criminal justice and a move towards the control of offenders, based on their assessed risk, for the benefit of public protection, which has become a central goal for the probation, prison and police services.

On the other hand, a more pragmatic literature has provided critiques of the character, strengths and weaknesses of partnership working, primarily for the benefit of policy-makers and practitioners (see, for example, Audit Commission 1998; National Audit Office 2001; Rumgay 2003; Berry *et al.* 2011). The two literatures are linked by the common theme of examining working relationships and modelling the agency interaction, albeit for differing purposes. To aid our analysis, we refer to Davidson's (1976) typology of inter-organizational relationships. Davidson developed a framework to assist planners to assess the viability of co-ordinated approaches to the delivery of services. He proposed a five-stage typology with each stage representing a more complex level of interaction between organizations, namely:

1   communication
2   co-operation
3   co-ordination
4   federation and, finally,
5   merger.

To ascertain the viability of an 'inter-organizational undertaking' and the best strategy to deliver it, Davidson identified a three-stage framework in which planners consider in sequence: environmental pressures, organizational characteristics, and inter-organizational planning processes.

Davidson's framework remains relevant, and his idea of a continuum or matrix of interaction has been used by many writers. For example, Poxton (2004: 16) identifies four types of partnership working (communication, co-ordination, collaboration and integration). Such typologies can provide a means of benchmarking the level of working relationship between criminal justice agencies (as demonstrated by Thomas 1994). They can also provide explanatory power. For example, examination of Davidson's three sets of factors can help explain the existence and nature of organizational interrelationships and the extent to which organizations and workers are prepared to negotiate and change, or 'mutually adjust' (Lindblom and Woodhouse 1993).

For an organization to be propelled into working more closely with other organizations, there must exist an environment of political, economic and/or social 'turbulence', such that 'individual organizations, however large, cannot expect to adapt successfully simply through their own direct actions' (Emery and Trist 1965: 24). But a 'turbulent field' is insufficient of itself to achieve closer working unless organizations can see clear benefits in terms of additional resources and, crucially, respect for what Davidson calls domain. 'Domain' is the implicit agreement on the nature and extent of respective organizational integrity, i.e. mutual acknowledgement and respect for such things as agency purposes, geographic areas covered, services offered and client characteristics.

Where one organization has expansionist ambitions and little respect for the domain of the other, there is likely to be resistance to closer working. But even when domain is respected, closer working will only happen when the 'limits of rationality' are acknowledged (Davidson 1976: 133). The existence of unresolved individual and group role conflict and the absence of leadership will prevent participants from acting rationally to achieve clear goals. Throughout the remainder of this chapter the concepts of turbulence, domain and the limits of rationality as here defined aid our interpretation of the relationships between probation, police and prison officer occupational cultures.

We now discuss probation–prison and probation–police relations pre- and post-1998, arguing that a potential tipping point was reached in 1998 when a political consensus acknowledged that the probation service's community-facing role was set to develop more strongly than its custody-facing role (a consensus that was to disintegrate within five years). We conclude that, while structural and cultural transformations in the three organizations presaged the emergence of a generic criminal justice worker, they ultimately failed to establish the polibation/prisobation officer because of the tenacity of cultural continuities in each organization. We turn first to our interviewees' perceptions of the state of relationships between probation, prison and police officers in the period from the 1960s to the 1990s.

Probation and prisons: from prison welfare to shared working

Culturally and historically, probation officers have felt uneasy about working in prisons, as though by doing so they were 'colluding with something harmful' (Nellis 2007: 44). They took over responsibility for prisoner 'after-care' (later 'through-care' and even later 'resettlement') from the voluntary organization, The National Association of Discharged Prisoners Aid Societies (NADPAS), in 1966, and prison welfare officers (PWOs) were appointed to every penal institution. The service was renamed *The Probation and After-Care Service* for about 15 years until the early 1980s. Throughout that period, there were fierce debates both within the probation service and between it and the prison service about whether or not there should be probation officers located inside prisons at all.

The debate was both ideological and cultural. Ideologically, the service stood accused of colluding with a politics of expediency by 'keeping the lid on' the cauldron of discontent that characterized many prisons in the 1970s and 1980s. As Stanton (1985: 107) argued, 'everybody knows what is wrong with the relationship between the probation service and the prison department, everybody knows that there is an essential difference of philosophy'. The primary task of the PWO, it was asserted, was to reduce prisoner anxiety (Othen 1975: 100), thus making the prisoner easier to control and inducing in him [*sic*] a state of 'false consciousness' about the reality (*political* reality, that is) of his plight.

Culturally, there were two issues. First, there was a fear that probation officers working in prisons would become institutionalized or culturally acclimatized to an environment that was anathema to everything they stood and had been trained for. Othen was in no doubt that 'the problem for probation officers is not whether we can work in such terrible places, but the unpalatable fact that when we do we are a part of the dependency-producing, self-respect-destroying regime' (1975: 102). Second, by defining themselves (or being defined) as 'The Welfare', probation officers were allegedly depriving basic grade prison officers of those aspects of their job that gave them the most satisfaction and stopped their role from being exclusively that of turnkey or jailer. In an interview for *Probation Journal*, John Bartell, the then new Chair of the Prison Officers Association (POA), expressed the fear that 'we could be reduced to merely doing the menial task of fetching and carrying prisoners' (Stone 1986: 85). Others have argued that this view is disingenuous and that the POA's real aim was to clear the prison of 'civilians' (Leech 1991).

What, then, were the tasks of PWOs in this era? Othen (1975) set the scene thus:

> Letters astray, forgotten or crossed; breaking of bad news and coping with feelings aroused; obtaining news of sickness, birth, death; why relatives/object of heart's desire has not visited; urgent visits, extra visits; coping and helping to reduce excessive anxiety; parole interviews; commiseration/'be patient my son' interviews in long-term establishments; flood of receptions and discharges in others.
>
> (Othen 1975: 99)

In sum, PWOs had three roles: working directly with prisoners, liaising with probation service colleagues in the community and co-operating with prison staff to ensure the smooth-running of the prison. Of these, it was the first that brought them into conflict with prison staff and the last that attracted criticism from probation service colleagues, especially those who belonged to the National Association of Probation Officers, whose policy became to withdraw probation staff from prisons and increase resources for prisoner after-care in the community (Glanfield 1985). The second role, that of liaising with probation colleagues in the community, was uncontentious in principle but criticized in practice because 'outside' and 'inside' probation officers were mutually accusatory about each others' competence and commitment to prisoners (Williams 1991).

Our research confirms that prisons were pretty unpleasant places in which to work in this era. Leaving aside the overcrowding, slopping-out and crumbling buildings, an atmosphere of thinly veiled violence was pervasive:

> My abiding memory is two uniformed officers grabbing me by the lapels, hanging me up against the wall, and I don't actually remember their exact words now but they were very threatening about do-gooding bastards.
>
> (CO1)

We heard stories about sexism (for example, the female PWO who was summonsed to the censor's office to give 'advice' about letters containing graphic sexual messages, women not allowed keys or on the landings) and racism (for example, the black gate officer openly known as 'Black Bob' and the wearing of National Front badges on prison uniforms).

Others recognized that being a prison officer wasn't perhaps the easiest of jobs:

> I'm not saying you had to kow-tow to them … but you had to respect their position because they were doing a difficult job, sometimes a pretty revolting job … you know, you had prisoners defecating in their cells … and riots … you know, some had witnessed hangings and I mean horrible things they had to deal with.
>
> (FPW8)

And that there were ways of getting what you wanted if you were prepared to swallow some of your professional pride:

> It was about how you treated them … if you talked down to a prison officer, you weren't gonna – it's not rocket science. But some of my colleagues didn't understand that you needed to be careful with the way you handled other professions.
>
> (FPW5)

Such views acknowledge Kreiner *et al*'s (2006) argument that being a prison guard ranks among the most pervasively stigmatized 'dirty' occupations. Kreiner *et al.* categorize prison guards as being *socially* tainted because they work with people despised by society, but they place less emphasis on the *physically* tainted work highlighted in the above quotation. Probation officers, while sharing some of the social taint of prison guards, historically enjoyed a somewhat higher social prestige (Ashforth *et al.* 2007) though, as we discuss in Chapter 5, this has diminished in recent years.

In 1972, Priestley analysed the situation of PWOs in terms of (a) society's ambivalence towards prisons, (b) the ill-defined role of the PWO, (c) role conflict and (d) institutional pressure. He offered four strategies for survival, redolent of the prisoner culture literature of the time: conformity, retreatism, innovation and rebellion. Pratt (1975) summarized the PWO's dilemma as that of *visibility* and *strangeness*. The role is both exposed and 'other' within the prison setting, resulting in both stress and opportunity. Contrary to Priestley's call for clearer role definition, Pratt argued for the role to remain undefined, at least for a while, so the PWOs could use their professional social work (note, *social work*) skills to develop innovative relationships that were appropriate to the setting. However, crucial to this development in a context of confrontational 'communication' and grudging 'co-operation' (Davidson 1976) was for the probation service to 'come to terms with its fear and distrust [of the prison service] and certainly abandon its arrogance' (Pratt 1975: 395).

Despite NAPO's policy to withdraw probation officers from prisons, it was clear by the mid-1980s that they were going to stay and that there had to be some resolution to the ideological and cultural conflict between the probation and prison services. Increasingly both services were experiencing public sector managerialism and by 1988, the Home Office Minister of State, John Patten, was arguing that 'we're all in the business of punishment' and that 'it is bizarre to scratch around for polite euphemisms for what is going on' (Worrall and Hoy 2005: 33–4). In 1985, a report by Jepson and Elliott proposed 'shared working' between probation and prison officers and this, for the next 15–20 years, is more or less what happened.

'Shared working' was defined from the outset as *not* being social work but 'through-care' with an interdisciplinary approach. There was no attempt to blur the boundaries between probation and prison officers but to get them working better together to achieve the same goals (Lacey and Read 1985), although it was conceded that this was an 'uphill struggle' (Fieldhouse and Williams 1986: 143). It took many forms but the uniting themes were, first, through-care (later resettlement) and, second, 'rehabilitation' in the specific form of 'what works' or 'evidence-based practice'. The term 'resettlement' was adopted by the Home Office in the late 1990s as an overarching term that covered sentence planning inside the prison and reintegration into the community on release (Maguire 2007). Models of resettlement consisted of varying degrees of welfare assistance, problem-solving skills and, crucially, responsibilization. The roles of prison and probation officers were viewed as being complementary and the development of cognitive behavioural programmes (such as *Reasoning and Rehabilitation* and the *Sex Offender Treatment Programme*) provided opportunities for both to work together in the same classroom (rather as probation and police officers were to work together in the community on prolific offender projects). Encouraging prisoners to accept responsibility for their actions, express victim empathy and improve their repertoire of responses to life problems was an agenda to which both prison and probation officers could subscribe and which necessitated their 'co-ordination' (Davidson 1976).

Although many probation officers still had no interest in working in prisons (and dreaded being required to do so), it was during this period that some of our interviewees recounted their most satisfying experiences of working in prisons:

> I got the job in the prison for six years, which was brilliant. It was a good move; it was worth waiting for. It was a wonderful time to be there. [My predecessor] had set up this really good system of working. Every [prisoner] on admission was seen at a board the next day with a senior [prison] officer or an officer and either me or one of my staff.... And then, you would pick up on what the problems were and then between us, we would act on it.
>
> (FPW5)

> We did quite a lot of joint work with prison officers. We did the offending behaviour group ... there'd be one probation officer, one prison officer. Some were very good, some were very bad but that generally worked quite well. Yeah, we worked well together, yeah.
>
> (PW9)

So much did some probation officers enjoy working in prisons that chief officers had difficulty in persuading them to take jobs elsewhere. For some, working in prison was (and still is) an escape from the pressures of work in the community (PW2; PW9) but some just became institutionalized:

> With staff I have seconded to prisons, I say, you come out after an absolute maximum of five years. And, of course, they don't want to. And I say, well you just become part of the institution … you get sucked in. It's a very invasive culture.
>
> (CO13)

But the cultural changes that facilitated shared working were not just in one direction. Prison officers may have felt freer to express an interest in offender rehabilitation, but probation officers were moving away from their image as 'the welfare' or 'care bears' and becoming increasingly comfortable with a 'disciplinary or enforcement approach' (PW9). And there was still a need for probation officers to tread warily in interpersonal relationships:

> You have to play a game and the game is, you're a civilian, they will treat you as a second-class citizen, you have no rights and there's no issue of professional courtesy … they will treat you as they see fit. So long as you know that … and you're basically nice, you pussyfoot around them and nicely-nicely, 'oh could you do that, oh cheers, that great'. And then you get what you want.
>
> (PW6)

> They had a general collective view that we were just a complete waste of space and they didn't know why we were there. Then there was a different view based on how good you were, whether you actually did anything valuable, you know, on the wing, in terms of the way the wing ran.
>
> (PW5)

The election of New Labour to government in 1997 was to force this embryonic and still fragile partnership between the probation and prison services on at a much faster pace than either side was comfortable with. The desire of the government to erase the concept of probation from the collective conscience as a term too closely associated with the tolerance of crime (Worrall 2008a: 117) led to the setting up of the Prisons-Probation Review to explore the possibility of integrating the two services. The consultation document reporting on the review and entitled *Joining Forces to Protect the Public* (Home Office 1998) rejected the merger of the two services, partly on grounds of principle (insufficient overlap of responsibilities) and partly on grounds of cost. It described the prospect of a full merger as being 'a bridge too far' and explicitly recognized that probation's role in the public protection agenda would involve it more in a range of inter-agency work in the community (not only police but mental health, local authorities, the Crown Prosecution Service, victim support and voluntary sector organizations) than in developing its relationship with prisons beyond that of the routine improvement of 'shared working'. Significantly, *Joining Forces* in 1998 acknowledged what the *Carter Report* (2003) later failed to grasp, namely, that the cultural tide for probation was already shifting towards a sense that it was the police and not the prisons who were its 'natural partners'. Here lay an indication that the structural future of criminal justice administration would perhaps be distinguished more by federation than merger. But the relationship between probation and the police had, if anything, been more hostile historically.

Probation and the police: mutual suspicion

The aforementioned antipathy felt by probation officers towards working in prisons was matched by their disdain for the police, which also had ideological and cultural foundations. Ideologically, probation and police officers were regarded as occupying contrasting positions in the criminal justice system. On the one hand the police, as crime fighters, apprehended criminals with the objectives of preventing and detecting crime. On the other hand, probation officers' work focused on the same group, but constructed them as 'clients' rather than criminals, and provided supervision with the objective of change and rehabilitation. With such different missions, it is not surprising that police and probation officers should come into conflict and develop distinctive occupational cultures based on contrasting worldviews.

The relationship in tension is alluded to in textbooks and memoirs from this period. Mott, who joined the probation service in 1960, generally praised the police but noted that police and probation officers would not always agree because they 'deal with mutual clients in different ways' (1992: 113). Parsloe (1967), writing for social work students in the late 1960s, advised:

> The probation service has a special and important relationship with the police. Any officer will know how much the local police can either help or hinder his [sic] work. The relationship between these two services is never likely to be easy, for they represent distinct parts of society's mixed attitude to offenders, and different kinds of people will be attracted to each service.
> (Parsloe 1967: 89–90)

Our more experienced interviewees, who joined probation in the 1960s and 1970s, recalled working their 'patches' and having little interaction with the local police officers, despite them covering similar areas on their beats. A significant feature of this period is that both services worked close to the same communities, though both were to retreat from them. First the police moved officers from foot patrols based around beats to motorized patrolling under the 'unit beat system' in the early 1970s (Weatheritt 1986). Subsequently this new system was held popularly responsible for damaging the traditional relationship between the beat officer and the public. From the late 1980s, the probation service was also to withdraw from being embedded in communities; the patch system gave way to office-based programme delivery and desk-bound risk management.

The patch system, which included undertaking regular home visits, as discussed in Chapter 3, enabled probation officers to build their field experience and to get to know families and individuals within relatively small geographical areas. Although the police were also working close to the community they were perceived as an oppositional force. One interviewee talked about working his patch on a council-owned housing estate in the mid-1970s:

> When I started, we let 'em out and the police locked 'em up, pretty much. And they hated us and we hated them ... we were namby-pamby social workers and, you know, all that kind of thing, do-gooders; and the police were rough, tough, you know, keeping people safe and lock 'em up and throw away the key. And there was a complete culture divide between police and probation.
>
> (CO11)

Other interviewees confirmed that the relationship was not just one of indifference, but one of suspicion and hostility, often mutual (CO3; CO12; FPW2; CO16). This is captured by one interviewee who survived a formative experience by deflecting the hostility of police away from probation officers to social workers:

> I was sent to do a talk to the police in about my second year of work ... I got shoved in this room [with] about 30 kind of really old, experienced police sergeants, who just wanted to destroy the probation service ... and the only way you survived was by mentioning social workers and then they all agreed that social workers were worse.
>
> (FPW6)

Suspicion existed at both individual and organizational levels. At management level this was evidenced by the absence of information-sharing protocols between agencies. At the operational level of probation officers there was cultural and ideological opposition to providing information on clients to the police:

> Police were very much kept at arm's length and you wouldn't share information with the police. I mean people would often tell you things but you would never have shared that. And there's probably an element of collusion with offenders, and obviously, that's something that changed.
>
> (PW16)

Thus far we have characterized the probation–police relationship in a way that suggests, at best, Davidson's first stage of inter-organizational relationships, namely 'communication'. However, although probation officers were wary of the police as an organization, some were building informal mutually beneficial contacts with police officers that were to prove the groundwork for later enhanced relations. For example, several interviewees talked about mixing with police officers around the courts and talking cases through with them and, similarly, liaising with the police over child protection cases. This informal, possibly aberrant, behaviour was to be sanctioned formally, if not by the respective occupational cultures, with the passing of the Crime and Disorder Act in 1998 which coincided with other influential factors including a change in training regimes.

We now turn to more contemporary perceptions of these relationships.

NOMS, the myth of 'prisobation' and the spectre of polibation

The emergence of NOMS in 2004 can be characterized by the desire of the government to eradicate the concept of 'probation' from the national psyche and erode the professional identity of probation officers, while at the same time creating a narrative of 'joined up' ('seamless', 'end-to-end') penal thinking and cost-effective delivery of both public protection (through risk assessment) and services to offenders (through contestability) (Worrall 2008a: 120). What the *Carter Report* failed to appreciate, however, was the cultural shift that had already taken place within the probation service, away from closer working with prisons and towards a 'federal' relationship with the police. In our research we have been interested in identifying the impact of NOMS on probation officer cultures and, specifically, on relationships between probation and prison officers. We would argue that the impact has been greatest at (a) senior management level and (b) at the level of probation officers and prison officers working together inside prison. The impact on probation officers working in the community has been either minimal (with experienced officers often refusing to use the term 'offender manager' in preference to probation officer), taken-for-granted (among those staff who have been recruited and trained since 2004 – 'I'm a child of NOMS' (PW4)) or resistant:

> [NOMS] was such a catastrophe … we're just poles apart … and all the fears are realized inasmuch as NOMS is run by prison staff, it's not run by probation staff … we've got people who know nothing about our job … making huge decisions about us as a service.
>
> (PW19)

The comradeship and solidarity of prison officer culture, as described by Liebling *et al.* (2011) is still very recognizable, even if it is not always easy to explain:

> The prison service are militarified and we're not – we're reflective thinkers. … Just the way they carry themselves, the way they speak … like prison talk is very curt and quick, 'da, di, da, di', you know, 'want it done, this is what's gonna happen', you don't get into conversations and things.
>
> (PW23)

In this environment, probation officers feel vulnerable in their role.[1] In the current financial climate, prison officers view them as being 'expensive and unnecessary' (PW8), and as 'middle-class tossers, competing for their jobs' (PW17). Burnett and Stevens (2007) found that prison officers believed they would need to make very little adjustment to become offender supervisors and one of our respondents agreed that they regarded probation officers as redundant:

> They basically hated us, like they didn't want us there, we were too expensive ... I think they thought that the offender management model was, 'this is it, we are probation officers now, you know, we don't need probation officers, we can do everything'.
>
> (PW6)

Additionally, the rise and rise of prison psychologists (many of whom now run the accredited cognitive behavioural programmes) has further threatened the role of probation officers in prisons. As we saw in Chapter 3, one interviewee told us that she was shocked that the governor could simply decide that probation officers were no longer to run programmes (PW1).

In some prisons at least, offender supervisors may be either prison officers or probation officers (suggesting the emergence of the 'prisobation' officer) but they don't necessarily do the job in the same way. Specifically, we were told that prison officers don't like, or don't have the skills, to write reports, so this task often falls to probation staff, who are also allocated higher-risk offenders who are likely to be subject to higher-level multi-agency supervision on release.

Other respondents were more optimistic and suggested that probation culture can mitigate the worst excesses of prison culture in ways that may not be immediately obvious. We were told that probation officers are often more challenging of prisoners than prison officers are. 'There's a lot of appeasement here' (PW3) one senior probation officer told us. She argued that this was not in prisoners' interests and was the result of laziness and fear on the part of prison officers. Probation officers, she argued, put in more time and effort to help prisoners resolve their problems instead of taking the easy way out. She felt that prison staff who worked alongside probation staff were gaining these skills.

At senior management level, there was some criticism of the failure of probation's leaders to penetrate the top echelons of the NOMS hierarchy. The predominant view of NOMS was of a 'command and control' culture which no longer has any probation voice at the top:

> The prison service is a service that is not institutionally and constitutionally capable of understanding that there's any other way of operating other than the way the prison service operates ... and NOMS is the prison service, it's got no probation thinking in it ... it's deeply frustrating.
>
> (CO2)

Probation is regarded as 'troublesome', we were told, because 'they don't do what they're told' (CO14). The implications of this are pervasive and reach beyond the scope of this chapter to the heart of the probation service's future. Arguably, relationships between the two services can no longer be accurately described as 'inter-agency' since they are now one and the same agency. On paper, they have reached Davidson's level five model, namely that of merger, but while a 'turbulent' environment has been readily identified, our research suggests that obstacles to a genuine merger remain in the form of a threat to probation 'domain', a failure to resolve individual and group role conflicts and a perceived absence of probation leadership within the merged organization.

In contrast, contemporary perceptions of relationships between probation and the police are generally more positive. Our research suggests that from the perspective of probation officers, relations with the police began to change from 1998. From this year the Crime and Disorder Act required local agencies, including probation and police, to work together and share information to identify and resolve crime issues. In practice this meant that police and probation employees would meet routinely and formally and would work together at strategic and operational levels. The closer working was given further nudges with the establishment of the MAPPA framework from 2000 and the widening of prolific offender projects from ad hoc area-specific initiatives to a national scheme in 2002, which extended to a national PPO Strategy in 2004. Many of our interviewees in senior management roles referred to the changing relationship with the police as their most significant changed relationship. Some compared the mutually beneficial relationship with the police with the less coherent relationship with prisons:

> I think relationships with the police are excellent ... I mean when I was a new officer, you know, the police were the enemy ... police officers didn't come into a probation office ... I think a huge change, you know, largely triggered by a whole MAPPA process. I mean not all of that is brilliant but ... and I think our natural allies actually are the police not the prison service. You know, I think the mistake was, if we had to go in with somebody, was to go in with the prison service, not the police; I'd much rather be in with the police.
>
> (CO13)

At the same time that agencies were finding their way in formal partnership working, new training arrangements for probation officers were also set in place, from 1997, that separated probation and social work training, with the creation of Trainee Probation Officers (TPOs) and the Diploma in Probation Studies (see Chapter 2). Treadwell (2006) argues that although the intention of the new programme was not to create an unquestioning enforcement mentality in TPOs, it did have that consequence for some. In terms of working relations with the police, this raises the possibility that some probation officers who have qualified since 1997 are more likely to accept the police as co-workers than their colleagues are, who trained under previous regimes. And indeed we did find that interviewees tended to characterize themselves and their colleagues in terms of the qualification framework that they trained under.

For some of the older, more experienced, interviewees, the irony of the turn-around in organizational attitudes towards the police was not lost. One interviewee recalled an incident from the 1970s when as a young probation officer she was chatting to police officers outside the police station behind the court:

> I can remember my boss saying to me, if I catch you talking to a police officer again, you could get sacked, whereas now, if I don't talk to the police, I could get sacked.
>
> (PW24)

The turbulence of the environment had contributed, therefore, to creating the conditions after 1998 in which probation-police co-operation and even feder-ation (in Davidson's sense of the term) was deemed both appropriate and desir-able. The Labour government funded the police to unprecedented levels and as probation retreated from the community due to resource constraints and the dominance of computer-based work, the police returned there through reassur-ance policing, neighbourhood policing teams and the introduction of Police Community Support Officers. Both probation and the police had different but converging motives for getting closer to each other and thereby to communities, united in the cause of public protection. In such conditions, the potential for mutual adjustment and respect for organizational domain is likely to be enhanced. There is evidence that probation–police partnership working can bring benefits for the effective management of offenders (see, for example, Mawby and Worrall 2004), especially when *complementary* skills are acknowledged. As one interviewee remarked:

> We've transformed our relationships with the police now in ways that were unimaginable when I came into the job. ... The reason why we work well with the police is because we're different to them, and from them.
>
> (CO2)

This point is reinforced by Nash (2008: 303, 307) who argues that multi-agency work should be about bringing different skills and knowledge bases together to add value when focusing on a problem or situation. Polibation, for him, raises the threat (and reality in public protection teams) of bringing together agency practitioners who become too similar and lose their distinct contributions and core cultural characteristics. The extent to which practitioners merge their prac-tices or cross over to take on characteristics of their partners has been a recurring theme in both UK and US literature (Murphy and Lutze 2009; Nash and Walker 2009). Corbett (1998) coined the term 'mission distortion' to describe practition-ers drifting towards their partner's way of seeing things. Our research provided examples of practitioners moving in the direction of their partner agencies.

Interviewees recounted examples of police officers who had become focused on rehabilitation which, when combined with their own 'can do' approach, sometimes had unfortunate consequences:

> [Of PPO officers] What always makes me laugh is, I became the bad cop and they became the good cop ... because the police are very much 'there's a problem, let's sort it' ... but I had the licence, I was the one with the power ... certainly in the offenders' eyes, I seemed to be the baddie.
>
> (PW6)

> [Of PPO colleague] He's a smashing guy but he's a bobby, you know, and he comes across as, you know [laugh]. He's ... he's a people person in a non-people person way. He's ... police are quite black and white, you know, just in the way that they approach stuff. You know, there's a problem, we can solve it. Yes ... a very pragmatic approach to it, you know; tell me your problem, I'll give you a solution or a way you can do it, and then go and do it, yeah. Without the subtleties of human interaction, you know. I think that's the thing about it [laugh].
>
> (PW17)

By the same measure, interviewees provided examples of probation colleagues moving in the opposite direction:

> The TPOs, no disrespect to the TPOs, they work completely differently ... they're into 'get 'em'. You hear them so often 'I've got 'em'. I've heard it so often. I'll say 'you've got who?', you know, and they say 'well, I can breach him now' ... I say 'is that what your job's about?' you know, grabbing hold of him, breaching him? 'Isn't it about like going out and negotiating and pulling 'em in a little bit?' And they don't see that, a lot of them.
>
> (PW23)

The structural transformations that enabled closer working relationships may have fed into the cultural transformations that we have described but this is not the complete picture, and we would argue that Davidson's model is thus oversimplified. Just as in the pre-1998 period we found pockets of co-operation amid the general mutual stand-off, in the post-1998 era there exists within the general spirit of openness and co-operation cultural continuities in both agencies that emphasize that these are two different agencies with separate missions that at times coincide and coalesce but at other times reinforce traditional suspicions. For example,as we discussed in Chapter 2, the excesses of police culture are still evident and were put forward by two interviewees as reasons for leaving the police and re-training as probation officers.

Equally, while interviewees working at an operational level provided examples of strong working relations with some police officers, there was an equivalent number of comments that referred to the tensions that remain, arising from, inter alia, police propensity to try and take over offender management 'because they're always much bigger and stronger' (CO14) and their perceived lack of empathy and understanding:

> They just don't get the whole softly-softly, catchee monkey approach. It's very much let's get in there and crack some skulls. So obviously, sometimes they can be a bit frustrated with our way of working in terms of the slower way ... I think some of them probably just don't see our work as any value ... I mean they're not really interested in people, are they, post-sentence, coppers? They don't really care.
>
> (PW15)

Conclusion

In this chapter, we have demonstrated that the political, economic and social landscape of the past five decades, but particularly since the late 1980s, has created a 'turbulent field' which no single criminal justice agency can navigate alone. The old regime of minimal communication between police and probation proved wholly inadequate for the demands of community safety, public protection and risk management. We argue here (see Table 4.1) that probation–police relations moved dramatically through Davidson's levels in the late 1990s to a relationship of 'federation' where formal joint structures exist for at least some objectives and tasks within the two organizations. The relationship between probation and prison is more complex, having been one of uneasy co-operation from the 1960s to the 1980s, followed by a gradual move to 'federation' and a forced move to 'merger'

Table 4.1 Adapting Davidson's model to probation – courts – prisons – police relationships

Probation relationships	Historically	Tipping point	Contemporary
With courts	Federation	1999 Specific Sentence ('fast delivery') Reports	Co-operation with (decreasing) elements of co-ordination
With prisons	Co-operation (The Welfare) moving to co-ordination (Shared Working)	1998 *Joining Forces to Protect the Public*	Federation (e.g. accredited programmes, resettlement) accelerating to Merger (Carter Report and NOMS)
With police	Communication (mutual suspicion) with pockets of Co-operation	1998 Crime and Disorder Act	Federation (Public protection partnerships e.g. PPO, MAPPA)

by 2004. In contrast, however, the historically close, or federated, relationship between probation and the courts has become increasingly distant as the perceived traditional skills and contribution of probation to the process and procedures of sentencing have been regarded as less indispensible.

There were potential 'tipping points' in the late 1990s. One of these – the introduction of fast delivery court reports – symbolized the drifting apart of a hitherto symbiotic relationship between probation and the courts. With the 1998 Crime and Disorder Act and the publication of *Joining Forces*, it seemed possible that probation, police and prisons might 'federate' but the turbulent environment swept probation (reluctantly) and prisons in another direction. Our research indicates that probation perceives itself to have suffered as a result, not least because its domain has been threatened by the merger, role conflicts remain unresolved and there is a perceived absence of probation leadership at the top of the new organization. However rational the merger may have seemed to Carter and to policy-makers, there are limits to rationality that were not taken into account. Despite the deeply embedded historical animosity between probation officers and the police, the former now 'fantasize' about what might have been, had they merged with the police.

Yet, as we have shown, there remain strong perceived cultural continuities in these organizations that create tensions which might be regarded as being healthy in co-operative or federated organizations but as being toxic in merged organizations. If our analysis has any validity, then healthy relationships between probation, police, prisons – and even the courts – require a realignment that ensures respect for the domain of each in the interests of the wider community.

5   Perceptions, misconceptions and representations

A lot of people don't know what probation officers do. And I find that quite shocking. Like when you tell people you're a probation officer, they don't know what that means and they go 'what do you do?'

(TPO1)

I'm not sure that the public's view of the probation service has changed substantially in all the 30 years that I've been doing it [laugh], the first response is 'what?' [laugh] And the second response is, 'oh well you're softer on crimes'. And actually, that probably hasn't changed too much in all that time.

(CO8)

Probation workers do not have a high public profile. They do not wear uniforms and do not perform a high-visibility role that marks out to the public what they routinely do. The probation service does not have familiar and recognizable 'talking heads' who articulate through the media the probation perspective on criminal justice matters. Media coverage of probation work is intermittent, but media organizations do broadcast negative news when probation workers are implicated in incidents of failure in the criminal justice system. However, our research established that probation workers feel underestimated and misunderstood not only by the media, but also by family members, friends and the general public. This chapter examines probation workers' perceptions of how they are regarded by family, friends, the wider public and politicians. The extent to which the job is regarded as 'socially tainted' in that it involves working with people despised by society in general, media representations of probation work and the near-universal failure of the service to manage its media image are analysed.

Family, friends and public

There was almost universal agreement among interviewees that the public know and understand very little about the probation service and what probation workers do. However, there were some differences between younger and older interviewees in their perceptions of the status of probation work when they embarked upon their respective careers.

Among our more experienced probation workers, interviewees recalled a certain public prestige attached to the job when they started their careers. FPW7 joined the probation service in 1964 and recalled that the public impression was respectful:

> In the early days, we were a bit priest-like, weren't we, so if you said you were a probation officer, people would say 'oh we must be careful what we say' and, you know, imagine you're taking a moral view of them, in a slightly humorous way.
>
> (FPW7)

Despite attributing an elevated status to probation work in the mid-1960s, FPW7 recognized that a significant characteristic of the job was that it constituted high-prestige 'dirty work', as introduced in Chapter 1:

> We are probably the only group that will work with people [in the community] who are doing evil and don't deserve help, aren't we? And there's something special about us doing that, you know.
>
> (FPW7)

While FPW7's comments acknowledge the relative decline of the almost sacred status of probation work, CO12, who qualified in 1981, talked about how the positive public status of probation, when compared to social work, convinced her that she had made the correct career decision:

> I think the perception that I had of the probation officer, as compared to the social worker, was of somebody who had a much more clearly defined role, and probably as a result of that, had an enhanced status in the eyes of the general public.
>
> (CO12)

This elevated status still held when FPW4 joined the service in 1990. He felt that at that point in time probation workers were revered as professionals with a status in the community:

> I think a probation officer, when I first started as a probation assistant, was somebody who was almost revered as … it had a status…. And it was somebody who was … you know, had a fair amount of standing, a fair amount of knowledge and, you know, standing within the community.
>
> (FPW4)

By contrast, in contemporary impressions of probation work, the clear references to sacred attributes ('priest-like', 'revered') are replaced by more worldly descriptions. Interviewees' comments suggest that respect and awe have been superseded by limited interest and knowledge, based on stereotypical impressions that the probation service works with the undeserving and is too 'soft':

> The public image isn't ever gonna be good because we do something with people who nobody wants to really think about … and we can never get recognition for what we actually do on the measures that they're using to measure it.
>
> (PW17)

> I still think there's something about the public [not being] particularly interested in probation; they just want to know somebody out there is doing something about it. And they become alarmed when they hear something's gone wrong.
>
> (CO4)

These perceived public views of probation work, as we argue below, can be explained partly through the routine processes of news gathering. Crime stories are selected and elevated into local, regional and national news through a combination of news values and the structural and organizational characteristics of criminal justice and media organizations (Jewkes 2008, 2010; Mawby 2010a). However, before further examining the widely perceived public image of probation work, we will consider how probation work is regarded by our interviewees' family and friends.

While the former probation workers spoke of erstwhile public awe and reverence, the most recent joiners, the TPOs, talked about the reactions and views of their families and how they varied from support to surprise and opposition. One TPO talked about the negative attitudes of her ex-husband (who worked in a hostel for ex-offenders) and daughter:

> He, actually, hates probation [laugh]. With the offenders, all my daughter kept thinking of was, yeah but mum, you've lived in [this area] all your life and if you work here, and then you're gonna know the people, oh! So it was all negativity.
>
> (TPO9)

Another TPO, a female from an Asian background, related how her family were disappointed with her career choice:

> I think some cultures have an expectation about what you do as a job, what's seen as appropriate or, you know, worthy. I don't know, I think there's a lot of snobbery maybe, I'm not sure. I know that a lot of my relatives, I feel like they look down on what I do, which really, really annoys me [laugh]. … They wouldn't even ask what I do, what's involved. They just think work in prison, work with offenders, that's all they need to know [laugh].
>
> (TPO1)

On the other hand, a TPO whose father had worked in the police and fire services was more supportive, despite being surprised at the choice of career:

> My dad was pretty sure that I would go into the police and thought … because he did a little bit in the police and the fire service. So he thought that would be my career path, and he was surprised when I said the probation service [laugh]. Because again, I don't think he knew anything about it. But you know, largely sort of support and … but again, sort of a bit of mystification as to what the whole thing is.
>
> (TPO10)

Beyond the family, the TPOs found that their friends were both supportive of, and intrigued by, their work even if they didn't really understand what it involved. TPO3 felt that people he met socially thought he was doing an important job, involved in 'maintaining law and order', though they were generally unaware of what the role entailed and wanted to find out more. Similarly, TPO7 spoke about how his friends in more conventional administrative jobs were interested in his role:

> Everyone I interact with socially thinks it's a really interesting job. They want to hear about it and they think it's really good…. Everyone thought this is just … yeah this is fascinating. They're kind of working in sort of marketing stuff and all these kind of administrative roles and human resources. You know, and it's like I work directly with people who go out and rob people – it's great, you know [laugh]…. But then again, you read the papers and we're supposed to be rubbish at our jobs and we're supposed to be the problem rather than the solution.
>
> (TPO7)

This mixture of support and mystification is not restricted to TPOs, as more experienced probation workers remarked on the lack of knowledge of family members that co-existed with admiring support. For example, one commented:

> My husband thought I had a cushy life but he was very supportive. My family is very proud even though they don't really know what I do. People don't know what probation is. When I say what I do they say 'But you're so small – how do you manage?'.
>
> (PW2)

This kind of comment was quite typical, and one interviewee provided further insight into the difficulties of sharing detailed aspects of probation work with partners and friends and how this reinforced bonds with colleagues:

> I still don't believe that anyone understands or knows what we do, including the people that we share our lives with [laugh]. That's why we stick

together, it's ... you know, we form close friendships because we know what it feels like to have someone kick off on you, to have someone commit a horrendous offence that you can't even bear to think or talk about, you know. We do look after our own. It's hard for a partner, a friend to understand that, because we don't ... obviously, we can't talk in detail, you know.

(PW7)

As we saw in Chapter 1, several interviewees admitted that they did not disclose their occupations in social gatherings to avoid the debates that were sometimes provoked. Some TPOs had learned the hard way that at social gatherings, interest was not the only reaction to their choice of career. One recalled a party where:

Actually, where I was challenged and I got really angry [laugh] because she ... she said 'how can you work with people like those?' And I'm like 'they're just people'.

(TPO2)

Thus far, we have discussed how probation workers feel their work is perceived by family, friends and the wider public. It is notable that there is a mixture of lack of actual knowledge about what the job entails combined with distaste over the people they work with. But there is also a frisson of curiosity concerning working with risky people. These are some of the consequences of doing dirty work and they hint at the lure of edgework (see Chapter 1) which we explore further in the next chapter. We now turn to examine another important source of public knowledge about probation work, that of media representations.

Media representations and corporate communications

Probation and the news media

When talking about public perceptions of probation work, our interviewees frequently mentioned the influence of the news media and there tended to be general agreement that while not usually interested in the routine work of probation, the news media were interested when notable cases or incidents came to light. This puts probation work in the position of being relatively invisible to the media in its routine work:

To be honest, I don't think it's a sexy story. You know, sitting down in an interview room, interviewing an offender, week after week, getting them to understand why they're behaving the way that they do and getting them to change, doesn't really grab the public appetite, and as I say it doesn't grab headlines. People traditionally talk about us being like the oil in the cogs of the criminal justice system. I think there's a lot of truth in that.

(PW5)

On the other hand, there was a commonly held belief that when the news media focused on probation work, they tended to perpetuate negative stereotypes and misunderstandings or, alternatively, left the service dangerously exposed when serious incidents occurred:

> The media portrays us so negatively, you know, the sentences, they think oh it's a rubbish sentence, short sentence, and they just don't have a clue. They don't have a clue the input that we have in safeguarding the public.
>
> (PW18)

> And people don't ... why don't people understand? I mean if the news can't even report it properly. I think you've still got a number of people out there, who think that we're the prisoners' friends, the offenders' friends, and we don't know ... you know, we're just woolly liberals looking after them, without thinking.
>
> (PW8)

> The public have a right to expect us to, you know, do everything we can to manage risk, and to do things properly, but they can't expect us to eliminate risk because you can't do that. But you know, *The Sun* doesn't wanna listen to that. I mean the *News of the World* doesn't want to listen to that. So the media have got interested, when the profile of the people we deal with has changed. So you know, they're interested in murderers, sex offenders and perverts, aren't they?
>
> (CO7)

A small-scale academic study by Jewkes (2008) confirms the experiential conclusions of the interviewees, namely that probation work, often invisible in the news media, has significant news value when serious cases blow up. She also notes (2008: 58) that people who work with 'outsiders' can themselves become demonized through negative media coverage, with consequences for their morale. Jewkes argues (2008: 59) that until the mid-2000s the probation service was not only un-newsworthy, it was (quoting Aldridge 1999b) 'stubbornly lacking in news value'. This, she contends, changed in 2005 and 2006 when a number of cases pushed the probation service into the media glare. She examines five 'mega-cases' (Peelo 2006), namely unusual crimes that particularly offend society, are subject to high levels of reporting and serve as reference cases to explain subsequent crimes. Like 'signal' crimes (Innes 2004) they attain a symbolic status. Jewkes contends that news coverage of these cases cast the service as dangerously ineffective; all involved murders by people under probation supervision.[1] To these we could add the murders of two French students in 2008 by Dano Sonnex, as examined by Fitzgibbon (2011). In considering the news values that propelled these cases into the headlines, Jewkes identifies the prominent coexistence of 'novelty' and 'predictability'. Representing the former, the previously invisible probation service was projected as at fault for some of the worst crimes committed in the period; representing the latter, the outcomes were projected as the natural consequence of feckless youth and a soft criminal justice system. Interpreting the dominant political discourses, Jewkes also posits whether the media hysteria was a co-ordinated distraction to soften up the probation service and to encourage public support for its reform.

In tune with Jewkes's analysis, probation workers recognized the changing media profile of probation work. The relative anonymity of probation until the mega-cases of 2005–6 did bring some benefits:

> I think probation have often wanted to keep under the radar of the public image … because the trouble was, you know, it was the bad news that would often be … and still is often, the bad news that causes significant downfalls. So, you know, there is still around very much a feeling of, we won't put our heads above the parapet because we might get shot down. And that's partly because we're not very skilled at handling the media. You know, we're small organizations, because each probation area's different.
>
> (CO14)

> I think partly, [in the early 1980s] we didn't have much press at all [laugh]. And I think that's probably been, you know, to a large extent, a recurrent theme over the years, that actually, we've tended to be a bit of a secret service; people haven't known a lot about the probation service, unless they've had first-hand experience of the service. And that's probably protected us in a way, except when you get the obvious, you know, high profile Sonnex and Rice, and whatever hits the headlines. And then, of course, we're all damned, aren't we? But those cases have been so few and far between, whereas, there's almost constantly something in the press about social services have failed here and failed there, and whatever.
>
> (CO12)

Others registered frustration with the low profile and with the acceptance of bad press when it occurs:

> I think we have a poor profile because we don't tell anybody what we do. I'm not quite sure why we never have really. Part … we're a bit self-effacing really, and it is sort of well, you know, we like to sort of quietly get on with it. And we're very defensive, to the point of ridiculous [laugh]. So we … you know, so we have a bad case, and we go out and say we're really sorry, which is fine…. But we are so defensive. And we've allowed ourselves to be done to over the years. Interestingly, we've survived, and I think we're much stronger than we like to think we are…. So it's almost like well if we just keep quiet, we'll sort of carry on doing this stuff [laugh].
>
> (CO10)

This situation is the outcome of cultural, structural and organizational dynamics that exist in uneasy tension in the current turbulent operating context. First, culturally the probation service has hitherto been largely willing to adopt a low public and media profile. The service has been comfortable to be a modest and self-deprecating secret service, doing good work quietly. Culturally, this links to a passivity and a willingness to apologize that some felt characterized the probation service. One chief officer, for example, commented that:

> I think probation culture is far too *mea culpa*; absolutely too *mea culpa*. And I think that being like that has allowed the Ministry of Justice, Home Office before, others, to lend blame on probation inappropriately ... it's like 'I'm Spartacus' and no one else owns up, is the analogy I use.
>
> (CO3)

Second, and structurally, the voice of the probation service is constrained in a way that restricts access to the media. Probation chiefs are restricted in communicating as leaders of probation by their structural position within NOMS and the oversight of the Ministry of Justice (MoJ). As individual chiefs, they can communicate about local probation issues relevant to their areas, but they do not speak on national policy, which is the domain of NOMS and MoJ. This can be frustrating:

> When the National Probation Directorate was set up in 2001, as a government agency, the national director became a civil servant, and so was then bound by the rules of the civil service, not to speak independently. So the probation voice disappeared publicly for a number of years. And that was, I think, probably unexpected; we didn't anticipate that would happen. We thought having a national voice, a national director would actually focus the voice of the probation service. And it did internally within government, but externally, they were completely unable to say anything. So all the awful things that happened, whether it was cases going wrong or whatever it was, never did you hear anything from the leadership of the probation service at that point ... I think, and it's still the case that, you know, there's nobody at the centre of NOMS who will be able to say anything around government policy. It can only be done through ministers.
>
> (CO8)

> The national voice of Probation has not been there over the years. In the old days with there being a sort of civil service, the Home Office unit and the Probation unit, civil servants aren't allowed to have a different role. And that's continued with NOMS, because their role is to protect ministers. So there isn't a national voice for probation, anybody nationally able to speak out on behalf of the service, because they're always protecting a minister, if they speak. And ... and even to the point where we're almost stopped from speaking at a local level sometimes, you know, we're not allowed ... we're

only allowed to comment on certain things under certain circumstances. So we have protocols ... they'll allow you to talk about local issues, but they don't like ... so for instance, London is a good example, of course, because what's local and what's national is a very fine line. Most issues in London are national issues; they get into the national press, even though they're about London Probation. So you know, there have been examples where there'd be something in the national press and the MoJ would not allow us to comment, and so they would handle it. But in their handling of it, all they're doing is protecting the minister, not protecting the reputation of probation.

(CO14)

To add to the frustration of the gagged probation chiefs, their lack of voice has left a gap which is filled by the MoJ and NAPO. The former are not regarded as a positive supporter of the probation service:

I get very angry that, our employers effectively, the Ministry of Justice, for example, the Home Office as was, never seem to make a positive comment about the probation service ... I mean at the moment, they're talking about probation because it's cheaper than prisons. A little bit they're talking about us, but mostly from emptying the prisons. You don't hear Ministers saying the probation service supervises umpteen thousands of people, of whom only this proportion reoffend, they manage these thousands of seriously dangerous people and we've had two serious incidents out of all that. We don't hear anybody saying what the probation service actually do with people is this, this, this and this. And I mean on an individual level, I can sit down and bore friends and acquaintances, but until somebody starts saying it out very loud, I can't see how the public's gonna have an idea of what we do.

(PW24)

The alternative voice is that of NAPO and in particular, the Assistant General Secretary, Harry Fletcher, cited by most interviewees as the most prominent probation voice. Fletcher is the *only* nationally recognized voice of probation. Some chief officers felt that he was not the most appropriate voice and sometimes communicated unhelpfully naive messages:

He's done a lot of work over the years, but you know, he wasn't the person who should have been speaking for the probation service, but he was the only voice ... and the media would go to him, because he was the only voice who was prepared to say anything, or able to say anything. And some of what he said was ... seemed to be off the mark, it seemed to be giving the wrong messages at the wrong time, very specifically from a union point of view.

(CO8)

Other chiefs admired Fletcher's presence in the absence of other voices: 'I'd say 95 times out of 100 he's bloody good … he's done what chief officers should have done 10 years ago and we didn't do it.' (CO2).

Third, an analysis of the organizational dynamics of external communications reveals the lack of resources that probation trusts allocate to reactive and pro-active media relations and to corporate communications more generally. Proba-tion trusts simply have not had the budgets or the will to invest in building their corporate communications functions. Again this can be related to both the struc-tural constraint on speaking out and the cultural preference that 'probation tends to keep its head down' (CO4). On the whole, the probation areas we visited had few resources for corporate communications. One area had recently lost its com-munications officer and the post had not been replaced. In another area the chief officer allocated some of his own time to work on communications issues with the assistance of his personal assistant. London Probation, as one might expect, does have a marketing communications team, but with approximately five staff at the time of our research, this compares with the resources that a medium-sized provincial police force would allocate to corporate communications. The small numbers of professional communicators also indicates that the probation service lacks specialist skills in this area:

> We haven't done a lot of engagement with the media, and there's not a lot of expertise in the organization really. There's a handful of people that have really got it, and it's a very different skill set. We will say things, I think, very openly and very genuinely, but they're not necessarily the things you should be saying to the media.
>
> (CO4)

Despite this minimalist approach to the proactive promotion of probation work, our research found some excellent examples of probation workers culti-vating local media contacts and succeeding in getting out good news, promot-ing probation workers as 'hidden heroes' (CO5). In the same vein the Probation Chiefs Association has become more active in communicating the profile of the probation service. It is important that it does so because the default probation position of adopting a low media profile is becoming less and less tenable.[2] The turbulent political conditions and an increasingly medi-ated society demand that all public-facing organizations develop the capacity and capabilities to defend their organizational position, to counter adverse pub-licity and to correct misinformation and misunderstandings. This is something that a partner agency, the police service, has done, though with mixed out-comes (Mawby 2007, 2012).

While the police and probation service are not comparable in terms of size they both operate in the same field, often collaboratively, and therefore it is worthwhile to briefly consider how the police have developed structures for com-munication. The police service in England and Wales is organized territorially across 43 police force areas. Each force has its own press office, or in one case,

Norfolk and Suffolk, a shared press office. These are resourced to different levels depending on the size and characteristics of the force, but they undertake similar core functions including reactive and proactive media relations, public relations and marketing activities and the development of communications strategies and policies. In recent years there has been a distinct growth in police corporate communications (Mawby 2010b), which has only been halted by public sector budget cuts (Cartmell and Green 2011). In addition to the force structures for corporate communications through which individual chief constables and their officers communicate, the police service has complementary, sometimes competing voices in the form of the Association of Chief Police Officers (ACPO), the Police Superintendents' Association (PSA) and the Police Federation. Each of these bodies has press or information officers and are regular contributors to public and media debates on policing and wider criminal justice issues.

While this framework for police service communications is not infallible, as the Leveson Inquiry and other investigations have established (Filkin 2011; HMIC 2011), there are elements of principle and good practice that could be considered for transfer to other criminal justice agencies, for example, a communications 'champion' at senior management level, a place for corporate communications in the organizational structure and provision for media advice and training (Mawby 2008). Nevertheless, even if the probation service were to commit greater resources to media relations and were to increase their capabilities and capacities to engage with the media, some interviewees pointed out that probation good news, compared to policing news, is not always plentiful or accessible:

> What I want to do is try and get beyond community payback and talk about the people that turnaround really crumpled, chaotic lives. And generally, offenders don't come back and tell us 'I'm a success story', because actually we were a moment in their life when it was troubled. So if they've completed their order, they walk off into the sunset and don't come near us again, and would like to forget about it because it wasn't the most happy part of their life. But somehow, we need to capture the drug addict that turns his life round, or the offender that learns to read and write, and can read to his kids now, gets himself a job, and bottle them.
>
> (CO4)

> I think it's a two-way street. First, you've got to present it, but then also your audience has got to … you've got to hook an audience and, and they've got to be wanting to listen…. But our intrinsic disadvantage in presentation is that we're so small and we sit alongside much bigger partners and in dealing with the media generally, whichever kind of media, generally, we have far less to give them. Now if you think about the police, you know, particularly in terms of the local media, the local paper here there's probably a story every day … the only organization in [this

county] that gets in the paper more often than the police is the football club.

(CO8)

Another aspect of communication is having a strong identity or image. This is something that the police have developed through several phases of 'image work' since 1829 when the modern police service was established (Mawby 2002). The police 'brand' has been built partly through fictional and factual media representations, and it is to this area that we now turn in relation to the probation service.

Factual and fictional representations of probation work

It is not only in the news media that probation work is marginalized or sensationalized. Probation also has a low profile compared to other criminal justice agencies in factual and fictional representations. The police have a long and rich history of media representations which have been popular with audiences and subject to academic study (Leishman and Mason 2003; Mawby 2003; Reiner 2010). Reiner (1994), for example, has shown how the debate about whether the role of the police should be essentially 'service' or 'force' based can be plotted dialectically through police drama series from *Dixon of Dock Green* to *The Bill* (see Leishman and Mason (2003: chapter 6) for an update of this dialectical discussion). More recently *Life on Mars* (BBC, 2006–7) contrasted the prevailing ethics of policing in the 1970s and 2000s (Garland and Bilby 2011). Equally, factual programmes such as Graef's 1982 observational documentary, *Police*, and Daly's *The Secret Policeman* in 2003 highlighted unacceptable policing practices and added to the pressure to implement change and reform.

Similarly the prison service is well established as a subject of films, television dramas, documentaries and reality programmes (Wilson and O'Sullivan 2004; Mason 2006; Jewkes 2006). Wilson and O'Sullivan (2004, 2005) have argued that prison films can fulfil a number of functions in pursuit of prison reform and television dramas, e.g. *Bad Girls* (ITV, 1999–2002) and documentaries, e.g. *Holloway* (ITV, 2009) have reflected arguments about women and imprisonment (Wilson and O'Sullivan 2004; Jewkes 2006).

In contrast there are relatively few films or television dramas, series and documentaries that have focussed on probation work. There are few, if any, fictional or factual probation officers that have caught the public imagination in the way that police or even prison representations have. As one interviewee noted, 'there is no equivalent of *Casualty* or *The Bill* for probation work' (TPO9). It is not surprising therefore that there is little academic research on how probation has been represented in film, literature, television and radio dramas and documentaries. In contrast, the ESRC has funded research into representations of policing (Allen *et al*. 1998) and the Esmee Fairbairn Foundation funded the Prison Film Project (Wilson and O'Sullivan 2004). Among the limited academic literature on media representations of probation, Bennett (2008) has noted that both factual and fictional media have focused on the 'front end' of criminal justice processes, namely police investigation and prison, with little attention paid to release and resettlement. In these circumstances, recent contributions to the literature by Saunders and Vanstone (2010) and Nellis (2010) are welcome.

Saunders and Vanstone (2010) examine four films concerned with rehabilitation through self-reform and formalized intervention. Just one of their choices focuses on the work of the probation service, namely *I Believe in You*, made in 1952 by Ealing and directed by Basil Deardon. The film's main protagonist, Henry Phipps (played by Cecil Parker) is a middle-aged ex-colonial civil servant who joins the probation service as a second career and the film tracks his progression from fish-out-of-water to accomplished probation officer. Symbolic of his progress is his inept initial court performance early in the film, when he is ridiculed by the presiding magistrate because he hasn't got sufficient knowledge, competence or confidence, compared to his accomplished and authoritative performance by the end of the film, when he has clearly earned the respect of the same magistrate.

In the Ealing film tradition, *I Believe in You* reflected the immediate postwar optimism of the emerging welfare state, but also strove to achieve social realism. As Saunders and Vanstone argue (2010: 379), although it is 'at quick glance, a box-ticking rag-bag account of day-to-day events in the life of a rigidly middle-class, middle-aged probation officer', which projects an idealistic and romantic view of probation officers and their role in society, on closer analysis it should be appreciated for its connections to the modern. Phipps is client-centred but challenging of behaviour, offers a pro-social model and seeks collaborative relationships. Crucially there is awareness of the importance of the personal relationship between officer and client (Saunders and Vanstone 2010: 385).

Despite Saunders and Vanstone's praise for the film, *I Believe in You* is not well-remembered and rarely reappears on television. Looking back on the film, Birkbeck (1982: 86) remarked that 1980s probation officers worked under pressures unknown to Phipps' generation, but they could learn from his regular and influential court performances. Nevertheless, the portrayal did not create a symbolic and lasting representation of the probation officer in the way that another Ealing film, *The Blue Lamp*, from 1950 and also directed by Deardon, created an enduring symbol for policing in the form of PC George Dixon. Despite being shot and killed in the film Dixon was resurrected and served from 1955 to 1976 in the spin-off BBC television series. Dixon became a symbol of, and benchmark for, a certain kind of legitimate policing and was revived for a BBC Radio 4 six-part series in 2005. While 'Dixon' is still called upon in political and media debates on policing, the name of 'Phipps' as a touchstone is absent from probation debates.

Notwithstanding that media representations can be misleading and inaccurate, as Nellis (2010: 2) somewhat ruefully points out, the viewing public have not been offered a popular narrative of the post-war evolution of probation work or 'fictional probation champions' in the same way that they have for policing.

Since *I Believe in You*, British probation workers have rarely featured as protagonists in films, though one exception is *The Parole Officer* (2001) which starred Steve Coogan. Culture.com[3] describes the film as being:

> about, well, a parole officer, called Simon Garden. Typically for a Coogan creation, he's socially inept, and totally useless at his job. His success rate is dismal – out of a thousand clients, Simon has actually convinced three to eschew a life of crime and to stick to the straight and narrow.

This description clearly plays to some of the stereotypes that perpetuate and the film was not well-received critically, though the Coogan character is likeable and sympathetic. During the interviews we made a point of asking the participants if they were aware of any media representations of probation work. Several mentioned *The Parole Officer* and PW17 remembered that Coogan was 'the kind of classic "assist, befriend and advise" because he was saying about scaling the hill of offending and, you know, coming back down the other side and stuff like that. So he was very, you know offender orientated'. Few had heard of *I Believe in You* though one chief officer, CO8, remarked that Cecil Parker as Phipps was his ideal probation officer.

Moving from film to television, again there is a dearth of factual and fictional programmes featuring probation work, compared to the daily programmes on policing and the regular programmes that feature prisons. Dramas around probation have been more common than documentaries. Between 1959 and 1962 the ITV series *Probation Officer* focused on the work of two male and one female probation officers. Shot in a semi-documentary style, the episodes were based on real court cases. Two of our interviewees remembered this series and for one it was influential in his choice of career:

> Another influential factor, there was a series called *The Probation Officer* that was around in '50s, '60s. I've forgotten the actor, but it played it straight, you know, it wasn't like the more recent ones, where they were playing it for drama and so on. It was more like a documentary, although it was a series of fictional situations … Looking back, they played the sort of cases I've dealt with, you know, and they played it seriously. … That influenced me in terms of, you know, I'd got the interest in medicine and working with people, but that sort of came to the fore in terms of giving me knowledge about the sort of thing I might be able to do.
>
> (FPW7)

Probation work did not feature again in a television drama series until the screening of *Hard Cases* (Central ITV), which ran for two series in 1988 and 1989. It was filmed in Nottinghamshire and followed a team of six probation workers based in a run-down Midlands office. Mike Nellis (2008: 213) has written that the series did not capture the public imagination but did articulate, through the main characters, contemporary probation concerns with 'care/control, idealism/

realism'. He concludes (2008: 214) that *Hard Cases* was an 'honourable piece of work' that presented probation workers as human, skilled and compassionate.

While the series may not have captured the public imagination, it was debated within the probation service. The March 1988 issue of *Probation Journal* included two articles reviewing the first series. Both considered that probation work was over-dramatized[4] but Mason (1988: 37) concluded that it was better than he expected and 'did have something of the feel for the job, from tedium to violence, absurdity to despair and back again'. Parkinson (1988: 36) commented that it was 'not bad' and portrayed recognizable characters 'with their feet on the ground and their hearts in the sky'.

Despite these mainly positive reviews, a letter in the same issue of *Probation Journal* complained that the series dangerously dramatized probation work and stereotyped the characters. Nellis also recalls (2008: 214) that Graham Nicholls (recently retired chief officer of Lincolnshire Probation Trust) received 'considerable flack' for his involvement in enabling the series. Nicholls devised the series with his friend, the writer John Harvey, and went on to act as technical advisor during production. Interviewed for this research, Nicholls confirmed the tension between showing the reality of probation work and the need to create a watchable drama:

> There is a temptation, and requirement, in TV drama to accentuate things, you've got to have an incident in every episode. And probation actually isn't like that really [laugh]. You might, if you're very unlucky, get one or two violent incidences in an office in a year. Even now, even in what you'd think of as being the hardest environment in which to work, levels of violence and assaults, and all the rest of it, are still, thankfully, relatively low. And in the '80s, they were certainly low. Of course, Ted Childs [the producer] was used to making stuff that was all cops and robbers and he looked at the scripts and he was horrified how, you know, how people just sat around. And so he then started to say to John [Harvey, the original writer], well you've got to put some more stuff in. So then, John would come up to me and say well could this happen? And I'd say well it could happen, it's very unlikely. And, so it was that kind of discussion. So what actually went in, in the end, some of it was based on my experiences, and some of it was based on the sort of context in which we were working. None of it actually was based on any real people, but there's one bit that everybody always says to me, oh well that was so-and-so, wasn't it? And I say no, it wasn't. What was interesting was that the probation response insofar as it reached me, the probation response was pretty hostile. The public response to it was actually pretty good. It got good reviews and it was thought of quite warmly outside of probation.
>
> (Graham Nicholls)

Although Nicholls was supported by his colleagues across the grades in Nottinghamshire, he admitted to being surprised by the negative feedback he received from probation officers across the country. Defensive and protective of their professional identities, they complained to him that the portrayal of probation was derogatory, an opportunity missed and misrepresentative. The weight of reaction left him bruised as his intentions had been honourable:

> My basic aspirations for the series were that it would tell people that we work with adults, rather than 12-year-olds, and that we didn't wear uniforms, and probably just something about the kind of broad context of what we did. I didn't have any great higher expectations than that ... It was trying to say look, this is a really difficult job.
>
> (Graham Nicholls[5])

Several of our interviewees remembered *Hard Cases* being screened. One chief officer, CO5, remembered watching it while a probation officer and found it convincing on one level:

> The bit I seem to remember, it conveyed really well was this commitment, probation officers' commitment to their offenders and their cases ... And how much it took over their lives, which probation does. I think it completely takes over your life. But I thought it conveyed it pretty well, actually.
>
> (CO5)

Others were not so convinced. One, CO9, clearly felt uncomfortable about the exposure of the usually closed world of probation, saying, 'well I suppose it's just opening up your world, isn't it really? We're used to it being kind of fairly anonymous.' Another chief officer remembered working close to where the series was being filmed. She was not impressed:

> Oh God, I used to watch it and cringe.... It's dull, isn't it [laugh]? Don't you think? I mean our day-to-day job is interesting in that we work with people, but to project it, it isn't flashing lights and cardiac arrests, and, so what it focused on, was the people, the stories of the people, which are interesting, they're always interesting. And then, it focused on the stories of the members of staff. But it was stereotypical ... But the bottom line is, it's not as interesting as *Holby City* or *A&E*, or *The Bill*. There's something much more interesting about watching emergency services.
>
> (CO16)

Since *Hard Cases*, probation has not featured regularly in television series. *Jack of Hearts*, starring Keith Allen, ran for six episodes on BBC in 1999 and sparked some interest and, more recently, *Misfits* (Channel 4 2010) has depicted probation workers as 'malign control agents' reflecting the sterility and remoteness of NOMS (Nellis 2010: 12). The main characters, five young people sentenced to community service, kill two probation workers, which spawned spin-off merchandise, including 'Keep calm and kill your probation worker' T-shirts. The importance and character of the probation worker–client relationship had certainly moved on since *I Believe in You*; as Nellis (2010: 16) bleakly concludes, the portrayal 'represented a new nadir'.

At the time of writing, the most recent drama has been BBC One's *Public Enemies*, screened in three episodes over consecutive nights in January 2012 and starring Anna Friel, as probation officer Paula Radnor, and Daniel Mays, as convicted murderer Eddie Mottram, released on licence after serving ten years in jail for strangling his girlfriend. Written by Tony Marchant, Harry Fletcher was enlisted as script and technical advisor, in which capacity he facilitated access for the production team to a hostel and probation office, this having been refused by the Ministry of Justice (Fletcher 2012).

The drama quickly shows its political and social conscience and through Friel's character ably demonstrates how idealism clashes with risk management processes. Memorably, Friel's probation officer, returning from suspension (in relation to a parolee who killed while under her supervision) and picking up her new case, tells her partner 'ten years ago this job was about helping people get their life back. Now it's about control, punishment, getting the crime rate down', (though see Chapter 8's discussion of the temporal inaccuracy of nostalgia).

Reviews reported a 'gloom-ridden drama about the inadequacies of the British probation service' (Patrick Smith in the *Telegraph*, 4 January 2012) and that 'our red-taped tick-box parole system simply doesn't work' (Euan Ferguson in the *Observer*, 8 January 2012). However, the most insightful review was Keith Watson's (*The Metro*, 4 January 2012), which berated the twist of Eddie Mottram determining to prove his innocence, rendering it a miscarriage of justice drama instead of a study of how a released murderer, supported by the probation service, struggles to adapt in an outside world that has moved on while he has been imprisoned for ten years. As Watson says, *Public Enemies* should have trusted its subject matter and challenged its audience.

Probation fares no better in print. As Nellis (2010) has mapped out, there is a relative dearth of probation-related books compared to novels with a police or prison setting. Similarly while there are many prison and police memoirs, probation life stories are fewer and far apart, some with the added twist of 'offender becomes probation worker' (and finds God) (Wigley 1992; Turney 2002). While not a memoir, the poet Simon Armitage (1998/2009) has written sparingly about his experiences while a probation officer. He captures something of the culture relating to encounters with the police, the myth of home visits and the fear of serious further offences (see Chapters 3 and 6). One of his early poems is also evocative of a bygone age of 'knowing' empathy. It is entitled 'Social Inquiry Report':

> I interviewed him twice: once at his home,
> once from the back seat of his shooting brake
> with his mangy dog on the soft-top roof,
> its tail curling in through the quarter light.

He'd bought the cars from a friend in Bolton
then sold them. He'd never done a wrong thing
in his life so imagine his surprise
when the law turned up and arrested him.

We sat and watched as the metal crusher
cubed a written-off Morris Traveller
and listened to the panel-beaters send
their muffled echoes into Manchester.

I lent weight to his side of the story
but they sent him down. In the holding-cell
he shook like a leaf but feigned a handshake
to palm me two things: a key to his house

to turn off the water, and a fiver
for dog food and a gallon of petrol.

(Armitage 1989: 58)

In terms of the characterization of probation workers in literature, it is worth briefly considering two novels from the United States. In David R Clarke's novel (2010), *The Parole Officer*, the protagonist is too good to be true. Pete Watson is an experienced parole officer; he is tall, athletic, has a beautiful wife and three well-behaved children, with whom he lives in a nice house in a good area. He is a church-goer, serving as a deacon at his local church and lives by the virtues that his parents passed on to him (honesty and the importance of family orientation). While he is saddened that most people he works with reoffend, he still has the attitude that 'if I can help one person ...'. This portrayal is notable for the character's edgework (2010: 104) when he ducks out of sight of his family and supervisors to do good work outside of his normal occupational processes and routines. In contrast to the clean-living Watson, in *Slow Motion Riot* (Blauner 1991) Steven Baum is a street-wise, 20-something New York City parole officer, who 'deals with the scum of the NYC underworld'. Nevertheless, despite his cynicism, he roots for the underdog, empathizes with difficult clients and confides (1991: 20) 'But here's the secret, which I almost never say out loud: every once in a while, you just might turn some of these guys around.' These are very different characters, but at their core is a humanity and a belief in the importance of the probation worker–offender relationship that harks back to, and draws a line of continuity from, Henry Phipps.

Representations of female probation officers

Images of female probation officers are even fewer. The literature mentioned in this chapter so far is notable in that the memoirs have been written by men and the protagonists in the novels are male. Female probation workers rarely feature in books (though see Todd 1964 and, more recently Ruth Dugdall's novels (2010, 2011) featuring Cate Austin). One that does is not a good role model. Nellis (2010: 9) discusses the novel *A Time for Justice*, published anonymously by Hodder and Stoughton in 1997. It includes a female assistant chief officer, Jill Hull. According to Nellis, this is 'one of the most malevolent portrayals of a woman professional in any modern novel – mean-spirited, arrogant, self-aggrandizing, pretentious, feminist/femocrat and zealous anti-racist'. Nellis concludes that Jill is emblematic of everything the author despises about the probation service.

Saunders and Vanstone (2010: 384) note that *I Believe in You*, through the relationship between Phipps and young Charlie Hooker, 'underscores the importance of disinterested care shown by older to younger men'. Yet the film also has a strong female character, Mattie Matheson, played by Celia Johnson (she of *Brief Encounter* fame) who acts as a street-wise mentor to the less experienced Phipps, though her cut-glass accent suggests a very clear (albeit inaccurate) class divide between probation officers and their clients (Worrall 2008b: 328).

The Probation Officer (1959–62) starred Honor Blackman as Iris Cope, one of three probation officers and *Hard Cases* has two strong female characters – the experienced and able Gill who has put her work before family life and the young-in-service Leonie. Paula Radnor in *Public Enemies* initially appears to be an accurate portrayal of a 'modern' female probation officer – efficient and caring, trying to do the right things within the confines of NOMS. But she develops into a weak woman who gets too emotionally involved with 'offender' Eddie Mottram. The implausible denouement of his innocence fails to ameliorate this gratuitously stereotypical portrayal.

A very different picture of a young female probation officer is given in Leonard's (1992/2007) humorous US novel *Maximum Bob*. Kathy works alongside a young police officer called Gary and, by the end of the novel, she decides to join the police herself. But Kathy and her young, female probation colleagues, take a 'no-nonsense' approach both to offenders ('He was a jerk, but I liked him') and multi-agency work. At one meeting with the police, Gary is left musing about 'these nice young girls in shorts and jeans who dealt with criminal offenders' (2007: 130–1). The taboo of sexual 'chemistry' between female probation officers and male offenders is, perhaps ironically, dealt with more realistically in this humorous novel than in the heavy-handed *Public Enemies*. We return to the broader issue of the feminization of probation work in Chapter 7.

Conclusion

In this chapter, we have examined how our interviewees feel probation work is perceived by their family, friends and the wider public. Family members are generally supportive though bemused, friends are admiring, inquisitive and/or incredulous, and the public are misinformed and contemptuous. The thread of dirty work helps to explain these perceptions because probation work with different kinds of offenders has the properties and responsibilities that give rise to intrigue, fascination, repulsion and admiration. This is a complex picture which has not been easily or adequately captured in film, the news media or in fictional and factual television programmes.

Some would argue that the nature of probation work does not fit well with film and television's dramatic structures. Saunders and Vanstone (2010: 388), for example, argue that 'it is hard to imagine a current blockbuster based on the redemption of a probationer undergoing a cognitive-behavioural programme'. Nevertheless, probation workers operate at different stages of the criminal justice process, deal with the consequences of highly dramatic crimes and manage conditional liberty. This work does not lack drama. In the next chapter we explore the desire of probation workers to follow the dramatic 'flow' (Czikzentmihályi 1975) of the work and respond creatively to it. We consider the problems they encounter in an organizational structure and culture that all but forbids any such creativity.

The final words in this chapter capture something of the complexity surrounding perceptions of probation workers. Paradoxically, as probation workers have emerged blinking in the spotlight of attention and have hesitantly faced a critical media and public, their standing with other criminal justice agencies with whom they routinely interact has steadily improved:

> There certainly is a public perception and media perception of probation, which is highly critical and problematic. I agree with that. But actually, in relation to those key professional groups in and around the court, and now I would include the police and prison service, I actually think that's gone full circle … I think we do actually have a very decent reputation, which is based upon knowledge and understanding of risk, which is better than it's ever been. I genuinely believe that. The problem is that those who don't actually understand risk, and public protection … I don't say that critically, because why should the general public understand … that's where the problem is. That's where the perception difficulties are; not amongst those who actually really do know and understand what we do.
>
> (CO1)

6 Job crafting, coping and responding to adverse working conditions

> But what about the 95.9 per cent who were *not* off work as a consequence of stress?
>
> (Collins 2008: 1174)

We have already argued that probation workers contend with turbulent social, economic and political conditions (Davidson 1976; Mawby and Worrall 2011) and are subjected to converging pressures from the government, management and the media. The probation service as an organization and front-line probation workers have to find ways to respond to these 'new realities of the workplace' (Naus *et al.* 2007: 684) if the organization is to survive and be successful and if employees' work is to be meaningful and fulfilling. In this chapter we consider the ways in which probation workers manage their careers and the extent to which they can exercise control over their work. We examine their coping mechanisms and the ways in which they manage their self-presentation. We will argue that the responses by probation workers to these pressures can be modeled by drawing on concepts discussed in Chapter 1, namely Hirschman's (1970) concepts of 'exit, voice and loyalty' plus 'neglect', extended by Naus *et al.* (2007) to include 'organizational cynicism', by McLean Parks *et al.* (2010) to include 'organizational expedience' and by us to include 'edgework' (Lyng 1990, 2005).

It is beyond dispute that the job of the probation worker has changed dramatically in recent decades and that this has resulted in a considerable degree of pessimism, negativity and distress about both the future of the work and the ability of individual workers to cope with multiple pressures. Nevertheless, our research suggests that many probation workers not only cope and survive in these difficult conditions, but actively gain job satisfaction. In this, they are not dissimilar to statutory social workers who, despite the often extreme demands of the work and unrealistic expectations of the media and the public, remain a group that reports relatively high levels of job satisfaction (Collins 2008; Collins *et al.* 2009). Taking pride in doing 'dirty' work that others might be too squeamish to undertake is also a factor (Simpson *et al.* 2012: 9). In this chapter we explore how probation workers 'craft' their jobs in order to remain motivated, cope with the inevitable demands of the job and respond to the adverse working conditions about which so much has been written. We start with the following working definition of 'job crafting':

> Job crafters are individuals who actively compose both what their job is physically, by changing a job's task boundaries, what their job is cognitively, by changing the way they think about the relationships among job tasks, and what their job is relationally, by changing the interactions and relationships they have with others at work.
>
> (Wrzesniewski and Dutton 2001: 180)

We argue that probation workers craft their jobs in three basic ways. First, they shape their careers physically to maximize the different experiences available within the organization (thus also aiming to avoid the aspects of the job that they least prefer). Second, they develop both individual and group strategies that enable them to cope with the routine pressures of the work. Finally, they respond in both positive and negative ways to the broader and longer-term changes to their role. As we explore 'job crafting', we are mindful that the internal role conflict (welfare versus punishment) that has been traditionally blamed for the stress within the work, may have been considerably overstated – at least for contemporary probation workers.[1] As Allard *et al.* (2003) discovered in Australia, the received wisdom that community corrections workers experience stress and dissonance as a result of role ambiguity and conflict between the welfare and punishment aspects of the work, leading to occupational burnout, no longer holds. On the contrary, they found that most community corrections workers can reconcile these demands *within* the role and that occupational burnout, where it occurs, may be related more to external organizational factors, such as the conflicting demands of managerialism and professional autonomy.

We have alluded in Chapter 1 to Carlen's (2008) concept of 'imaginary penalities', asserting that probation has become an area of criminal justice work that requires its practitioners to distinguish (and then reconcile) the demands of (a) knowing the rules and (b) using the rules to achieve meaning. In contemporary probation work, the key conflict is no longer that of 'welfare versus punishment' but rather one of 'rhetoric versus reality'. But instead of exposing the dissonance between rhetoric and reality (or providing a critique of policy) the practitioner's skill now lies in acting 'as if' rhetoric *were* reality (Carlen 2008: 5). Alongside modern police and prison personnel, probation workers:

> [C]harged with the authorization, development and/or implementation of a system of punishment address themselves to its principles and persist in manufacturing an elaborate system of costly institutional practices 'as if' all objectives are realizable.
>
> (Carlen 2008: 6)

Yet, as Carlen herself insists in relation to prison officers, many practitioners are fully aware of this 'imaginary' and (we would argue) can nevertheless construct an identity and culture that provides them with meaning and reward, albeit within constraints over which they have little or no control.

Shaping careers

Probation workers historically and currently, as we traced in Chapter 2, join the service with life experience gained, for example, through volunteering or through previous careers in a variety of settings. Subsequently, employment by the probation service involves a willingness to work in a variety of settings, whether or not one is promoted within the organization. Generally workers value the opportunities to move between posts and to develop different skills and specialisms during their careers. Typically, more experienced interviewees had worked in a number of probation roles in different locations:

> I've been really lucky in terms of moving pretty much every four years, different offices, different tasks, etc., etc., to keep my job as interesting as possible.
>
> (PW1)

At one extreme, one (PW23) had trained as a probation officer in England before moving to Australia to work as a probation officer, before returning to work as a probation officer in a different area of England. More often, probation workers told us about careers that had started as assistants or volunteers working in offices, day centres and hostels before qualifying and working as generic case officers:

> We used to have an activity centre, with a pool table, table tennis table, all the coffee area, etc. And I used to run that, and do small pieces of work with individuals, or transport people. That was another thing, take a family on prison visits, which, you know, is unheard of these days, isn't it? And just really be involved with different pieces of work that probation officers might think I could help with. I helped run a women's group, I think an alcohol awareness group as well, I did some work with that, but not running that, just sort of helping out. Those kinds of things.
>
> (PW1)

Once experienced in generic caseloads, most participants took the opportunity to take on more specialist roles in prisons, community service or with specific groups (e.g. sex offenders, prolific and priority offenders) or on secondments to, or initiatives involving, other agencies (see Chapter 4). Many experienced workers also worked with Family Court welfare cases before the separation of this work and the creation of CAFCASS (Children and Family Court Advisory Support Service). Working with non-offending families, negotiating child custody and access – and even reporting on the suitability of adoptive parents – may seem very strange to contemporary workers, but it was perceived to fit with the role of 'servant to the court' and it presented its own challenges, as these two former probation workers illustrate:

We were still doing adoptions, which was lovely – visiting people who were in the final stages of the adoption process. And you were visiting them, to check out that everything was fair, legal, above board, nothing untoward had happened, they were satisfactory. And you'd go to court with them and the judge or registrar would say 'this is your child'. That was very [rewarding].

(FPW5)

I think as an SPO in court welfare, you're dealing with all the complaints and, you know, I've never had complaints [before], you know, I don't remember complaints. But I mean I'd be getting one a day sometimes in court welfare. Because of this aspect ... I mean parents don't like to be told they're wrong about their children, do they, or to read that in what you're saying. So I was ... I was forever dealing with complaints.

(FPW7)

The movement between roles and posts did not always suit our interviewees, and a number resented being moved from positions in which they felt they were performing well and had more to offer:

No choice, no. I was angry, because the idea was that, at the end of five years, maybe people are getting a bit, you know ... maybe they're getting a bit sort of tired and, you know nothing's changing, nothing's happening. And that wasn't the case.

(FPW5)

Others took the chance to move roles because of difficulties they were experiencing. However, many of our interviewees relished the rich experiences and the diverse opportunities that a probation career makes possible. It allowed them to develop their skills and a career that may involve promotion. It also satisfied a need to find creativity and fulfilment in their work. For example one chief officer recalled the excitement of moving from a prison position to a new day centre team in the 1980s:

We did one-to-one work ... me and this other guy developed some work around working with men and masculinity and offending, and everything, which was really interesting. So it was a great three years, a really exciting, creative period ... you had a blank sheet of paper and you could almost do what you wanted.

(CO5)

Another chief officer captured the fulfilment of doing probation work when talking about recently visiting a prison to interview a prisoner:

I really enjoyed it. It was an investigation, he was complaining, but I just thought, oh this is what ... it takes me back, this is what it's all about. Yeah, it's much more rewarding than managing staff [laugh]. It's easier as well. And I did, I kind of had that nostalgia for it, thinking oh God, I used to love this job. And I did, I loved it; loved being a probation officer, more so than I've loved any other job that I've done.

(CO16)

Among the younger and/or less experienced interviewees, some made no secret of their ambitions to move upwards into management positions. Some eschewed management but couldn't imagine another career, 'I can't see anything comparing to what I get from this job' (PW17). Others recognized and anticipated that their careers would need variation if they were to last the course, for example:

Do I wanna be a probation officer to the day I die? Bearing in mind I'm 27, started at 24, that's 40 years plus of being a PO in the trenches. I don't wanna be a PO for 40 years. I don't think it's healthy to be a probation officer for 40 years straight, I really don't.... Move around, I'd like to do a bit of groups one day, I'd like to move into different areas. Certainly as well, I think that's important, I think you need to move around a bit, keep your practice up-to-date, keep your mind fresh.

(PW15)

The service was described by a number of participants as having a 'flat' or 'shallow' hierarchy with only three management grades – senior, assistant chief and chief (or equivalent terminology) – and most workers would not expect to be promoted beyond the senior grade. The desire to be promoted was not universal and some acknowledged that seniority might bring more stress than prestige. Only one of our 'children of NOMS' (post-2004 recruits) had been promoted and she described 'having a shot' at applying for a managerial role when it became available in her specialism, rather than following any premeditated career plan. She had found it particularly difficult being a team member on Friday and a team manager in the same office on Monday. She felt unprepared, untrained and unsupported but survived because she was highly motivated in a very uncomplicated and unambiguous way:

I'd always wanted to be good at my job. I wanted to be somebody who … and I still do want to be somebody who, whatever job I'm doing, I want to be seen as somebody who's good at their job and is well respected in that role.

(PW4)

As an interviewee, she gave the impression that, while being fully committed to working with offenders (because that was the job she was employed in), she would have been equally successful in any public sector job she turned her hand to.

Overall, across our sample, interviewees had enjoyed, and were enjoying, the variety of a career in probation and contributed to a widely experienced and multi-specialized workforce. Being a specialist in a number of different roles within the organization was one of the ways in which probation workers coped and made their work meaningful. We now turn to other coping mechanisms.

Coping

Probation work is stressful. The TPOs we talked to who were on the cusp of completing their training spoke with some trepidation about beginning work as fully fledged probation officers. During their training they had worked long hours to balance the academic and practical components and there were clear anxieties about the workloads they would soon take on. More experienced workers told us about the stresses associated with balancing contact time with probationers, doing effective work with them, with the demands of satisfying the paperwork trail and keeping computer systems updated. Some probation workers were apprehensive about taking annual leave due to the amount of work that would accumulate while they were away.

It is not only the amount of work that can cause stress, but the type of work undertaken and the type of people that probation workers work with. They engage with an 'undeserving' group and the work can be emotionally taxing:

> I'd come home and sit for an hour or two hours and say nothing, while I put myself together … and I've had colleagues, who they … they won't talk to anybody 'til they've read the paper for half an hour or so, you know, just to unwind.
>
> (FPW7)

Much of the stress experienced by our interviewees came from within the organization. In particular, workers felt unsupported by management and made to feel that their inability to cope was due more to personal shortcomings than organizational failings:

> I was made to feel that workload pressure was my fault. If there's one word I hate it's 'prioritization'! We're told to prioritize but they never tell you what NOT to prioritize.
>
> (PW2)

> I did have a period off with stress, but when I came back a little bit later, I started looking … at the workload measurement tool that was negotiated nationally … And I started going through [laugh] myself, I think … they publicize it in the NAPO bulletin, and I just sat down and ran off my caseload and worked out how long, and it was a simple … you could work it out without the tool … 150 hours in a month and I was expected to do something like 250 hours work … So I actually found that it made me feel better … because I could say well it's not me not coping, yeah, it's too much work.
>
> (PW12)

Perceived lack of support coupled with constraints on professional autonomy and high levels of accountability resulted in some participants feeling bullied or, to use Waldron's (2009) term, subject to 'emotional tyranny'. As we shall see below, PW10 likened her experience to being in an 'abusive relationship' and argued that it was dangerous for the organization as a whole if its most experienced front-line workers were feeling demoralized and deskilled. Feeling and expressing emotion play an important part in the performance of many jobs and the concept of 'emotional labour' (evaluating and managing workplace emotions) is widely understood (Hochschild 1983). In probation work, recognizing (and managing) the emotions that influence one's moral and professional judgements is a central component of training and supervision. Nevertheless, what some of our participants said they experienced was a loss of confidence in their own judgement as a consequence of 'the use of power to distort the process of moral evaluation' (Waldron 2009: 21).

In addition, probation workers currently operate in a criminal justice context in which budgets are tight and the future is uncertain. How do they cope with doing difficult work in turbulent times? We identified a number of responses. At the individual level, these included inner responses such as praying, silent meditation or intellectualizing being a probation worker, and more expressive responses, for example talking problems through with colleagues, families and friends, or 'speaking up' at work through involvement with NAPO or UNISON. More physical responses included taking sick days, experiencing stress-related illnesses or, in extremis, leaving the probation service. More positively, as we shall see, probation workers also cope by seeking to bring meaning and creativity into their work and by testing their professional skills in difficult cases. At the group level, probation workers cope by developing strong group solidarity involving the use of humour and at times an 'us and them' mentality. This was particularly helpful in situations where bullying by management or a blame culture was felt to exist. One interviewee likened his team's group of desks in an open plan office to:

> a raft in the middle of the sea and you're hanging onto it for dear life, because if you spin away ... if you sit in another OMU [offender management unit] ... it feels so alone, you know, so you rely on your colleagues around you.
>
> (PW20)

In the following section, we use our research data to explore six responses presented in Chapter 1 – exit, voice, loyalty (from Hirschman's 1970 model), neglect, cynicism and expedience. To reiterate briefly, 'exit' is when a worker physically leaves the organization or psychologically withdraws from it; 'loyalty' is the response of workers who keep faith with the organization, openly support it and wait for better times; 'voice' is a more proactive response where workers speak up, voicing their dissatisfaction and promoting change. The fourth response, 'neglect' is seen in absenteeism and lax, uncaring performance. Fifth,

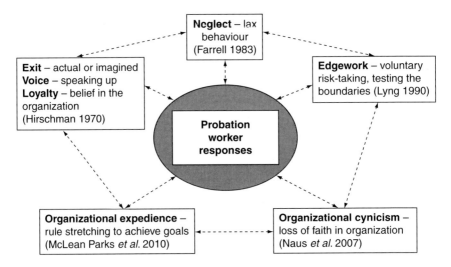

Figure 6.1 Probation worker responses.

organizational cynicism (Naus *et al.* 2007), presents in two ways: workers either become disillusioned and alienated or adopt a more positive stance as a caring critical voice of conscience. Sixth, organizational expedience (McLean Parks *et al.* 2010) is seen in behaviours where workers break, bend and stretch rules to achieve organizational objectives. Having considered these responses, we argue that this model alone does not entirely capture some aspects of the data we have collected. While the concept of 'organizational expedience' comes closest to providing an explanation of contemporary probation work, we suggest that there are some elements of the work that can only be explained in terms of 'voluntary risk-taking' (Lyng 1990). In an organization obsessed with risk assessment and risk management, we argue that it is not inappropriate to draw upon the socio-logical concept of 'edgework' to extend our understanding and add a seventh response of 'workplace edgework'. Figure 6.1 provides an overview of these responses and their interconnectedness.

Applying exit, voice, loyalty, neglect, cynicism and expedience

Among our participants were those who *exited* the service at retirement age, those who left to move into academic posts, those who were on the verge of retiring and younger workers who had decided that they were unlikely to spend many more years in the service. Those in the first category talked about careers of fulfilling work in different posts, adapting to change (giving examples of loyalty) and then as managerialist practices dominated, experiencing a gradual wearing down and mental exiting, referring to themselves as 'dinosaurs'. FPW1 talked about the service leaving her rather than vice versa when she left in 2001 after almost 20 years:

My partner said 'oh it's not that she left probation, it was that probation left her'. And so, there must be something then, that means that I felt that the job was changing.

(FPW1)

Those who moved to academic posts were more positive, feeling that they could retain their attachment to the service without compromising their principles or values:

So I wouldn't say I was disillusioned but I was demotivated. I didn't have the enthusiasm for the job, in the same way that I'd had in the past. I saw too many changes … I thought this would be a real opportunity to get into the training and positively shape that.

(FPW4)

Those on the verge of retiring were among our most disillusioned interviewees, expressing cynicism (see below) about the organization's integrity and its treatment of experienced workers. PW8 talked about her determination to be a rebel to the end, acknowledging that she was 'difficult to manage':

I think the service will be delighted to see me go [laugh]. Hurray she's gone, thank the Lord for that [laugh].

But there were younger workers, even trainees, who were already thinking about their exit if things did not improve:

Well, I … I think, for the next few years, I'm happy to be a probation officer and get the experience. Depending on how much further the organization changes, especially in terms of how you work with offenders, I'm not sure how it's gonna change. If it changes in a way that I can't work with or I don't like the working style, then I might leave and look for something else.

(TPO1)

More sadly, perhaps, was the response of one mature TPO who had achieved her ambition of training to be a probation officer, but was already showing signs of psychological exit:

It is a big disappointment, because I think, all these years I've wanted to do it, finally done it, sacrificed quite a lot, and it's not even what I wanna do. That is … when I've told my friends, they said to me well, the bottom line is, you've done it; you know, you can say you're a probation officer, you wouldn't have known if you hadn't done it. But no, I would be shocked if you saw me in five years and I said to you I'm a probation officer … so I don't know, I really don't know what I'll be doing. And I think I'd hate to be a probation officer just because it's … I don't know what else to do, because it's people's … you know, it's not like oh you're processing goods, it's people.

(TPO9)

The absence of *voice* at every level within the organization was one of the most frequent complaints we heard in interviews and one of the reasons that some felt unable to remain in the organization. As we have seen in Chapter 4, there was a concern among chief officers about the absence of any significant probation voice at the highest level within NOMS. This absence of organizational voice within NOMS was reflected within the organization itself, with some workers feeling there were no opportunities for the individual to voice their concerns. PW10 became very emotional when asked about her view of herself as an experienced worker within the organization. 'I would really like this noted down', she said:

De-professionalized, demoralized … told how to think, told how to feel. Very, very unhappy towards the end of my career, professionally, very unhappy. Very, very unhappy. I haven't left though, but very unhappy.

Some participants found their voice through union membership. As we examine in more detail in Chapter 7, interviewees who were probation workers in the 1970s and 1980s remember NAPO as being a powerful influence on probation cultures, providing an alternative and critical vision of the service. Being a NAPO member, for some interviewees, was an important part of establishing and expressing their working identities. More recently the influence of NAPO has declined and some workers have turned to UNISON in the hope of finding a 'voice'. One active UNISON representative of PSO grade explained how his union role enabled him to speak up:

I'm part of a union group that sees quite frequently my chief officer. And one of the comments I made just last Thursday to her was that it's my belief, or UNISON's belief, that they don't … they've never developed their staff properly. You know, and she were telling me that the business decision is that they're gonna keep the probation officer grades because they've invested in their development; it cost £50,000 to train a probation officer. And I said to her yeah, … you've spent 200 quid on me, you know, over the years.

(PW20)

Despite this absence of voice, most of our participants were, by definition, displaying *loyalty* by remaining in the organization and, by and large, speaking very positively about their work with offenders. Even those who disliked the general direction of change were finding ways to cope, survive and achieve job satisfaction. They were drawn to the job through common values which include a desire to 'make a difference', a conviction that people can change and a belief in the worth of working directly with individuals to effect change. Although the overt religious faith of the past was no longer apparent (as we explore in Chapter 7), an ethos of service or vocationalism remained. In embarking on probation careers, our interviewees were seeking meaningful work which they thought deeply about.

Some probation workers joined the organization only to find that aspects of their personality or part of their set of values were not sufficiently attuned to the dominant organizational values and ethos. However, they demonstrated loyalty through being prepared to adapt and change. This was the case for one 'laddish' male (PW15) who adapted, not without difficulty, to a feminized culture (discussed in Chapter 7) and also for people that joined an organization that was more enforcement-oriented than they had anticipated:

> It has changed. Because I'm more … you know, when there's talk about advising, assisting, befriending, I'm more of that person. But then again, it has changed, so you have to change with it.
>
> (TPO2)

Others were happy to enforce the new ways of doing things:

> This guy, he had probation officers way back … he's like 40-odd … and he used to come to me and say, 'you're very different from the people I used to have, you know, they used to let me just do what I want' … I said you need to understand it's changed. You know, like two misses and you're in breach, and you go back to court. So that is changing; that's fine with me.
>
> (TPO10)

In general the trainee probation officers had an optimistic spirit, a loyalty towards the organization. Certainly they were worried about the caseloads they would face, the long hours and difficult cases, but there was an acceptance that this is the organization they joined and they were learning, adapting, experiencing some highs and lows, aspiring towards specializing or climbing the hierarchy. They lacked cynicism, they valued humour and some had spotted that probation workers could be moaners.

We did not hear many stories about *neglect*, in the sense of the deliberate withholding of effort. However disillusioned our participants might have been with the organization, they saw themselves as having a higher loyalty to offenders. They would work long hours and endure the tedium of spending 70 per cent of their time in front of computers if they could justify it as being in the interests of their 'clients', as many still insisted on calling offenders. Where lax behaviour did exist, it took two predominant forms: taking sick leave and being lazy or abusing professional autonomy. The former was explained as a mechanism for coping with stress:

> Yeah. Yeah, and some people, they just … they just take sick leave or just, you know, it's like you're tired out, it's like you can't give any more [laugh].
>
> (TPO3)

The latter was something that happened in the 'good old/bad old days':

> Some people got away with a lot that you wouldn't get away with now. Some people didn't ever do any records, for example, and it wouldn't have mattered. And actually, you do need to keep a certain amount of information, you know, a running record. Some people [laugh] would, you know, see people once every blue moon; if they were particularly lazy, they'd come in late, go for a long lunch down the pub, go early. You know, there was a lot of that going on, and you can't get away with that now; it's much more professional. And it needed to … we needed to get more professional in our approach.
>
> (CO16)

Some interviewees were undoubtedly *cynical* about the organization and 'management', but they would also emphasize that they were doing things their own way to retain the integrity of probation work. They expressed dissatisfaction but at the same time did their utmost to 'do the right thing', acting as the conscience of the organization. One TPO in his fifties who had been a PSO and had a vast range of experience of social and youth work, took confidence from his accumulated years and the self-belief that this generated:

> I think it becomes more and more difficult. But I think certainly, if I didn't have the experience I've got, and the fact that … I'm old enough now [laugh], I'm not scared of huge organizations like probation or whatever, because I know that I do my job. But I think within … the boundaries, we're still able to do a lot of work with individuals and you can still have an effect on people, if you're prepared to actually give it that little bit extra and just say 'I don't really give a shit what they're telling me to do, I've seen this particular person and I know that I can work with them.'
>
> (TPO8)

One former probation worker was willing to defy management over what she saw as the unfair treatment of a colleague who was subject to disciplinary proceedings:

> She got suspended on full pay but it was the stigma of that. It was awful. And we were all told we weren't allowed to have any contact with her at all, which we totally ignored. We all rallied round her, because she was more important to us than what management told us. They couldn't sack us all.
>
> (FPW8)

Another experienced worker was furious that she had been disciplined for attending the funeral of an offender's mother. She was told that she should have sought permission first:

Do I go and ask 'can I go to the funeral?', to be told 'no, you can't?' Do I go and ask 'can I go to the funeral?' to be told 'yes you can but we must accompany you?' Do I not go to the funeral? Or do I go to the funeral and just make sure that nobody knows about it and hope that I don't get found out? What sort of a dilemma is that for a professional person? I'm nearly 60 years of age, I have to go and ask permission.

(PW10)

Those who expressed cynicism about the organization did so partly because they were holding on to a vision of the job that could no longer be accommodated by the organization. Attempting to maintain a level of integrity that they believed the organization no longer valued was very stressful. But what appeared to have dawned on some workers was that it no longer matters *what* you do, provided the appearance of *how* you do it meets organizational requirements. Consequently, they became increasingly instrumental or *expedient* in their attitude to the rules, which proved liberating for some, though unsatisfactory for others. The completion of risk assessment reports was perceived to be regarded by the organization as being more important than their content and the meeting of breach proceedings targets more important than working with an offender to avoid breach proceedings. For some interviewees, this resulted in an undermining of their sense of professional integrity:

I want to do good work but I've been told that I must try to be comfortable with 'good enough' work. When I was a TPO, my friend and I used to spend ages discussing and planning our work with offenders but no-one noticed us. But we had another friend that everyone thought was wonderful. She said 'I've learned that no-one is interested in offenders, they're just interested in OASys, so I make sure my OASys forms are immaculate.'

(PW2)

But for others, the challenge of reconciling the meeting of organizational objectives with carrying out meaningful work with offenders was motivating in itself. We heard many stories of workers who took pride in bending or even resisting the rules in order to work effectively, while avoiding organizational censure:

So you can be creative because the way I see it, when I'm in that room, nobody knows what I'm doing. They know what … they think they know what I'm doing and I tell them what I'm doing when I write it on the computer.

(PW15)

Much of our research data can be adequately analysed in terms of loyalty and expedience, with pockets of exit, neglect and cynicism, and a somewhat alarming absence of voice (though see Chapter 7 for an extended discussion). Nevertheless, there remains data that cannot be captured within this framework. In the next section we argue that some elements of probation work can only be understood as examples of edgework.

Edgework in probation

Many of our respondents expressed their desire for 'action' and 'autonomy' – a chance to put their skills to the test 'on the edge', or engage in 'responsible creativity'. In Chapter 1 we discussed the concept of edgework and its possible applicability to probation work. Here we discuss a number of examples of probation workers identifying elements of their work that we would describe as forms of workplace edgework.

Probation edgeworkers enjoy controlling the boundary between getting close to offenders (establishing rapport, showing empathy and concern and so on), in order to do effective work, and maintaining distance or behaving 'professionally' towards someone who has broken the law and is disapproved of. This involves actively choosing to *like* offenders and, despite the tedium of much routine work and disenchantment with the organization, it was the face-to-face work with offenders/clients that kept these workers motivated (Annison *et al.* 2008; Canton 2011: 208):

> I think offenders are great. We still have some probation officers who don't like offenders. I really worry about that. At induction I say to people … if you're meeting offenders, like them for goodness sake, because if you don't like them, this will be a miserable job and you'll be scared of them and they'll know.
>
> (CO 15)

Taking a step further towards the 'edge' were those probation workers who suggested that it was not only *offenders* that they found attractive, but *offending* itself. Drawn towards behaviour regarded as deviant or 'other', they control this through working with offenders while not crossing the boundary into illegality themselves:

> What is it about people who break the rules that is the appealing thing that brings probation officers together? I think, for me, I'm not a person who breaks the rules … I've got a super-ego the size of Jupiter. So I do my rule-breaking vicariously.
>
> (FPW 1)

What is being alluded to here and in the previous quotation is the edgework that offenders themselves engage in (Katz 1988, Milovanovic 2005). Probation workers have to engage with that reality so, at the least, they engage in *vicarious edgework* and, at the most, that engagement is itself a form of edgework.

Although they are not expected to put themselves in danger or 'harm's way' – indeed are discouraged from doing so – in the same way as police or prison officers, probation workers are often in the position of negotiating the boundary between controlling a 'risky' offender and the situation getting out of hand, resulting in violence, harm or loss of professional face:

> There were a couple of occasions when I was under threat but actually your skills carried you through. You learnt ... how to read people and when it was right to confront and when it was right to sort of just be a bit more conciliatory. You very much relied on those innate kind of interpersonal skills to manage some very difficult individuals.
>
> (CO12)

While most interviewees said that the risk of personal violence in the job was overestimated and that it was controlled more by personal skill and authority than by formal risk assessment, we heard several stories of violent incidents, often in hostels (approved premises) or day centres, involving workers being attacked or threatened and sometimes being rescued by other residents. So the imaginary of confronting violence remains powerful. For example, one experienced female PSO recalled working in a day centre and being harassed over a period of months by a drinker who not only threatened her with a Stanley knife, but also:

> He used to set his dog on me ... everybody used to be ringing up, oh he's coming, he's coming. And he took a door off to get at me. I still kept going back to work every day [laugh] ... and he was the only person that did frighten me really out of all of them.
>
> (PW22)

Others regarded being threatened for the first time as a sign of doing your job right (PW15). Dealing directly with an aggressive offender, rather than breaching them gives some workers 'real highs':

> My boss would just say 'well you just wanna breach them or recall them or, you know, send them back'. But people are communicating something ... because they're being at their most open sometimes when they're kicking off. And if you can work through that with somebody ...
>
> (PW17)

Talking about controlling the boundary between safe and risky physical environments included balancing (or controlling the boundary of) confidence in one's own professional ability with the instinct to take the safe option of a secure environment. In Chapter 3, we examined how the buildings that housed probation workers were once heterogeneous and 'risky' in their locations and physical design but now are often bleak and anonymous. In these buildings, workers are located behind locked doors and offenders are seen for their appointments in secure interview rooms. Thus, refusal to conform to the rules of building usage constitutes voluntary risk-taking. One worker refused to use 'secure' interview rooms because he felt they inhibited communication and gave 'a real barrier to doing anything'. In his most intense interviews, he became conscious of his own body language:

> [S]till having to push people as well. And thinking 'right, where's your limit, how close can I get you to that limit, to do something properly, without actually the fact that you're gonna kick my head in?'
>
> (PW17)

Pushing an offender to their limits meant pushing oneself to one's limits with its consequent excitement. Despite this, we had not anticipated that even the most committed probation officer would describe their work as 'fast and exciting', but a number did. Nor was this enthusiasm for edginess confined to the nostalgic recollections of COs and experienced officers – some trainees also used the same vocabulary. Some career-young probation workers appear to get a kick out of being on their mettle, using their skills to control a situation that could fall apart if they mess up. But it is hard work and involves 'emotional management' (Hochschild 1983; Lois 2005). One trainee who had previously worked with the police used a deliberately dramatic voice to describe the kind of encounter he enjoyed in the magistrates' court:

> I think I'm attracted to 'fast and exciting', which is why I liked [being in the police]. And every now and then it can be [in probation]. I've had emergency things happen, like emergency recalls to custody. Or the magistrate wants that oral report done in 20 minutes and you've only just finished interviewing the offender, and you gotta think on your feet and you've gotta stand up in court and deliver that assessment in 20 minutes. I like that.
>
> (TPO4)

In situations that verge on the edge of chaos, where things might just fall apart, professional skills are tested to keep things together. The work may be intensive, there may be a need for creativity and it requires intellectual and emotional investment. *Creativity* was apparent in both old and new contexts. Older workers recall having the freedom to recognize and adapt to the needs of clients, for example, by developing courses for sex offenders:

> [In the days before accredited programmes] we ran offending behaviour programmes ... all of which we had to devise and develop for ourselves.... A fantastic opportunity, in terms of creativity.
>
> (CO12)

Younger workers may choose to operate outside the NOMS framework, feeling deskilled, oversocialized and alienated in the current organizational structure. Through taking risks and being (responsibly) creative, probation workers regain agency and achieve feelings of authenticity and self-actualization. They are being true to themselves and their occupation and 'making a difference', realizing some of the motivations and hopes that led them into the career in the first place:

I find myself doing all my extra phone calls at 7.00 in the evening. I've gotta phone that person because he had a crisis this week ... is there anything I can do to help? Because you don't get to do that in the supervision time.

(TPO5)

I've got guys who kind of ... who don't like conforming in a room, particularly people like just out of prison, they don't like being sat in an interview room. I'd much prefer to be able to get them out and have a walk with them.

(PW17)

The thinness of the line between 'responsible' and 'irresponsible' creativity was brought home to us when we presented some of our material to an invited audience of academics and practitioners. While the examples given above were deemed acceptable, the following example produced the angry response that it simply reinforced negative media and managerial stereotypes of inappropriate behaviour:

I took one of me blokes up through the woods, because he was a bird spotter ... I can't record it on the CRAM system because I'll get a bollocking.... We were talking about all sorts of stuff in his life, and about offending.

(PW17)

Attempts at unconventional work with an offender raised ethical as well as organizational anxieties. Sticking to the script for a supervision session not only provides security for the worker but allows the offender to consent and participate on an informed basis. 'Going off script' could be viewed as 'sneaky' (TPO4) or catching the offender off-guard. Thus the traditional skill of 'engaging' with an offender and establishing a relationship with them could be interpreted as being manipulative, much as 'rehabilitation' was vilified in the radical social work and political literature of the 1970s and early 1980s (Walker and Beaumont 1981).

The *intensity* and pace of probation work is also much greater than often appreciated. There is a need for an adrenaline rush just to get through many days' work, but burn out is a real danger. Those who had worked in approved premises had many stories about the intensity of the work:

It was quite different [working] in the hostel. You did everything, from helping clear the rooms and making the beds to doing the accounts ... but single cover at night, so you were on call all the time. I think you can do a couple of years. The adrenaline is wonderful but you can burn out or get addicted to it.

(CO10)

Even those undertaking 'ordinary' work in offices found the days full of pressure:

The pace was fast, appointments all day. You had to grab time to do reports, OASys etc. There were crises, more pressure. I don't think anyone was completely sane. On a scale of one to ten for anxiety, everyone was routinely at seven, so it didn't take much to tip the balance.

(PW2)

Some were able to articulate the bodily sensations that accompany this level of intensity and the need to manage it through the process of 'winding down' during periods of leave:

If I'm having a period of leave, my body knows the day before I'm going on leave, my body will start to withdraw all the adrenaline and then two days after I've finished, I'll just be completely unable to do anything, just completely without energy.

(PW17)

Despite the excitement, the concept of edgework involves the possibility – however slight – of failure. Probation workers live in fear of 'getting it wrong', of miscalculating the risk of an offender reoffending, either in terms of frequency or, more significantly, in terms of the harm done. It is the spectre of the 'serious further offence' (SFO) that inhibits routine voluntary risk-taking by probation workers. In situations such as the Dano Sonnex case, the repercussions for practitioners who have not followed risk assessment procedures to the letter may be dire (Fitzgibbon 2011), despite the paradox that 'only a willingness to work outside the tick-box methods and grasp the "situational context" in which … offenders are located, enables reliable estimates of real risk' (2011: 144). For this reason, there is a distinction between edgeworkers for whom the consequences of failure affect only themselves and those 'service-oriented' edgeworkers for whom failure can harm others as much, if not more, than self (Lois 2005). For these edgeworkers, the retrospective management of negative emotions and the regaining of the 'illusion of control' are essential parts of managing the boundary between order and chaos (Lois 2005: 148). Fear of getting it wrong outweighed examples of actually getting it wrong, though one interviewee had experienced severe criticism by an organizational inquiry and had subsequently decided not to take risks:

If there's a conflict between what I should do as a professional and what I need to do to survive, I will reconcile it in favour of surviving … because if I don't survive, I'm not here.

(PW9)

But this defensiveness or precautionary culture drew passionate anger from another interviewee about what she saw as the abuse of experienced practitioners:

It feels like an abusive relationship, where the more it goes on and the more it's allowed to go on by higher managers, the more you become a victim.

And it's dangerous because you're making decisions ... on the front line ... I'm not saying you should be over-confident ... but you shouldn't be sitting there, after 18 years, questioning your ability.

(PW10)

Armitage (1998/2009) reflects on what would now be called a suspected serious further offence, using the compelling analogy of a 'monstrous bird of guilt' hovering above those involved, like a vulture ready to pounce on any sign of (administrative, not moral) weakness:

> The son of a woman on your caseload died in an incident involving a bathful of scalding water. They took all your files away for inspection, but you'd done everything by the book. The monstrous bird of guilt circled above the town looking for somewhere to strike, but those in the open kept their nerve when they stood in the cold of its shadow and those who could offer it a thick skin or a pair of tight lips to home in on kept well under cover, and it flew off over the red-brick houses, robbed of its kill.

(Armitage 1998/2009: 8)

Conclusion

In this chapter, we have continued to challenge the view that the probation service is an organization in irredeemable decline. We have not disputed that it is struggling to contend with turbulent social, economic and political conditions that threaten its 'domain', or traditionally recognized field of expertise. Nor have we disputed (see Chapter 5) that it is regarded by the media and the public more generally as a socially tainted occupation, but we have argued that there is a general, if implicit, acknowledgement that dirty work is *necessary* work and that those who undertake such work are not to be denigrated.

More significantly, we have argued that probation workers respond to adverse conditions in a variety of ways and that not all of these ways are negative, passive or fatalistic. Recognizing the imaginary, probation workers are skilled at crafting their job in ways that allow them to meet the organization's demands while maintaining their identity as honourable professionals who 'make a difference'. Building on the extension of Hirschman's model of exit, voice and loyalty (which now includes neglect, cynicism and expedience), we have suggested the addition of 'workplace edgework'. This enables probation workers to fulfill their desire for action and to practice this not recklessly, but through what might usefully be termed 'responsible creativity' (explored further in Chapter 8), unacknowledged by the organization and yet contributing to its objectives. These responses are neither mutually exclusive nor unchanging over time. We found workers combining responses and having utilized different responses at different stages of their careers. Those who were cynical might exit in future, be neglectful or, more positively, learn to assert their voice. Being loyal to the organization did not mean that workers would not also engage in behaviour that was expedient or 'on the edge'.

7 Diversity and different voices in probation work

The probation service has been committed since the 1980s to what used to be termed 'anti-discriminatory practice' (ADP) and is now called 'valuing diversity'. Qualifying training programmes strongly featured ADP, which was sometimes criticized as being 'too oppositional and concentrat[ing] primarily on issues of gender and race' (Hilder 2007: 10). With the creation of the National Probation Service (NPS), the discourse of ADP was replaced by one of 'diversity', which embraced and celebrated difference and was perceived as being less threatening to the mainstream (Hilder 2007: 10). *The Heart of the Dance* (National Probation Service 2003) was one of a series of strangely named policy documents (invoking a choreographical analogy) that sought to position equal opportunities at the centre of the service's culture, incorporating sexual orientation and disability in its remit. Despite these good intentions, Canton (2011) regards the outcomes of various policies and initiatives as disappointing. Drawing on earlier work by Thompson (2006) he identifies 'occupational culture' as one of three levels of discrimination (the others being 'structural' and 'personal'). He argues that culture can be a 'carrier' of discrimination, with office dynamics, politics and work allocation practices feeding into and sustaining conventions of 'how things should be done' (2011: 38).

In this chapter we consider four of the diverse voices that exist within probation and discuss their impact on probation workers' occupational cultures. In drawing on Hirschman's concept of voice, we extend his rather narrow use of the term. While Hirschman conceived voice as a reaction, namely a means for employees to speak up and to signal their dissatisfaction to managers, later writers have developed the concept to explore organizational inequality and exclusion more broadly (Simpson and Lewis 2007). The voices we are considering are: the voice of religion, the voice of the union, the voice of ethnic diversity and the female voice. We discuss the extent to which these four voices not only reveal organizational discrimination but, more positively, create and sustain identity in probation work. We conclude that it is the female voice – theorized as 'gender capital' (Ross-Smith and Huppatz 2010) that is the most pronounced in shaping contemporary identity within the service. But first we consider the tenacity of religious motivation.

The voice of religion

The religious (or, more specifically, Christian) roots of the probation service are well-documented (Vanstone 2004; Whitehead and Statham 2006; Canton 2011; Mair and Burke 2012). Indeed, while some histories trace the origins of the service in the late-nineteenth century to its earlier American counterpart, Phillips (2010) argues that there is a clear distinction between the two histories, with the latter being rooted more in concepts of choice and free will:

> [P]robation in the US began with a more pronounced neo-classical criminological focus ... whereas the missionaries in the UK saw their clients as able to be saved with their behaviour stemming more from godlessness than poor decision-making.
>
> (Phillips 2010: 8)

By the time the probation service was established in law in 1907 it was officially a secular organization, yet the role of religion was still sufficiently a matter of debate to warrant the following commentary in the 1935 *Handbook of Probation*:

> It is not in dispute that the foundation of successful probation work must be the religious spirit in the best sense. It seems probable that an officer who has succeeded in adjusting his own life satisfactorily will be able to communicate something of his own harmony to his probationers, as to all others with whom he is brought in contact. It may be done consciously or unconsciously. The danger to be most carefully avoided is forcing the subject of religion on people who for one reason or another are not ready for it. This can only result in producing hypocrisy or rousing antagonism.
>
> (Le Mesurier 1935: 62)

While all histories of probation emphasize its religious roots, all assume that religious motivation has steadily declined and is no longer a significant feature of probation culture. Mair and Burke, for example, suggest that 'it is difficult today to appreciate the significance of religion in Victorian Britain' (2012: 8). We also made this assumption when we started our research and were therefore rather surprised to find that, even within a small sample, there was evidence of religious motivation, albeit of a more subtle kind than may have existed in the past. This evidence emerged initially without direct questioning. For example, one of our first interviewees described the start of a typical day thus:

> I'm a very early person, so my day starts at like 4.00/5.00 in the morning [laugh]. I say my prayers and when my family come up about 6.00 a.m., we'll all pray together, have a shower, then off we go.
>
> (TPO3)

Another trainee probation officer volunteered the importance of Buddhism to him in the context of reflecting on the service's commitment to diversity:

> [I]t's a diverse organization; more diverse than most, I would say, in terms of ethnicity, in terms of perhaps sexuality. Not so much on the faith but ... I'm a person of belief myself, I've practised Buddhism for the last ten years and I've come into a very Christian organization. I haven't had any problems with that, I haven't had any issue, I don't take issue with it. But I think ... you have to be careful what you say, but I just think that there is a kind of ... in some offices, there's an overload of Christianity in your face. And I know colleagues who've had homophobia, they're homophobic. You know, homosexuality versus Christianity debate, and problems, staff problems with that. I've never experienced that as a gay man myself, but I know of people that have and have had to move office or there have been grievances. Not rife, but I've heard about it. And even when I started and my boss said to me, there has been some homophobia, even in my first office, so be aware of that. And people will tell you and people will tell offenders about God and enforce those values. I've heard of that happen. Again, it's not everywhere but pockets.
>
> (TPO4)

An experienced worker cited a well-known prayer as illustrating her approach to stressful times:

> 'God grant me the serenity to accept the things I cannot change, courage to change the things I can, and the wisdom to know the difference.' Just get on with it.
>
> (PW10)

Being made aware that religious motivation may still be alive in 'pockets' of the service, we began to seek the views of longer-serving and former workers. One former worker reflected thus:

> When I first started, I think Christian motivation was explicit and was there, as we've talked about, the prayers at morning and so on. We then went through a phase, where ... and I remember this happening explicitly ... that if somebody sat in an interview for social work training to be probation, and they started to talk about reforming offenders ... we wouldn't give them a place. Then ... and I don't think it's as neat as this ... but then, when there was a focus on black probation officers coming into the service, we must increase, we must recruit black social workers, black workers, they brought with them, in some cases, extremely strongly, a kind of religious motivation, and suddenly ... you couldn't [reject them] then, because you were deemed to be racist ... and the attitude seemed to change towards it, I thought ... it was quite interesting ... during that period.
>
> (FPW 6)

We have included these two lengthy quotations because they demonstrate – as did the quotation from Le Mesurier (1935) – that religious motivation is inextricably entwined and sometimes in conflict with other values. Historically, the concept of redemption has conflicted with the secular notion of free will and choice (Phillips 2010). In a contemporary context, toleration of religious motivation may be an unforeseen consequence of ethnic diversity, while conflicting with other values such as non-discrimination on grounds of sexual orientation. We discuss below the concerns expressed by the National Association of Asian Probation Staff that its members experience discrimination on grounds not just of skin colour but also of religion. Far from being a thing of the past, religion remains an influence on probation culture – perhaps its last taboo.

The voice of the union[1]

As we write, the National Association of Probation Officers is celebrating its centenary (NAPO 2012). Founded in 1912 by Sydney Edridge, it has described itself throughout its history as both a trade union and a professional association and has been a central influence on the probation service's sense of occupational identity and its relationship with other workers – not just those in the criminal justice system.

During the 1970s, NAPO developed from a 'cosy' professional association to a trade union representing an increasingly well-trained profession. Politically, increasingly left-wing and concerned to promote an ideology of radical social work within criminal justice and beyond, it campaigned on ideological grounds to withdraw from prison welfare departments (see Chapter 4), to refuse to write social enquiry reports in 'not guilty' pleas and for the right to demonstrate in solidarity with workers not directly concerned with criminal justice (participation in the Grunwick dispute leading to the suspension from NAPO of its London branch). Bitter wranglings in NAPO over the issue of *ultra vires* (that NAPO was acting outwith its authority or legal mandate) led to new objectives to broaden the legitimate interests of NAPO in social as well as criminal justice (Worrall 1997).

Interviewees who were probation workers in the 1970s and 1980s remember NAPO as being a powerful influence on probation cultures, providing an alternative and critical vision of the service. Branch meetings and national conferences were significant networking sites and allowed for debate that was at times both intellectual and stimulating – an opportunity to get away from the demands of the daily routine. As CO14 put it, 'the people I wanted to respect me were other NAPO members, not my managers necessarily – you got your cred from NAPO'. But that influence has faded, and some cited the over-zealous promotion of anti-discriminatory practice in the late 1980s as one (possibly minor) catalyst, causing workers to feel intimidated and anxious about expressing their views. In particular the presence of monitors at conferences who censored language deemed inappropriate caused some consternation. One participant recounted a nervous elderly female member using the phrase 'work like a donkey' then adding 'can I say that?':

[A]nyone could go to the monitors afterwards and say 'I was outraged ... they used the word "donkey"' or whatever. And so it was a bit menacing, to be honest, for some people. And other people thought 'good, about time'.

(CO3)

The covering of statues of bare-breasted angels in a conference hall was recounted by a few interviewees as being a 'final straw' moment:

And [one speaker] made the point, 'Have we really gone this far [laugh] that somebody has climbed up [to the statues] because it would be so offensive if we, as a load of adults, were able to see these bare-breasted angels?' Isn't that ridiculous, you see? But it kind of caught the moment. You can imagine it. And they cleared the hall, while the exec decided what to do [laugh] and everyone was outside drinking coffee, saying 'well I don't think you should show bare-breasted angels', and oh ridiculous, you know. And it was a moment where it had gone a bit too far, yeah? And anyway, then we got the signal to all come back in and there were the angels – they'd been revealed, you see. Anyway, it got in the *Daily Telegraph*. Can you imagine how that looked for probation?

(CO3)

Most experienced workers that we interviewed were members of NAPO, even if they were no longer active and felt that it had lost sight of the bigger picture (for example, domination by the prison service) in favour of fighting domestic battles over relatively minor matters. Those who remained active were clearly committed: 'I really do believe it punches above its weight. We're a very small union. You know, I think we've got a very good publicist, who keeps us on the front page' (PW7). One experienced worker talked movingly about how he became involved in the Edridge Fund, NAPO's benevolent fund that assists probation workers who become ill or in debt:

I feel very privileged to be in a position to be part of a group that can say well at the end of the day, here's £400 or something, because it'll make a substantial difference in a short period of time, obviously not in the long, but in a short period of time, you can access a reasonable amount of money quite quickly for people who are in a bit of a state of desperation. So although that won't be a full answer, it certainly is helpful.

(PW11)

The same interviewee talked at length about the importance of NAPO to health and safety issues, citing hostels and unpaid work as two areas of obvious potential health and safety risks. Less obvious issues relate to the ubiquity of open-plan offices (see Chapter 3) – noise and workstation-related injury:

[W]e sit at computers three quarters of the day, heaven knows what we're doing to our spines or our eyes, both of which are suffering, spines particularly. So there are a lot ... and repetitive strain injuries, the upper limb disorders, they're quite prominent.

(PW11)

As we saw in Chapter 6, one consequence of disillusion with NAPO has been that some workers have turned to UNISON in the hope of finding a 'voice':

I'm gonna effect some change. I don't know at what level and where, but that's why I'm in the union, I suppose, when you're an elected representative, your voice needs ... your voice has got to be heard. They don't need to take your advice but they certainly need to hear you. And that's what I like about the [UNISON] union role I've got – they're not able to dismiss me.

(PW20)

Few recent recruits that we interviewed were active in NAPO. Several did not belong at all and those who did saw membership largely in terms of personal protection (and obtaining *Probation Journal*) rather than collective solidarity:

And that's another thing that seems to have changed, because I was talking to the trainees about whether they'd been involved in NAPO and they ... almost all of them said, oh no, I suppose I'd better join NAPO but I haven't been involved, I suppose I ought to. But it was very instrumental; it was about needing to belong to a union for your own protection.

(FPW4)

TPO7's view was more hostile and he felt that 'they are just opposing everything for opposing's sake ... hang on a second, grow up, we're professionals, do a job'. Nevertheless, when discussing probation's media presence, almost all interviewees cited the NAPO Assistant General Secretary, Harry Fletcher, as the most consistent and publicly recognizable voice of probation. While some complained that he naively damages probation by saying how bad things are, most admired his willingness to speak up and contrasted this with the absence of any other probation voice in the media (see Chapter 5):

Harry, of course, is very good, Harry Fletcher. I mean it's funny when I got this job in [here], I met somebody on the platform in the station and I said, I've got this job in [here] now in probation. And they said 'oh, have you taken over from that Harry Fletcher?' And you think cor ... you know, that's the voice of probation.

(CO14)

Although NAPO produced a newsletter from 1913 (Whitehead and Statham 2006), it was not until 1929 that the journal *Probation* was launched. Vanstone

(2004) considers this to have been, 'symbolically ... of critical importance because it inaugurated the professional voice of the service' (2004: 76). The first paper in the journal was a call for the service to adopt more scientific methods of working, thus heralding the era of the probation officer as 'expert' in human psychology. In the ensuing 80 years, the journal has provided a chronicle of critical practitioner and, increasingly, academic, reflection on the role of probation in criminal justice and methods of working. Its more general influence on the cultures of probation work has not been explored in any detail, but we found that interviewees regarded it with affection even if they did not read it regularly, as though it provided a kind of 'comfort blanket' of reassurance about the values of the profession. We have already noted that some workers joined NAPO at least in part because they were then entitled to receive *Probation Journal*. Others commented that the quarterly journal and the monthly newsletter made them feel 'part of the probation community' (CO4) with articles having credibility because 'it's academic stuff from people actually doing the job' (CO9). As the journal has increasingly sought academic respectability, it has become a peer-reviewed journal and one participant wondered whether that had changed its cultural influence:

> I think what we've done in that process is we've scared off practitioners from writing for it in the way they used to in the past. But having said that, the quality of it is so much better than it was. [There are] some fantastic articles written by practitioners now, but they're people who clearly are gonna go on and go into academia.
>
> (CO2)

Probation Journal has possibly now become more of a vehicle for those with academic aspirations who regard it as a first step to publication. It also continues to attract articles from academics who were former probation workers. It constitutes both an archive of changing attitudes within the service and an artefact – or visible element – of probation cultures (Schein 2010).

The voice of ethnic diversity[2]

Goodman (2012) recalls that, when he was a probation officer in London in the late 1970s and 1980s, 'probation officers were all white, working with a predominantly young black client group, disaffected and with suspicious relationships with the police' (2012: 4). Despite the commitment of staff to working in non-discriminatory ways, 'practice was individualistic and idiosyncratic and often idealistic' (2012: 4). One consequence of the increasing awareness of discrimination in criminal justice (Phillips and Bowling 2012) was an attempt to increase the recruitment of black and minority ethnic probation staff, though this was far from straightforward. Worrall (1995) argued that the recruitment of black men and women was hampered by (1) perceptions that the probation service was part of a system that oppressed black people, (2) cumulative educational disadvantage that rendered disproportionate numbers of black people ineligible for training, and (3) unfair and irrelevant recruitment procedures and selection criteria. But above all, she argued that no attempts to address these problems 'will be sufficient to retain black staff unless they feel that (a) the job is worth doing and (b) the working environment is supportive and free from discrimination' (1995: 40).

Latest available figures (Ministry of Justice 2011) indicate that members of BME groups represented 14.1 per cent of all probation service staff in 2010, a slight increase on the previous year. Staff from a Black ethnic background represented 8.3 per cent, those from an Asian background represented 3.5 per cent, Mixed 1.8 per cent and Chinese or Other 0.5 per cent (2011: 85). The situation was very different in the 1980s when the concerted recruitment of BME staff began. Despite (or because of) their increase, BME staff found that existing structures within the service and NAPO failed to provide them with the 'voice' they needed to secure support and to change cultures (Phillips 2005; NAPO 2007).

The Association of Black Probation Officers (ABPO) was formed in the early 1980s in the West Midlands with the dual aim of supporting black[3] staff and 'holding service management and NAPO to account in relation to the experiences of black staff' (NAPO 2007: 84). One of our interviewees recalled the early days of ABPO:

> I was also involved in ABPO, Association of Black Probation Officers, and they held regular support meetings across London and the south-east, which I used to attend. So yeah, there was a structure there, an infrastructure there that was quite supportive for practitioners to network, to share ideas, share experiences, and be imaginative about … at that grass roots level, in terms of work with offenders.
>
> (FPW4)

Later in the 1980s Asian probation staff considered that they needed a separate 'voice' and the National Association of Asian Probation Staff was created. In recent years, with the new criminal justice focus on terrorism, a survey of members has suggested that Asian staff experience discrimination not only in respect of skin colour but also their language, culture, dress and religion (Heer 2007; Singh 2007: 174; Heer and Atherton 2008).

By the 1990s, under Section 95 of the 1991 Criminal Justice Act, there were regular government publications providing statistics about both race and gender and criminal justice, intended to alert practitioners to possible discrimination. One consequence of these publications was that resources began to be allocated specifically for programmes for women (run by women) and for black offenders (run by black staff). The following account gives a flavour of the enthusiasm felt at the time by black probation workers:

> So there was a group … a ten-week programme that was put together for black offenders to come to a group, to look at issues around identity; to look

at issues around lifestyle; to look at issues that linked with the community; education; employment; and some issues around sort of how they might rehabilitate themselves within the local community. It was voluntary. We set up a referral system, so that each probation officer could refer, saying whether they refer for employment, training or education. They could refer their offender, if they felt that they could benefit from it. We set the criteria quite loosely and quite inclusively around offenders who identified as black and who felt that they could benefit from attending the group. And we got a good number of recruits, we had groups of like 25/30 ... on a rolling basis. Yeah, there was so much optimism around at the time, and there was resources being devoted to it. This was supported by management. And this was grass roots. This was practitioners. This came from practitioners, this was owned by practitioners and they were being supported by the local management. So I think that's why it worked and it was quite positive. It kept my motivation and [that of] many other practitioners at the time.

(FPW4)

Although 10 per cent (six) of our interviewees identified themselves as black or Asian, five of these were trainee probation officers and all six were based in the south-east of England. While one former probation worker talked enthusiastically about the early days of working specifically with black and Asian offenders, none of the trainee probation officers appeared to regard themselves as specialists in working with minority ethnic offenders. As with female interviewees, we did not ask what appeared to us to be a rather clumsy question about experiences of being a probation worker from a minority ethnic background and we did not find any evidence that these workers regarded the job in ways that were fundamentally different from white interviewees. Given the very small and geographically specific sample, however, our comments here must be treated with caution, though to omit them would, we felt, fuel the unacceptable view that they were 'too few to matter'.

The female voice

The culture has been changed by the current training regime – less people on second careers and not enough men. Most of our entrants are young women in their early/middle 20s with no life experience.

(CO13)

And then they come and they're sat behind a desk with a computer, and they're absolutely fantastic [but] get somebody shout at 'em, and they're in floods of tears ... and they've got stress, because they've no life experience.

(PW22)

Over half of the probation workers that we interviewed were women and one of our key findings was that the probation service has been 'feminized' over the past 20 years. But what might that mean – beyond the obvious point that the majority of probation workers are now female?

Morris (1987) argued that 'criminal justice professions are seen quite simply as male professions; it's man's work requiring the characteristics of men' (Morris 1987: 135). And some might say, why not? With 80 per cent of recorded crime and 90 per cent of serious crime being committed by men, and the prison populations of almost all countries around the world being between 91 and 98 per cent male (Walmsley 2012) there could be an argument for saying that the current proportions of women in criminal justice organizations (approximately 25 per cent in the police and prison services) are not unreasonable and reflect the nature of the work, which overwhelmingly involves dealing with deviant, difficult and, at times, dangerous men.

On the other hand, as Heidensohn observes, 'women have always and everywhere played some part in the maintenance of order in society' (1992: 19). Maintaining order in society is not only about dealing with criminal men. It is about civilizing and socializing and women play a crucial role in achieving this: in the family, in the community and in certain so-called 'caring' professions such as teaching, nursing and social work. In these professions, their role has only ever been partly about caring. It has also been about having responsibility for keeping the peace, moderating men's potential for aggression, civilizing the next generation of citizens, policing other women and, finally, implementing the grand plans and ideas of men – generally making the unworkable work.

Historically, we suggest that it is possible to see three very broad eras of women's contribution to criminal justice. Until the late 1960s or 1970s, women police, prison and probation officers worked exclusively with women and children. This era, which we refer to as the 'women as symbolic mothers' era, has been interpreted in a number of ways: women's skills were regarded as being particularly suited to work with families; working with men was regarded as beyond the competence of women and/or too dangerous for them; and women were employed by men to 'police' families in the broadest sense by establishing disciplinary alliances with mothers (Donzelot 1979; Mahood 1995; Worrall 2008b; Annison 2009). Although that era is long passed, there remains a legacy of a 'maternal' approach to the work:

> I used to think, well if I can just teach … not teach, that's the wrong word … people to say 'please' and 'thank you', it's something, isn't it? And I hate bad manners, I don't like bad manners at all. And they get to know me and they know that. And I'll challenge anybody in reception for swearing, effing and blinding. I'll just say 'it's not necessary that'. I don't shout and rawk at 'em but I just say it's not necessary to swear like that.
>
> (PW22)

The second era was one in which equal opportunities discourse dominated the 1980s and 1990s. It was the period when women were given the opportunity to act like men in the police, prisons and probation. The main concerns were: how to increase the recruitment of women while maintaining selection standards; how and where women should be deployed; how and when they should be promoted to senior posts; and what modifications should be made to working conditions to accommodate the family responsibilities of women. In the year when women overtook men as probation service employees (Annison 2007), Kay (1993) wrote about the ambivalent attitudes of women maingrade officers towards promotion. This article, and McFarlane's (1993) response to it now read as historic debates, with both authors predicting that the cultures and styles of management in the service will only change when more women are promoted.

This era has been characterized as consisting of a 'fix the women' approach (Ely and Meyerson 2000), in which the root problem was still perceived to lie with women's inability to behave like men and in which the solution lay in accommodating (or compensating for) women's 'weaknesses'. Little was done to dismantle a work culture that promoted long hours, compulsory social networking, neglect of families and an aggressive, competitive approach. The aim was to make these things more accessible to women rather than to question their validity and relevance per se. Women who wanted to succeed found themselves minimizing or denying discrimination or even difference. It was the era in which women became aware of what Ross-Smith and Huppatz (2010) term 'female capital', as opposed to 'feminine capital' which we discuss later:

> [F]emale capital is the gender advantage that is derived from being perceived as female, but not necessarily feminine, whereas, feminine capital is the gender advantage that is derived from a skill set that is associated with femininity or from simply being recognized as feminine.
>
> (2010: 556)

In our research we interviewed a wide range of probation workers, including chief officers, half of whom were women. These were women who, by definition, have been successful within the organization and, in many ways, one would be hard pressed to find any fundamental differences in values and attitudes to the job between them and the men. Nor was it immediately obvious that their styles of management or leadership were markedly different from those of male chief officers (and if they were, that this was necessarily attributable to gender differences). Clear-cut gendered differences between 'transactional' (command and control) and 'transformational' (consultation and participation) leadership styles, such as those found in the police by Silvestri (2007), were not apparent (at least, not in the ways the female chiefs talked about themselves). The only example we found of explicit democratization of status (arguably a 'transformational' act of leadership) had indeed been introduced by a female chief, but her motivation appeared to owe less to gender-consciousness than to a desire to reduce hierarchies in general and make job titles more comprehensible to other organizations. Indeed, one might argue that she was contributing to the de-professionalizing of the service:

I don't use the term 'probation officer' at all, because people think there's a hierarchy and actually there are differences ... but people are trained to do a specific job ... I mean, it's a cultural thing, because it's actually valuing what other people do.... So what we've said is, this is the job you do [e.g. offender manager, tutor, director of X], and that's your job title.

(CO10)

But there was a sense that these women had somehow had to work harder to get where they were. Their backgrounds were marginally more humble than those of the men; they didn't take their education for granted; they worked part-time while bringing up their children and were denied promotion for a number of years, not directly as women but because they were working part-time and certain career opportunities were closed to them.[4] Some recounted alarming stories of sexism, especially but not exclusively those who spent time working in prisons. They were women who joined the service in the 1970s as 'bright young things' and worked alongside older ex-armed forces and ex-police men, some of whom were clearly unable to relate to them as equal colleagues. But these women have helped to transform the organization because they were a generation that benefitted from 'equal opportunity discourse' (Ross-Smith and Huppatz 2010: 557). It was female capital that put them in the spotlight but, as will be argued later, it has given them only limited room for manoeuvre (Skeggs 1997), offering a tactical rather than a strategic cultural resource.

Many might argue that this second era is far from over. As Kerfoot (2002) has argued, being a 'professional' all too often remains synonymous with being a man. But there are some interesting things happening in the twenty-first century. Diversity in organizations is justified no longer so much in terms of the rights of individuals but more in terms of the benefits to the organization. The business case for what Hallsworth (2005) has called 'corporate effeminization' is compelling in these days of corporate responsibility, ethical auditing, greening and softening, and the probation service has not escaped this influence. In addition to benefitting from 'equal opportunity discourse' or 'female capital' (Ross-Smith and Huppatz 2010), women in probation have been able to benefit from 'feminine capital' in that qualities and skills perceived to be feminine (for example social skills and the ability to compromise) have been increasingly valued within the organization. Overlooking the fact that attributing such qualities to all women is itself reinforcing of stereotypes, more women are being promoted, though sometimes to the most precarious leadership positions – the 'glass cliffs' that men do their utmost to avoid (for example, leading the already failing department or the most dysfunctional staff group):

Within this climate of challenge and transformation, it is possible that these women, and particularly that new women chief officers [of probation], may find themselves on a 'glass cliff', and in fact over-represented in precarious leadership positions.

(Annison 2007: 157)

A possible example of a glass cliff promotion in criminal justice in England and Wales was that of Eithne Wallis, the first Director of the National Probation Service, appointed in 2001. History (and our interviewees) may have judged her harshly for failing to secure a national voice for the service and 'selling out' to the male-dominated prison service, with which the National Probation Service was forced to combine in 2004 to become the National Offender Management Service. She paid a heavy price for the feminization of the probation service, but her legacy of almost 50 per cent female chief officers remains:

> In 2001 ... 50 per cent of the chiefs left ... so we had 50 per cent new chiefs, of which a large number were women and EW was the national director [but] she bought in wholesale to the Westminster high civil service culture. So she lost contact with the operations and became a political animal ... that enjoyed the power.
>
> (CO7)

Although we have no direct evidence, we might speculate that the near-universal despair about the absence of a probation 'voice' at senior levels in the prison-dominated, male-dominated NOMS is at least in part due to the probation 'voice' being increasingly a female one. The disadvantage of both female and feminine capital is that they reinforce stereotypical views of women leaders as women who are leaders, rather than leaders who are women. While the probation service, with its well-established respect for women managers, may have a sophisticated understanding of gender equality, there is little evidence that the same is true of either the police (Silvestri 2007) or prison services. Consequently, 'women's gender capital may only manipulate constraints rather than overturn power' (Ross-Smith and Huppatz 2010: 562).

Reaching a critical mass of women in management in the probation service (despite the associated problems outlined here) has only been possible because 70 per cent of probation staff and 80 per cent of trainees are now female. On the surface, this may sound unexceptional. After all, surely the history of probation lies in social work, which has always been a female-dominated 'caring' service. From 1970 until the mid-1990s, probation officers were required to hold social work qualifications. But it isn't that simple. Unlike other branches of social work, probation was male-dominated until the early 1990s. It wasn't until 1993 that female qualified probation officers outnumbered males (Annison 2007) and a national review of training (Dews and Watts 1994) bemoaned this state of affairs. As a result of this, and other reports criticizing the training of probation officers, the requirement for a social work qualification was dropped in 1995 and a specific Diploma in Probation Studies was established, with a greater emphasis on criminology, psychology and the administration of punishment (see Chapter 2). However, far from increasing the proportion of men entering the service, the opposite has happened.

Moreover, the work for which these women are being trained has become increasingly 'masculinized' in the sense that penal policies and public perceptions of criminals have become increasingly punitive and the administration of criminal justice has become increasingly managerialist. Public protection, enforcement and a very specific form of rehabilitation based on cognitive behavioural psychology replaced the traditional motto of 'advise, assist and befriend', and the probation service became subject to the KPI (key performance indicator) culture of public sector management, along with the police and prison services.

So how is this particular form of 'corporate effeminization' to be explained? One explanation gives credence to populist myths about women being fascinated by the psychology of the criminality of men. The toughening up of community sentences has been accompanied by an emphasis on cognitive behavioural psychology. University undergraduate students on programmes of both criminology and psychology in the UK are overwhelmingly female and there is now a distinct occupational group of prison psychologists who are predominantly young and female. Even those who enter probation training without a background in psychology will find a strong element of cognitive behavioural psychology in their training, thinly disguised as training in the management of offending behaviour programmes:

> The women who are coming in now are mostly sort of 25ish, young psychology, criminology graduates and they don't have a social work base. And yeah, they're not union-minded either, because we would say they're Thatcher's children, they grew up under Thatcher's regime, and therefore wouldn't be particularly interested in the unions, which were given a very bad name, people dropped out of them pretty fast. And yeah, they're far more technologically advanced than some of us dinosaurs effectively, with their computers and their iPods and mobile phones. I mean it is interesting. And we've got quite a bit to learn. They're also twice as fast on the computer as we are, and so able to work, in many ways, better than us in terms of speed. But yes, it's a very different culture, it's a different generation, in fact. It's not [just] there are very many more females, but they're also 20 or 30 years younger than ... there seems to be a sort of gap between a lot of 25 to 30s and then the sort of 50-plus. I'm not sure how many there are in the middle sometimes.
>
> (PW11)

Second, at recruitment level, women would appear to be performing better than men within a managerially focused work environment – they have become 'daughters of NOMS'. Contrary to the received wisdom that women work best in environments where they can use their intuitive, nurturing, caring strengths and their emotional intelligence, it seems that women also work well in structured environments with clear goals, where good preparation, good organization and a methodical, reliable approach are valued. The more the task of administering criminal justice becomes one of *administration*, the more likely it is that women will shine.

A third explanation is an increase in interest in women as offenders. This trend has been overwhelmingly led by women practitioners and academics over the past 30 years (Annison 2009; Worrall and Gelsthorpe 2009). Attitudes towards women offenders have changed out of all recognition, and that particular story has been recounted many times elsewhere. However, as the numbers of women being sent to prison increase it is becoming obvious to all that this is a particularly inappropriate environment in which to rehabilitate most women. Alternative provision in the community – predominantly by women for women – has finally become mainstream in criminal justice in England and Wales. Fragile though the funding is, the establishment of 'one-stop shops' where women at risk can access all the services they are likely to need, from health to housing, education to debt advice, life skills to cognitive behavioural therapy, is now part of the criminal justice landscape – thanks to decades of struggle by women working in criminal justice, both in the statutory and voluntary sectors (Corcoran and Fox 2012).

A fourth explanation is that the presence of women challenges male-dominated criminal justice cultures in a perhaps unexpected way. Evetts (2012) suggests that, as increasing numbers of women become managers in professional occupations, men are leaving management because it is viewed as 'less interesting and powerful' (2012: 17). In her research on prison officer culture, Crawley (2005) suggested that women prison officers undermine the 'masculinity' of prison work:

> Women disrupt the association between the prison officer role and the performance of masculinity; if women are allowed to do the job, and if they can do it as well as their male counterparts, the job is no longer a viable resource for constructing masculinity.
>
> (Crawley 2005: 195)

Probation has perhaps never been seen in quite the same way as an arena for 'doing' masculinity. Nevertheless, with the occupational identity changing dramatically, as it has in the past 15 years, it may be becoming a less attractive career, both for young male graduates and for older, second-career men who find that the skills they acquired in their previous more 'macho' occupations are not valued as highly as in the past. This is what one young male probation officer said to us in interview:

> I had a problem fitting into the organization as a young man. I'm a bit of a going-out type of lad, bit boisterous, I stand out. I had complaints that I was a bit loud, a bit this, a bit that, even sexist. I found I had a lot of self-reflection to do.... It is a bit difficult being a boisterous male because it comes across a bit boorish.
>
> (PW15)

But a final explanation penetrates to the heart of what it means for female probation officers to work with high-risk male offenders. Over the past ten to 15 years, the victim of crime has assumed a greater political significance in debates about criminal justice and the discourse of penal policy and crime prevention has increasingly become one of public protection with both the actual and symbolic victim taking centre stage. Within that debate, female victims have assumed greater attention and particularly female victims in intimate relationships. Now, whether or not those victims have actually benefited from this focus is an entirely different discussion. But our argument here is that it may not be fanciful to suggest that women working in probation no longer play the role (in terms of Freudian 'transference') of symbolic mothers, but increasingly take on the role of symbolic victims, 'seeking to impress on offenders the damage they have caused, exacting retribution or overseeing a process of regulatory restorative justice' (Worrall 2008b: 331).

Petrillo (2007) addresses precisely this issue in her study of women probation officers who work with violent and sexual offenders. Such offenders are likely to display stereotypical attitudes towards gender relationships and part of the job of a female supervisor is to challenge such views. But the emotional labour involved in doing this is often underestimated and unsupported by management, and female officers are aware of the dissonance created by the conflict between the requirements of supervision and the patriarchal assumptions still widespread within society that women are subordinate to men. Petrillo's participants described 'various techniques men will employ to [undermine their authority], from flirting and trying to charm the officers to physical and psychological intimidation' (2007: 398).

Additionally, Petrillo examines the impact of such work on the personal lives of female officers, identifying four areas: impact of and on motherhood; heightened awareness of personal vulnerability; impact of constant exposure to harrowing material; and the effect on personal relationships (2007: 400). Most of the women we interviewed who had been involved in such work spoke positively about it and saw it as both fulfilling and as an opportunity to make a real difference to reducing future victims. As one of our interviewees told us, 'I was known as "the paedophile lady" when I worked with sex offenders in prison' (FPW8) – a phrase that was a mark of respect and an acknowledgement that she meant business. Nevertheless, some reflected on the dangers inherent in undertaking the 'dirtiest' of 'dirty' work. One chief officer recalled:

> I can vividly remember this probation officer saying to me 'I feel like I'm working in a sewer. I need to go home and shower every night' – I remember her words and they still stick in my mind.
>
> (CO3)

An experienced female officer spoke graphically about 'the smell of sperm … horrible … goes into your body' (PW10) and her loss of sexual interest in her personal life. She expressed a concern that was expressed by a few other experienced officers (both male[5] and female):

You're regularly exposed to unpleasant information and I don't believe that it can't have some sort of effect on you ... maybe you don't know how the work's affected you until it's affected you ... I do worry about younger colleagues in their 20s, early 30s, with small children.

(PW10)

As though to confirm her concerns, a younger woman worker confessed:

It does give you a kind of warped sense of the world. And I have found that, in personal life, things like taking my daughter to the swimming pool, I'll be watching to see if there's any people who I feel don't look quite right there, and you're more aware of risks.

(PW14)

Morran (2008: 144) found similar 'hyper-awareness' among women working in domestic violence offender programmes.

So women are combining their interest in the criminality of men with their concern for victims and public protection to produce a new and gendered approach to work with offenders that is rehabilitative but at the same time confronting and enforcing. It is a kind of 'fix the men' approach that is neither maternal nor macho. But there is an emotional price to pay unless 'you become desensitized' (PW14) to the 'dirt'.

Conclusion

In this chapter we have extended and linked Hirschman's concept of 'voice' to the probation service's commitment to diversity by examining four different voices within the organization. The discussion has been neither comprehensive nor symmetrical. Had we written this book 100 years ago, the dominant cultural voice might have been that of religion. It no longer is, but we have been surprised that it remains recognizable as a voice. Had we written the book in the 1970s, the dominant cultural voice would probably have been that of the union and, in the 1990s, possible that of anti-discriminatory practice focusing on the voice of ethnic diversity. The categories are also not mutually exclusive or static over time. We interviewed BME women who were religiously motivated. We interviewed chief officers who had joined the service from religious motivation, had become politically active and now, despite their experience and seniority, considered themselves to be lacking a voice to such an extent that they are, or will soon be, retiring – or exiting – the organization (see Chapter 6).

But in this research, the dominant voice in the probation service is now the female voice. The feminization of probation work has wide-reaching and not always obvious implications. Simpson and Lewis (2007) have theorized the gendering of organizations by constructing a model that accounts for both the 'voice' and the 'visibility' of women at both a 'surface' and a 'deep' level of conceptualization. The former refers to the *state* of being – a snapshot of how an

Table 7.1 Voice and visibility in probation

	Voice	Visibility
Surface conceptualization	Women's voices are the norm within probation because women have access to both female and feminine capital	Women are highly visible in probation and no longer have 'token' status
	Women shine at work that involves addressing the psychology of male offending and speaking for the victim	Women shine by being well-prepared, well-organized and competent, especially at IT
	Probation is committed to discourses that claim to value diversity and equal opportunities	Women are increasingly successful within probation and gender differences at management level are not pronounced
Deep conceptualization	The meaning of offender management is constructed by a male- and prison-dominated hierarchy	Power is maintained within NOMS by white (prison service) men still being the norm
	Women's voices remain silenced by the dominant (NOMS/political/media) discourses of masculinity within criminal justice occupations	This masculine norm is invisible within a criminal justice model that universalizes the male criminal and the male worker

Adapted from Simpson and Lewis (2007: 85).

organization *appears* in terms of the voice and visibility of women. The latter refers to the underlying *processes* whereby the status quo is maintained or, of course, changed. In Table 7.1 we adapt this model to tabulate the surface and deep conceptualizations of the gendering or the feminization of probation work.

Applying the model in Table 7.1 to our data, it would seem to us that women in probation are more visible and have a greater voice than at any time in the history of probation. But it might be argued that that voice and visibility are very much at the surface level. At the deeper level of genuine cultural transformation their voice may still be silenced and their visibility limited. We could speculate that this stunting of the growth of the impact of women in probation might be in part due to the creation of NOMS. But NOMS itself has been a symptom of a wider discourse of masculinity within criminal justice and penal policy, which brings us full circle to the role of women in a system that is still seen as man's work, requiring the characteristics of men. Nevertheless, there is ample evidence from our research that women regard probation work as a 'domain' in which they can construct an identity that is not merely *valued* by the organization but *defines* the organization.

8   Doing probation work
Cultures, identities and the future

At the beginning of this book we stated our intention to explore the meaning of 'doing probation work' from the perspective of retired, former, new and experienced current probation workers across the range of grades. In our 60 interviews we explored what motivates people to become probation workers, how they make sense of their work, how they respond to turbulent political times and media criticism, and what stories they tell about the value of their contribution to society.

We also set out to challenge the position held by some of our academic colleagues that the story of probation is one of decline. Our research suggests that while working in a much-changed world, probation workers retain a strong sense of their roots, tradition, cultures and professionalism. Modern probation workers can handle the 'imaginary'. They can do what is required of them – they can be competent offender managers – while constructing identities that allow them to believe that they are still part of an 'honourable profession' (PW3).

In this final chapter, we discuss first the extent to which it is possible to identify probation culture(s) and we outline cultural characteristics under five broad headings: motivation, artefacts, job satisfaction, meaning and (re)presentation. We then address the pervasive themes of nostalgia and the narrative of decline, suggesting that nostalgia, far from being a 'defence of the weak' (Mathiesen 1965) or an escape from an intolerable present, provides a means of dealing with that present and reinforcing a positive identity in the face of an organizational and external environment that is perceived to be largely hostile. Next we revisit the three case studies we introduced in Chapter 2. We combine the key characteristics of these case studies with other features of probation work that we have discussed in other chapters. From this we build three 'ideal types' of probation worker, identifying their contribution to probation cultures. Finally, we consider the implications of our arguments for offender management and the future of probation work.

The characteristics of probation cultures

The foregoing chapters setting out the main findings from the interviews provide insight into who probation workers are and how they perceive themselves and their role. This data enables us to posit the characteristics of probation cultures. Before we identify these characteristics, it is important to clarify that our research has confirmed the presence of cultures; there is not a monolithic probation culture that pervades the organization. Indeed it is clear from the interview data that different cultures exist in rural and urban locations; for example, generally rural probation workers tend to be more autonomous but less embedded in particular communities. Further, there are cultural differences between neighbouring probation areas and between different offices within the same probation area. For example, we were told of differences between offices within London and also between London as a whole and other areas of the country. Second, cultures can reflect the type of work being undertaken and therefore it is not unexpected that probation workers in prisons, approved premises and unpaid work settings will develop a different culture to those working in community offices. Third, cultures are not static; they change over time and as our sample includes interviewees from the 1960s to the present, generational differences in cultures emerge. For example, as we will illustrate below, one interviewee (FPW5) in his seventies described himself as a 'culture carrier' who retained ways of thinking and working that were challenged during his later years of probation employment.

In identifying some of the characteristics of probation cultures, following Morgan (2006) and Schein (2010), the components that we anticipated might emerge included stated and unstated values, explicit and implicit expectations of behaviour and attitudes, symbols, rituals and myths, the physical work environment and use of language. Aspects of these dimensions of culture are evident, implicitly and explicitly, in the previous chapters and these are elaborated upon below. However, one aspect worthy of mention is the lack of visual cultural symbols compared to other criminal justice agencies. The police, courts and prison services have clear visual symbols. The police, as Manning memorably documented, are 'fraught with symbolism' (1997: 23), having a distinctive helmet, uniform and assorted gadgetry for officers and a blue lamp for their buildings; prison officers have a uniform and notably carry keys; courts have architecture and wigs – 'the majestic regalia of the Law' (Parker 1963: 145). Probation has nothing comparable, other than a dated caricatured image of a sandal-wearer that was imposed externally rather than generated and accepted from within. Our interviewees often found it difficult to identify distinctive components of their culture. One TPO, for example, like others, found it easier to identify values than images and iconography:

Um [pause] I'm trying to think of something that jumps out. I don't think there's [pause] ... anything strong that jumps out in terms of what probation ... I think [pause] what I see in terms of probation culture is, it is more like the old values; you're there to help them, you're there to support them, and yeah you're there to reduce their risk of reoffending and harm, but you're also trying to support them in their goals in life, where they wanna be, where they wanna go.

(TPO1)

This lack of cultural symbols is interesting in itself for what it connotes about probation cultures, and it points to the finding that probation cultures are characterized by the implicit rather than the explicit. As we examined in Chapter 5, this has consequences for the representation and public understanding of probation work.

While probation cultures differ and change over time, this does not mean that it is a fruitless or pointless exercise to investigate this area. Indeed, despite the differences and the difficulties of pinning down explicit components, there are family resemblances and common threads that run through and act as cultural locators or indicators against which probation cultures can be identified and analysed. The first of these is *motivation*. Probation workers are drawn to the job through common values which include a belief in the possibility of change and their own ability to effect it (to 'make a difference'); a faith in both offenders and colleagues which may be, but more often is not, a religious faith; and an ethos of service or vocationalism (that the work is a 'calling').

The second is what Schein (2010) terms *artefacts*. These are the most visible elements of organizational cultures and include such things as physical space, the layout of offices, the outputs of work, written and spoken language and the overt behaviour of group members. As we have seen in Chapter 3, probation work typically involves some or all of the following: an open-plan office on an industrial estate with separate bookable interview rooms and video links to prisons; long hours in the office doing computer-dominated risk assessment, reports and records; little time spent outside the office except for arranged events, e.g. multi-agency meetings and court attendance; a female-dominated environment; mutual support, chatter, humour and pleasant communal staff areas. Almost every element of these cultural artefacts has emerged in the past 30 years.

Third is the seeking and achieving of *job satisfaction*. We have argued that probation workers are 'socially tainted' (Kreiner *et al.* 2006) because they work with groups of people who can be difficult and are regarded by society in general as undeserving of their efforts. Successes are limited and hard-won. Nevertheless, as we saw in Chapter 6, probation workers seek and achieve job satisfaction in a number of ways: by constructing themselves as professionals with a legitimate desire to be autonomous (though that desire is often perceived to be thwarted by the organization); by drawing on an institutional memory that values a golden age of probation when workers *were* autonomous (while at the same time acknowledging that not all autonomous practice was best practice); by constructing for themselves moments of action when they are called upon to test out their professional skills in situations that are potentially chaotic or dangerous; and finally, by introducing into their work a creativity (or departure from the script) that they believe the organization prohibits (but which the organization is implicitly dependent on).

One common feature of job satisfaction is the belief in working and building relationships with individual offenders. Interviewees old and young, inexperienced and retired, and in different grades illustrated this core belief, which goes some way to explaining the general frustration over the contemporary dominance of the computer over personal interactions. As one recently qualified probation officer pointed out, most people are drawn to probation:

> because of the interest they have in working with people … and that bonds people together. Yeah, and I think there's not a lot of people that are motivated or enjoy working towards the targets that are brought in, and things like this. I think the majority of people are motivated, again, by individuals that they work with, who are on their caseload. So I think that kind of bonds people together as well, common shared experience of … and exchange of practice as well, about how you worked with so-and-so … what kind of approaches have you tried to engage whoever, and what's your idea about working with this particular type of people, or who have committed this type of offence.
>
> (PW26)

During their training and formative years, our more experienced interviewees were inculcated with the centrality of the relationship. One retired interviewee, FPW3, felt there is a '*sine qua non* of probation culture in its original state, it was the relationship and the genuineness of it, and that a lot of the work was done through authentic contacts between people'. This was reiterated by another retired worker who trained in the 1960s:

> My training was telling me that what I needed to do was find out and learn and see, and use relationships … all of my training was about relationships really, apart from the academic side, the learning about psychology, sociology, all that stuff. The skills were largely around the use of relationship, understanding relationship. There was a strong psychodynamic element within it … and it was all about understanding, using the relationship, hearing what people aren't telling you, the elephant in the room, all that stuff. It was complicated.
>
> (FPW5)

The most recent recruits recognized that it was important to build relationships with people on their caseload, but had found it was not straightforward:

> Every TPO in our cohort I spoke to has said the number one problem has been, you're never really taught how to interact with people, you're never taught how to engage with them really in supervision and how to work with them on a one-to-one basis. We're given a lot of theory about how cognitive behavioural approaches work and why we've got these groups, and what they're supposed to tackle, and why you should do this, and why you should do that, but I don't think you're ever really taught the skill of how to engage people and work with them.
>
> (TPO6)

We found that all our interviewees valued 'the relationship' with an offender and saw it as being crucial to the organization's objective of reducing reoffending. Where they differed was in their views about the purpose of the relationship, positioning themselves along a spectrum from 'rehabilitation', through 'rehabilitation and risk assessment' to 'risk assessment and offender management' (see also Durnescu 2012 on staff characteristics). While 'lifers' and 'second careerists' tended towards the former positions, 'offender managers' tended towards the latter positions.

The fourth element of probation culture is that of *meaning*. The job remains a vocation to some, and even cynics and world-weary workers regard probation as more than just a job; they need to make sense of why they do probation work. They need to do meaningful work and the cultural locators or filters for this include: an intellectualism that values thinking and reflection; a commitment to social equality and a respect for social diversity; a political positioning that historically has been overtly left-leaning (though is less so currently);[1] and a protective stance on the threatened 'domain' of probation work.

In sum, we would argue that probation workers find meaning through *professionalism*. The definition of professionalism is highly contested and has warranted a large body of academic literature in its own right. For our purposes, the most appropriate working definitions involve credentialism (recognized qualifications), expertise (recognized field of knowledge) and autonomy/legitimacy (recognized right of intervention in the world) (Eadie 2000; Fournier 2000; Freidson 2001). All of these *boundaries* that distinguish between occupational groups, between an occupational group and lay people/clients and between an occupational group and the market create a professional identity (Fournier 2000: 69). However, Fournier argues that in recent decades, the 'logic of the market' with its ethos of targets, performance and managerialism has dismantled these boundaries and threatened professional identity (2000: 77). Yet, she continues, it is possible to 're-make' professionalism by taking advantage of the 'malleable' and 'constitutive' (we have used the word 'creative') nature of professional boundaries (2000: 83). There is, of course, a danger that when the discourse of professionalism is imposed from above it becomes a mechanism for justifying change and controlling workers (Evetts 2012), but our research suggests that it can be used positively from within the occupational group to strengthen work identities. Above all, according to Freidson, professionalism will survive if those claiming it can persuade others that they can be *trusted* to put the good of the clients, the public or the development of an idea above their own economic self-interest (2001: 214).

In this regard and in the context of an uncertain future, many of our interviewees emphasized the unique position of the probation service as experts in the management of high-risk offenders; in this domain, they felt they had no credible challengers among the increasingly fragmented providers of criminal justice services. Whether this is adequately communicated is another issue. Freidson's emphasis here on the importance of 'successful persuasion' (as opposed to purchasing power or violent coercion) by an occupational group in convincing the public and the state of its value brings us to our next element of probation culture.

The fifth element of probation culture that we have identified is that of *(re) presentation* in the turbulent conditions of the external environment. Cultures develop as a means of integrating new group members into ways of working and are a resource for adapting to the external environment. Probation workers deal with uncertainty by adopting: a self-effacing/apologetic/non-aggressive/unthreatening position in relation to public and media criticism; a long-sufferance that redefines success and lives with or rationalizes failure; a sense of solidarity and isolation ('nobody understands us') ameliorated by humour (often dark), blame, arrogance and moaning masochism. There is also, importantly, a sense of liminality or 'bridging' – a willingness to work on the threshold, to span the worlds of law enforcement and law breakers ('we sit with judges and we shake hands with offenders' [FPW7]), and gaining satisfaction from being 'tricky to pin down'. This bridging is based on reconciling the formal position of 'servant of the court' and latterly 'offender manager' with the fundamental belief in the 'unassailable or irreducible worth of the offender as a human being' (FPW3) and the 'constant inclusion, the Christian bit about hating the crime, not the criminal; the passionate belief in change, in the value of the individual; the importance of respect; of giving people another chance' (CO4). As such probation workers are, as one interviewee (FPW3) observed, individuals with 'an entrée and a position' within, but not necessarily of, the courts and the community and with offenders. To achieve this balance, probation workers have to succeed in gaining credibility with, and the confidence of, offenders and at the same time maintain the confidence of their criminal justice partners. In the past, this might have led to collusive behaviour, as one chief officer recalled:

> And I was probably pretty collusive and well looking back, I think aspects to my practice which were ... I talked about prison officers as 'screws', and I suspect I colluded with the idea that crime was commonplace and, therefore, didn't challenge some of the thinking behind it at the time as well as I should have done.
>
> (CO15)

This balance has changed over the period covered in this book. The probation service's outward-facing presentation has come to emphasize enforcement and risk management and working as much with partner agencies and victims as with offenders. In itself this raises an issue of identity for probation workers that requires ongoing negotiation:

> We are constantly walking this path of both care and control, and we do want to have our cake and eat it, because that's when we're successful. But the people that like to hear lots of control don't wanna hear about the caring. The people who wanna hear about the caring don't wanna hear about the control. So you end up getting it wrong, whichever way you jump, because we don't get the middle ground across.
>
> (CO4)

Nostalgia and the narrative of decline

In Chapter 3 we quoted Armitage's account of a home visit which may or may not have been true but which had found its way into the folk memory of probation workers. Walker and Beaumont (1981) told a similar story of dogs sniffing up probation officers' skirts and demented budgerigars sitting on their heads during home visits for the preparation of social inquiry reports. And every seasoned probation officer can tell you about the office drunk:

> I knew everybody on the homeless scene. So you'd have people crashing into the office, drunk – they'd probably pissed themselves. There'd be people standing aghast and you'd say 'It's alright, I know Billy, he's okay, don't worry about it' and all the rest of it. So there was always something going on ... quite a bit of anarchy.
>
> (CO2)

Stories like these are part of a culture that enables hard-pressed professionals to cope with their adverse working conditions. They are not unique to probation work; Waddington (1999), for example, has written about the role of storytelling in police cultures. But they have been disregarded by a probation service that has always taken itself very seriously because it fears that, if it doesn't, nobody else will. However, this has resulted in a defensiveness that is not always healthy, as Pease has observed:

> I have found probation managers over the [past] decade to have been very sensitive to external criticism, far more so than the police over the same period. Some conflict in organizations is healthy but ... many conflicts surrounding probation management do not feel good.
>
> (Pease 1992: x)

In this book, we have aimed to challenge that allegation of defensiveness by opening up probation work to a critical, but sympathetic gaze. Our bias is clear. We could not have written this book, or undertaken our interviews in the way we did, if we had been fundamentally hostile to – or even disinterested about – probation work. Of course we think it is a 'good thing', without which the criminal justice system would be much the poorer. To use the catch-phrase of one of our interviewees (CO15), 'why wouldn't we?' We cannot predict what will happen to the probation service as we know it but, even if Mair and Burke (2012) are right and it disappears in the next decade, it is important that its cultures and the identities of its workers are not lost to a narrative of decline that harks back only to a 'golden age' when autonomous probation officers walked the earth, advising, assisting and, above all, befriending, villains – but failing to protect victims.

So we turn to the role of nostalgia and, in particular, the work of Strangleman (2012) on the effects of nostalgia on work identity. We already know from Pearson's seminal work *Hooligan* (1983), that golden age theory posits the existence in the narrator's memory of a crime-free, neighbourly community when young people behaved themselves, approximately 30 years before the present – whenever that 'present' is. The notion, if not the reality, as explored by Brogden (1991), Weinberger (1995) and Loader (1997) of a policing golden age is particularly strong, embodied by the character of George Dixon and the television series *Dixon of Dock Green*, which act as 'binding agents sending messages of security and reassurance' (Mawby 2002: 187). We found a similar memory in our interviewees but, rather than being 30 years ago, we found that the golden age of probation, as described above, existed whenever the participant entered the probation service. So it could be any time from the 1960s to the early 2000s, and it did not necessarily align accurately with external service developments. For example, several interviewees talked about the late 1980s as still being a time of 'traditional' probation practice when a glance at any history of the service will confirm that managerial changes to the service and the mooting of a 'correctional' service (Haxby 1978) had been under way from the late 1970s. The 1988 TV series *Hard Cases*, which we discussed at length in Chapter 5, arguably presented a picture of 'traditional' probation work that was already obsolete.[2] In contrast, FPW4 described being excited about the creation of the National Probation Service, which he viewed positively, as happening when he joined the service in 1993, although in reality it happened nearly eight years later (and after he had left!).

Many of our former and more experienced probation workers looked back on their careers proud of their occupation and the work that they had done, but frustrated that they could not and did not do more:

> As I got more experienced, there was a lot of frustration at seeing what I could have done with me knowledge and me skill, but couldn't do because I didn't have the time. Not just my cases. You'd be working with an officer and thinking we could have predicted that was gonna happen if we'd just done such and such and … almost as if the more knowledge you got, the more dissatisfaction there was in being inadequate and coping with things and that was true for everybody. Going back to when you start, you're idealistic, you think you've got the answers to everything and whatever you do is gonna work. And then with experience, you find it doesn't, but something else might and … leaves you feeling partly frustrated and partly inadequate.
>
> (FPW7)

So how do we explain (sociologically, rather than psychologically) this consistent cultural memory of good things happening in the early years of one's career and bad things happening more recently? Strangleman, in his studies of railway workers, and others (Williams 1973; Davis 1979; Bonnett 2010) have argued that (a) nostalgia is not about hankering for the past but about making sense of the present and (b) it is about a search for stability, predictability and reassurance at times when one's own values are being challenged by change, rather than a claim that the past *really was* better. Nostalgia, therefore, is a way of reflecting on, and controlling, change in the present. It is a way of retaining the 'moral order' and distinguishing between those who 'really cared' about the job (the old guard) and those who are 'instrumental and pragmatic' (the new guard). Elements of this are present in the statements of our former and more experienced probation workers who realized that times, and probation, were changing. For example, FPW5 recalled that towards the end of his career, his fit within the organization was becoming problematic and cultural tensions were common:

> We were still trying to do a job on the old rules, and the rules were changing. And I think my personal problem was that I was regarded or referred to myself as one of the dinosaurs. We were the people who believed in casework, relationships, the dignity of everybody. That wasn't flavour of the month any more. We were being managed by people who have got MBAs, and who were power dressing [laugh] and poncing about.
>
> (FPW5)

As such, nostalgia should not be dismissed too readily as being mere false consciousness. It enables workers to position themselves as being certain 'types' of worker, with skills, values and aspirations that are indispensible to the organization. In our research we found that even those who might be viewed by 'lifers' and 'second careerists' as being instrumental and pragmatic (the 'offender managers') had a very clear set of values and beliefs about what the job *should be*. They were not nostalgia-free but their 'golden age' might have been five years ago, or less. It was a time when they felt optimistic and self-confident.

As for the most recent recruits, the TPOs, whom we interviewed some months before their qualification as fully-fledged probation officers, they were unconvinced by the narrative of decline and looked forward to a potentially fulfilling career in probation. There was considerable agreement on the uncertainty of the future of the probation service; many predicted the continuing dominance of risk assessment. Most anticipated long hours, high caseloads and chaotic offenders. Yet just like the lifers before them, these young-in-service probation workers had aspirations. Some aspired to management, others looked forward to specialist roles in the future, others saw their futures outside probation; it was not necessarily a career for life. For example, TPO5, even at the point of qualification reflected that probation for her might be 'a bit of a stepping-stone' if there was insufficient scope to meet her creative needs to make a real difference to communities and criminal justice. She pondered that she might need to step outside the probation service to achieve that. But, in contrast, TPO3 looked to the more immediate future:

> I want to do my best in the job. I don't want to be just a probation officer. I want to make an impact, you know. If the sky's the limit, I wanna get there.
>
> (TPO3)

Typologies of probation workers

In Chapter 2 we introduced three of our interviewees in some detail because we considered that they were representative of three fairly distinct types of probation worker. We did not suggest that all probation workers would belong to one of these types, nor that it would be possible to 'read off' whole careers, attitudes and values that would neatly correspond with the types. Nevertheless, as our analysis progressed, we found sufficient distinctions emerging to make it possible to construct three *ideal types* that would help to explain some of the complexity of probation cultures and their implications for understanding the impact of probation work on the criminal justice system.

'Ideal types' are a well-established methodological device in the social sciences, originating with Weber's work on bureaucracies (Hughes *et al.* 2003) and having been used in many disciplines. They are constructs that extract the key features from sets of data in order to highlight the similarities and differences between those datasets. They do not claim to replicate reality, nor do they produce testable hypotheses and they are not normative (they don't suggest that 'this is the way things *ought* to be'). Thus, as Hughes *et al.* (2003: 131) explain, 'the ideal type explicitly distorts reality, giving a logically extreme, rather than an empirically generalized, depiction of the things it covers'. It is a way of organizing data that gives focus to the 'unmanageable complexity of actual cases' (2003: 131). With all these caveats, we now proceed to construct three ideal types of probation worker – the lifer, the second careerist and the offender manager. These people do not exist in this pure form in real life, but there was sufficient evidence of these characteristics and experiences to enable us to categorize most of our interviewees.

Lifers

Lifers are predominantly over 40 years of age and have spent all, or most, of their working lives in the probation service. They demonstrate a combination of some or most of the following characteristics:

- Relatively privileged backgrounds with a sense of duty (often religious) towards those less fortunate
- University at an early age, studying sociology or an unrelated subject (e.g. English, theology, physics)
- Worked as volunteer or in hostel
- Postgraduate CQSW
- Structural understanding of society, social work approach to individuals (belief in the importance of the 'relationship')
- Community- and court-based, centrality of court duty and home visits
- Historically not security-conscious, willing to take risks
- Historically committed to NAPO, union-minded
- Historically wary of police

- Ambivalent about prisons
- Frustrated about NOMS
- Hurt by changes in public perceptions
- Retain a belief in creativity and engaging with offenders.

Lifers have had to contend with huge changes, but remain loyal to the principles of the organization and are determined to make things work. They are more optimistic than pessimistic about the future for probation. They recognize that things are changing and difficult but believe in the fundamental need for probation and will argue for 'a place at the table'.

By definition, they have expressed loyalty and their exit is most likely through retirement. Some have made an effort to exercise voice through NAPO and the PCA, the latter in particular being a recent attempt to rectify the absence of voice at a senior level in the service. Edgework was arguably in their nature; these were people dedicated to making a difference and fighting inequality at a societal level – pushing the boundaries when probation work was less controlled, less reliant on computers and probation workers identified themselves as autonomous professionals.

Second careerists

Second careerists exist across the age range and their defining characteristic is that they have forged a significant previous career in an unrelated, or only marginally related, occupation. They demonstrate a combination of some or most of the following characteristics:

- Relatively unprivileged with some experiences of crime and poverty – first careers in the armed forces, police, church, social work, teaching, etc.
- University as mature student with concomitant financial hardship – related degree
- Experience as unqualified (low-paid) worker in hostel or related occupation
- Non-graduate or postgraduate CQSW or Diploma in Social Work
- Want to make a difference and contribute transferable people skills from previous careers (belief in the importance of the 'relationship')
- Community- and court-based, centrality of court duty and home visits
- Common-sense approach to security and risk assessment, trust own experience and judgement
- Historically committed to NAPO, union-minded
- Pragmatic about working with police and prisons
- Mixed, pragmatic views about NOMS
- Aware of changes in public perceptions
- Feel thwarted by the organization in doing the job as they would like.

Second careerists have been affected by change and do not feel in control of it. They lack voice but remain committed to offenders/clients. They are unwilling or unable to exit, though some may involuntarily withhold effort temporarily or permanently through stress-related illness and a few may begin to contemplate leaving if things don't improve (imagining exit). This group has the maturity and confidence to be expedient and to engage in edgework. If they are cynical, it is because they care about the direction the probation service is moving in. They are mixed in their hopes for the future. The majority are pessimistic about the loss of role and identity, the workloads and paperwork, the dominance of prisons, the punitive turn, the reliance on computers, the shrinking courts' role. However, others are positive. They are ambitious to progress, are getting 'stuck in' during difficult times, they recognize the enduring social welfare heart of probation work and want to change things for the better.

Offender managers

Offender managers are predominantly under 40 years of age and have joined the probation service in the past 15 years. Their most common characteristic is that they have been trained through the Diploma in Probation Studies route (i.e. since the late 1990s). They demonstrate a combination of some or most of the following characteristics:

- Diverse backgrounds, some evidence of residual religious motivation
- University at early age or as mature student, studying related subject (e.g. law, criminology, psychology, criminal justice)
- Instrumental approach to volunteering and gaining experience in order to be eligible for training
- Public protection ethos with little investment in social work culture (some ambivalence about the 'relationship')
- Office-based, centrality of risk assessment and IT skills
- Security-conscious, routinely risk averse but want to be creative
- Pragmatic view of union membership related to self-protection rather than credibility and conscience
- Comfortable working with police, prisons and other agencies
- Take NOMS for granted
- Accept negative public perceptions as part of the job.

Offender managers are realistic about change and want to do a good job, but that includes being creative and engaging with offenders. They are willing and able to exit if the job becomes too constrained. They may tend towards expedience, though some, where confidence exists, have embraced edgework as a means of seeking creativity. Offender managers are generally positive about the future. They see the difficulties of reduced budgets and market-driven futures, but are pragmatic. There will be chances for promotion, they are good on self-management and, if things don't work out, they will move on – this isn't a vocation and they are not on a mission.

Having undertaken this exercise, we are left with the social scientist's perpetual question, 'so what?' We suggested in Chapter 1 that 'doing probation work' had to take account of at least four elements – its status as dirty work, its context of turbulent conditions, its collective workplace cultures and its individual responses to adverse working conditions. Similarly, we are suggesting now that each ideal type of worker has something important and irreplaceable to contribute to probation work: for example, the idealism, vocationalism and intellectualism of the lifer; the life experiences, transferable skills and commitment to 'making a difference' of the second careerists; the victim empathy, concern for public protection and willingness to challenge offending behaviour of the offender managers. Taken together, these are the characteristics of the 'perfect' probation worker. On the basis of our sample, it would seem that each type of worker is well represented in the service at the present time. Unsurprisingly, we would argue that such proportions need to continue if the service is to maintain its unique contribution to criminal justice.

Implications for offender management

Our research has aimed to hold up a mirror to ways in which probation workers make sense of their work and sustain themselves in working conditions that are politically turbulent and socially tainted. It has been a relatively small study that has produced disproportionately rich data, only a fraction of which we have been able to include in this book. Our primary goal has been to suggest the characteristics of a group of criminal justice workers who have been overlooked in the literature on occupational cultures.

This task is important in its own right, but we should not evade the obligation to speculate about the implications of our research for offender management. This imperative is all the greater in light of the latest government consultation exercise, *Punishment and Reform: Effective Probation Services* (Ministry of Justice 2012). This sets out the government's intention to increase the scope for organizations from the private, voluntary and community sectors to compete at a local level to provide probation services for offenders, with providers increasingly paid for the results they achieve. While the move to make probation work more locally accountable (thus implicitly acknowledging the failure of NOMS) is likely to be welcomed by our interviewees, undoubtedly the main consequence of this policy, if implemented, will be to fragment the provision of services. The government proposes to allow the public sector probation trusts to retain certain core tasks or 'public interest' decisions, such as the preparation of court reports, initial risk assessment, the management/supervision of high-risk offenders, recalls and breaches (enforcement), and participation in Multi-Agency Public Protection Arrangements (MAPPA), but to allow other organizations to bid for the management of lower-risk offenders. Such proposals raise numerous policy and practice issues but, for our purposes, the most crucial is the impact on probation workers' identity. We have already noted in Chapter 2 that the new training arrangements will be available to any organization that wishes to fund individual staff for qualifications in working with offenders. The consultation paper is also proposing 'less prescriptive' national standards and 'further discretion' for the delivery of services. While the withdrawal of probation officers (as opposed to less qualified probation service officers) from work with lower-risk offenders has been steady and increasing over the past 30 years, it is far from obvious that offenders fall into neat (and static) low-, medium- or high-risk categories. Our interviewees spent so much of their time in front of computers precisely because risk assessment is a dynamic process and one that can be crucially affected by the nature of probation work intervention itself.

We believe we have shown that probation workers are highly educated, skilled and deeply motivated people – a fact that is grudgingly acknowledged in the government's consultation paper (Ministry of Justice 2012: 11). They are committed to the worthwhileness of working with offenders in the community but we found no evidence of the caricatured 'sandal-wearing, tree-hugging' welfare-oriented probation officer. It is disingenuous of the government and – to a greater extent – the media to perpetuate this stereotype. None of our interviewees questioned the importance of risk assessment and public protection. What they did question were the methods by which these honourable goals should be achieved.

We believe that our most important finding has been the need to recognize, encourage and support the desire of workers for 'action' – or what we termed, in Chapter 6, 'responsible creativity'. Like all other occupations, probation workers find ways of 'easing' (Cain 1973) or coping with the pressures and tedium of routine work, but one of these ways is being innovative or working 'on the edge'. This is emphatically not about behaving recklessly or disregarding the organization's objectives. Though sometimes expressed as a nostalgic desire to return to a mythical golden age of probation (such as that portrayed in the film *I Believe in You* or even in the TV series *Hard Cases*), we have argued that nostalgia is a powerful mechanism for resisting a narrative of decline and maintaining a positive work identity *in the present*. Liminality and working on the edge are about putting professional skills to the test for the good of the offender, victims, the public and the organization. Acknowledging this resourcefulness in its workforce is perhaps one way in which the organization could itself be a model of 'responsible creativity'.

Our second important finding has been the feminization of the organization. The implications of this for offender management are far-reaching and by no means obvious. Certainly, we found no evidence of probation work reverting to a stereotypical social work or 'caring' profession as a result of it being female-dominated. Instead, we found that being highly organized, computer-literate, team-playing and victim-focused were valued attributes. Being the 'symbolic mother' to offenders (Worrall 2008b) was seen as inappropriate. We might argue that some women saw their role as being the 'symbolic victim' in confronting and holding offenders to account for their actions. In many ways, women are more vocal and more visible within the organization than ever before and that is not always comfortable for male workers, as we have demonstrated in Chapter 7. At a deeper cultural level, both within NOMS and in relation to other male-dominated criminal justice organizations the absence of voice and visibility remains (Simpson and Lewis 2007), but the organization is increasingly being defined by its female 'voice'.

Our third major finding is that probation workers are multi-specialists who recognize the importance of inter-agency work and relish working alongside the courts, the police and the prison service (as well as other community organizations). We have evidence that this co-operation, co-ordination or even federation (Mawby and Worrall 2011) is stimulating and rewarding. What has demoralized many probation workers, however, is being *merged* with the prison service and losing their identity and respect for their *domain* within a 'command and control' culture. Although the term 'contestability' featured little in most of our interviews, it was also apparent that probation cultures value co-operation above competition when it comes to making provision for work with offenders in the community.

We conclude that probation cultures are complex but, if properly understood, do not undermine the objectives of offender management nor need they be feared by management, the government or the media. However, attempts to dismantle or dilute these cultures by fragmenting probation work and parcelling it out to the lowest bidders, may be counter-productive by loosening the 'ties that bind' probation workers to what was described to us as an 'honourable profession' and thus devaluing their commitment to their core universal value of reducing crime by working with offenders who are conditionally at liberty. It would be courageous for both NOMS and the government to respect that this work inevitably involves a willingness to work holistically and optimistically, though not naively, with uncertainty, ambivalence and (to a degree) failure. Someone has to do it.

Appendix A

Our participants

Interviewee	Age	Gender	Ethnicity	Grade	Years experience
TPO1	31–40	Female	BI	TPO	
TPO2	31–40	Female	BC	TPO (former PSO)	5
TPO3	41–50	Female	BA	TPO (former admin grade)	5
TPO4	25–30	Male	WB	TPO	
TPO5	25–30	Female	BA	TPO	
TPO6	31–40	Male	WB	TPO	
TPO7	31–40	Male	WB	TPO (former PSO)	2
TPO8	51–60	Male	WB	TPO (former PSO)	5
TPO9	41–50	Female	BC	TPO	
TPO10	25–30	Female	WB	TPO	
FPW1	41–50	Female	WB	Former PO	18
FPW2	51–60	Female	WB	Former ACO	20+
FPW3	51–60	Male	WB	Former PO	19
FPW4	41–50	Male	BC	Former PO	9
FPW5	71–80	Male	WB	Retired SPO	30+
FPW6	51–60	Male	WB	Former SPO	19
FPW7	71–80	Male	WB	Retired SPO	30+
FPW8	61–70	Female	WB	Retired PO	21
CO1	51–60	Male	WB	CEO	30+
CO2	51–60	Male	WB	CEO	30+
CO3	51–60	Female	WB	CEO	29
CO4	51–60	Female	WB	CEO	31
CO5	51–60	Male	WB	CEO	30+
CO6	51–60	Male	WB	CEO	29
CO7	51–60	Female	WB	CEO	30
CO8	51–60	Male	WB	CEO	30+
CO9	51–60	Female	WB	CEO	30+
CO10	51–60	Female	WB	CEO	20+
CO11	51–60	Male	WB	CEO	35
CO12	51–60	Male	WB	CEO	30+
CO13	61–70	Female	WB	CEO	35+
CO14	51–60	Female	WB	CEO	30+
CO15	51–60	Male	WB	CEO	35+
CO16	41–50	Female	WB	ACO	25
PW1	51–60	Female	WB	PO	20
PW2	31–40	Female	WB	PO	6

Interviewee	Age	Gender	Ethnicity	Grade	Years experience
PW3	51–60	Female	MO	SPO	10
PW4	31–40	Female	WB	SPO	7
PW5	51–60	Male	WB	SPO	25
PW6	31–40	Male	WI	PO	6
PW7	51–60	Female	WB	PO	20+
PW8	51–60	Female	WB	PO	20+
PW9	51–60	Male	WB	SPO	20+
PW10	41–50	Female	WB	PO	18
PW11	51–60	Male	WB	PO	20+
PW12	41–50	Male	WB	PO	10
PW13	41–50	Female	WB	PO	20
PW14	25–30	Female	WB	PO	4
PW15	25–30	Male	WB	PO	2
PW16	51–60	Female	WB	PO	31
PW17	31–40	Male	WB	PO	5
PW18	31–40	Female	WB	PO	2
PW19	31–40	Female	WB	PO	10
PW20	51–60	Male	WB	PSO	15
PW21	31–40	Female	WB	PO	5
PW22	61–70	Female	WB	PSO	26
PW23	41–50	Male	WB	PO	13
PW24	61–70	Female	WB	PO	40
PW25	51–60	Female	WB	PO	26
PW26	25–30	Male	WB	PO	2

Ethnicity codes: BA, Black African; BC, Black Caribbean; BI, British Indian; MO, Mixed other; WB, White British; WI, White Irish.

Appendix B

Project information sheet and schedule of interview questions

Probation officers, their occupational cultures and offender management

Information sheet

Anne Worrall, Emerita Professor of Criminology at Keele University and Rob Mawby, Senior Lecturer in Criminology at Leicester University have been awarded a grant by the Economic and Social Research Council (ESRC) to undertake independent research on the occupational cultures of probation officers. The research runs for 20 months from April 2010.

The research will explore and seek to understand the ways in which probation officers perceive themselves and their role in the criminal justice system. The key research question is:

- What are the characteristics of contemporary probation cultures and how do probation officers and their managers construct their occupational identities, values and cultures?

We also aim to address two subsidiary questions:

- How might such cultures contribute to, or undermine, the effectiveness of offender management?
- To what extent is an understanding of probation cultures essential to achieving change within NOMS and related criminal justice agencies?

This research is a small-scale exploratory study which may develop into a larger study in the future. It is a *reflective* study that focuses on the ways in which probation officers and their managers *make sense* of their routine work and handle the demands and emotions involved in 'doing probation work'. Given the widely recognized historical changes in the role, we want to explore whether probation officers and their managers need to have different personal qualities and ways of coping than they have had in the past. We want to try and identify the conditions under which probation officers and their managers feel they do their best – and worst – work, what sustains them in their work and what they find the most rewarding and debilitating aspects of their work. The Probation Chiefs Association supports this research and has assisted in identifying contacts but has no financial or managerial investment in it. The researchers are accountable only to the ESRC.

The interviews will last around one hour and will take the form of a conversation based on a pre-seen schedule. We would like you to give as much thought to the questions before the interview as possible. With your permission, the interviews will be tape recorded and tapes or transcripts may be sent to you for comment, if you wish, before they are analysed. We aim to ensure that all participants remain anonymous in the research report. Where this is problematic (e.g. if you have a role that is easily recognizable) we will discuss with you how you wish your views to be presented.

We are not undertaking observational research in this project. We will be relying on what participants *tell* us about their work because we are interested in the way that probation officers *perceive and reflect on* their work. It is not the purpose of this project directly to *evaluate the effectiveness* of probation work.

The findings of the research will be reported to the ESRC and in a 'plain English' paper for policy-makers and practitioners. The project will also produce conference papers, journal articles and at least one seminar/workshop. The researchers will also be available to address workplace meetings and conferences.

On completion of the project, in accordance with normal practice for ESRC-funded research, we will, subject to your consent, submit the interview recordings and transcripts to the UK Data Archive (UKDA) (www.data-archive.ac.uk). Before doing so, personal information will be removed. Access to all research data archived at the UKDA is regulated through a licence system. Archived data are therefore not in the open public domain but are available for research and education purposes to authorized users.

Anne and Rob are very experienced criminal justice researchers who have published widely on a range of topics including offender management, women offenders, and the police. They will conduct the whole of this research themselves, including undertaking all the interviews personally.

Interview schedule for current POs, PSOs, TPOs and managers

I would like to have a conversation with you around the following themes:

- Why you became a PO/PSO, what motivated you
- What you thought the job was about
- What you did before you became a PO/PSO
- How your training changed you
- How your career has developed, the type of jobs you've done
- Your daily and weekly routine – in detail (from waking to sleeping)

- One or more examples of an unusual day/week
- One or more examples of a crisis
- Where you do your work – physically and emotionally (including at home)
- Who and what gives you strength when the work gets overly demanding
- What rewards you now and keeps you motivated
- Any hardship (material or emotional) you have experienced in the job
- What your family and friends think about you being a PO/PSO
- How strangers respond in a social setting when you say you are a PO/PSO
- How you think police, prison officers, magistrates, judges, solicitors see you – and vice versa
- The extent, if any, to which these perceptions have changed during your time as a PO/PSO
- How the work of POs/PSOs has changed, if at all, during your career
- Your perception of 'offender management'
- Whether you regard yourself as a 'typical' PO/PSO, what you have in common with other POs/PSOs, how you are different
- Your experience of involvement in any unions/staff associations
- How promotion and experience of management has affected all of the above (if relevant)
- What keeps you awake at night
- What aspects of the job sadden/anger/frustrate/depress you
- Your view of the future of probation work
- Whether you think probation work has its own distinctive culture e.g. values, language, routines, visual symbols

Interview schedule for former POs and managers

I would like to have a conversation with you around the following themes:

- Why you became a PO, what motivated you
- What you thought the job was about
- What you did before you became a PO
- How your training changed you
- How your career developed, the type of jobs you did
- Your daily and weekly routine – in detail (from waking to sleeping)
- One or more examples of an unusual day/week
- One or more examples of a crisis
- Where you did your work – physically and emotionally (including at home)
- Who and what gave you strength when the work got overly demanding
- What kept you motivated
- Any hardship (material or emotional) you experienced in the job
- What your family and friends thought about you being a PO
- How strangers responded in a social setting when you said you were a PO
- How you think police, prison officers, magistrates, judges, solicitors saw you – and vice versa

- The extent, if any, to which these perceptions changed during your time as a PO
- How the work of POs changed, if at all, during your career
- Your perception of 'offender management'
- Whether you regarded yourself as a 'typical' PO, what you had in common with other POs, how you were different
- Your experience of involvement in any unions/staff associations
- How promotion and experience of management affected all of the above (if relevant)
- What kept you awake at night
- What aspects of the job saddened/angered/frustrated/depressed you
- How you made the decision to leave the Probation Service
- How sad/happy you were to retire from the Probation Service (if relevant)
- Your view of the future of probation work
- Whether you think probation work has its own distinctive culture e.g. values, language, routines, visual symbols

Notes

1 Probation – a tainted but resilient concept

1 Probation workers are hereafter abbreviated to PW, chief officers to CO, trainee probation officers to TPO and former probation workers to FPW.
2 Organizationally, until 2001, each of over 50 area probation services was managed autonomously, although most of the service's funding came from the Home Office. Each probation service had its own chief probation officer and, like the police, there was no centralized organization or spokesperson for the service.
3 Damien Hanson was jailed for 36 years for the murder of banker John Monckton, committed in November 2004 while he was under probation supervision having been released halfway through a 12-year sentence for attempted murder. His accomplice, Elliot White, was sentenced to 18 years' imprisonment; he was subject to a Drug Treatment and Testing Order at the time. Anthony Rice murdered Naomi Bryant in August 2005 while he was being supervised on a life licence by Hampshire Probation Area. Dano Sonnex was convicted of the murders of two French students in 2008. At the time he had been released from prison subject to a licence supervised by London Probation.
4 We define the term 'domain' as the implicit agreement on the nature and extent of organizational integrity (Davidson 1976).
5 Jon Venables was one of two ten-year-old boys who murdered two-year-old James Bulger in 1993. He was released in 2001 with a new identity and supervised under the terms of his licence by the probation service. Following the recall to prison and conviction of Venables in 2010 for child pornography offences, a case review was undertaken by Sir David Omand (2010).
6 A state of 'flow' involves activity where the actor can 'concentrate their attention on a limited stimulus field, forget personal problems, lose their sense of time and of themselves, feel competent and in control, and have a sense of harmony and union with their surroundings' (Csikszentmihályi 1975: 182).
7 Savage and Williams (2008: 5) note that the 'classic tradition of elite studies' was disrupted in the 1960s by the rise of survey analysis that meant 'elites' became underrepresented in research samples. Nevertheless, the value of interviewing those in senior positions with a wealth of experience is not uncommon in criminal justice research. See, for example, Reiner (1991) and Caless (2011) on senior police officers, Loader on policy-makers (2006), Mair on chief probation officers (2004), Phillips (2005) on the chairpeople of black and Asian professional associations, and Rutherford on 'working credos' (1993). Our research is *not* a study of elites but we are comfortable with our over-representation of 'chiefs'.
8 Based on the Ministry of Justice's response dated 2 February 2011 to our FOI request.
9 All interview transcripts are archived, through the Economic and Social Research Council, with the Economic and Social Data Service at www.esds.ac.uk. See study SN 7086: *Probation Workers, their Occupational Cultures and Offender Management, 1960–2011*.

2 Lifers, second careerists and offender managers

1 We use the term 'baby boomers' to refer to those people born in the decade following the Second World War, 1945–55.

2 Throughout the book we use the terms 'offender manager' and 'offender management' as generic terms to describe the policy, processes and attitudes that have driven the supervision of offenders leading up to and since the establishment of NOMS in 2004.

3 *Borstal Boy* was published in 1958 and recounts Brendan Behan's progress through the criminal justice system and his time in Feltham Boys' Prison from 1939 to 1941. Remaining on the book theme, CO2 was inspired by Tony Parker's *The Unknown Citizen*, published in 1963, which followed a 50-year-old habitual offender for a period of one year following his release from prison. Common themes are humanity, a search for understanding underlying issues and, probably, rooting for the underdog.

4 *Life on Mars* was a BBC television drama series first screened in 2006. Set in 1973, it both parodied and glorified the excesses of 1970s policing, embodied in the character of Detective Chief Inspector Gene Hunt, a violent, sexist, drunken, homophobic thief-catcher (Garland and Bilby 2011).

5 Probation officers have the power to 'breach' offenders who do not comply with their sentences or conform to the expectations of supervision arrangements. Offenders who are breached are returned to the courts for resentencing. In the past, probation officers were often reluctant to breach and stories circulate of POs who never breached an offender throughout their careers.

3 There's a time and place

1 Old-style records consisted of Part A (factual information), Part B (periodic assessments) and Part C (diary of contacts and other action). They were notoriously out-of-date, especially the Part B sections.

4 Probation's changing relationships with courts, police and prisons

1 This was justified in one recent case we came across in which a prison governor had thrown a probation officer out of his prison on the grounds of 'winding-up my officers' (CO16) and, during the writing of this book, a governor in South Yorkshire locked probation workers out of three prisons because the local Probation Trust had collaborated with a private sector firm, G4S, to bid to run the prisons in competition with the public sector (*Guardian* 1 March 2012).

5 Perceptions, misconceptions and representations

1 The murders of: jeweller Marian Bates in 2003 (the sentencing was in 2005) by Peter Williams; banker John Monckton in 2004 by Damien Hanson and Elliot White; teenager Mary-Ann Leneghan in 2005 by Adrian Thomas, Michael Johnson, Jamaile and Joshua Morally, Llewellyn Adams and Indrit Krasniqi; Naomi Bryant in 2005 by Anthony Rice; and lawyer Tom ap Rhys Pryce in 2006 by Delano Brown and Donnel Carty.

2 We note the existence of the Probation Association representing probation employers and GMB SCOOP representing chief officers within the GMB union but these did not feature in our research.

3 Culture.com (accessed 31 July 2012) *Parole Officer, The*: Interview With Steve Coogan http://culture.com/articles/546/parole-officer-the-interview-with-steve-coogan.phtml.

4 Illustrating that the series is fictional Mason (1988: 36) gives the example of an Assistant Chief – 'an entirely fictional character if only because he seems to know precisely what is going on'.

5 We are grateful to Graham Nicholls for waiving his right to anonymity in this section.

6 Job crafting, coping and responding to adverse working conditions

1 While this may hold for probation workers, we note that Naus *et al.* (2007) found in their study of employees of a Dutch trade union that role conflict was a predictor of exit and cynicism, as was low autonomy.

7 Diversity and different voices in probation work

1 We refer here to 'the union' as being NAPO, because this has had the greatest historical influence on probation culture, although we are aware that probation staff also belong nowadays to other unions, such as UNISON, a trend that, of itself, contributes to the decline of NAPO's influence.
2 We have omitted discussion of sexual orientation and disability because our research did not address these questions directly; only one of our interviewees volunteered that he was gay and two informed us that they had disabilities. Consequently, we have overlooked the voice of the Lesbians and Gay Men in Probation group (LAGIP) which is an informal grouping within NAPO that provides a support network for lesbian, gay, transgendered and bisexual individuals working in the probation service (Dale 2007).
3 The term 'black' is used in its political sense of 'non-white' rather than indicating particular ethnicity (www.abponoms.com).
4 A recent survey of women in NAPO (Kirton 2012) found that women's ability to be active in the union was hampered not by any ideological or 'in principle' barriers but by the sheer pressure of balancing work and domestic demands.
5 The taint of such work also deeply affected one of our male interviewees:

> When I was running that sex offender programme, I'd finish the group at seven or eight o'clock, and then I'd go home, and my wife would be putting the kids to bed, or they'd be in the bath and … I'd just feel dirty. I had to wash my hands almost symbolically before I left the office, and I did because what I'd been hearing was just so upsetting … and the rationalization and justification the men were giving for it was just ridiculous. But there was no counselling at all. It was just horrible.
>
> (CO5)

8 Doing probation work: cultures, identities and the future

1 More than one of the older interviewees commented that in times gone by, their colleagues' political sympathies were clearly discernible and had been a factor in them choosing probation as a career. More recently they found it harder to read the politics of newer joiners. CO8 thought that new recruits did not have the same sense of mission as his own generation 'I think the shift over time has been … this kind of underlying sense of social justice, motivates less people now than it did. Which isn't to say people don't… you know, aren't sympathetic and it's a good idea, but it's less likely to be at the forefront of why they came into the service.'
2 This was also the case with the portrayal of policing in *Dixon of Dock Green*, the television series which ran from 1955 to 1976. Even in its early days it was hanging on to a vision of community and policing that was slipping away. By the time of its final series in 1976, it overlapped with the harder-hitting *Sweeney*, which began in 1974 and with its focus on fast cars, violent crime and a less consensual society, better captured the mood of the times.

References

Aldridge, M. (1999a) 'Probation officer training, promotional culture and the public sphere', *Public Administration*, 77, 1: 73–90.

Aldridge, M. (1999b) 'Poor relations: state social work and the press in the UK', in B. Franklin (ed.) *Social Policy, the Media and Misrepresentation*, London: Routledge, 89–103.

Allard, T.J., Wortley, R.K. and Stewart, A.L. (2003) 'Role conflict in community corrections', *Psychology, Crime and Law*, 9, 3: 279–89.

Allen, J., Livingstone, S. and Reiner, R. (1998) 'True Lies: changing images of crime in British postwar cinema', *European Journal of Communication*, 13, 1: 53–75.

Annison, J. (2007) 'A gendered review of change within the probation service', *Howard Journal of Criminal Justice*, 46, 2: 145–61.

—— (2009) 'Delving into *Probation Journal*: portrayals of women probation officers and women offenders', *Probation Journal*, 56, 4: 435–50.

Annison, J., Eadie, T. and Knight, C. (2008) 'People first: probation officer perspectives on probation work', *Probation Journal*, 55, 3: 259–72.

Armitage, S. (1989) *Zoom!* Newcastle upon Tyne: Bloodaxe Books.

Armitage, S. (1998/2009) *All Points North*, Harmondsworth: Penguin.

Arnold, H., Liebling, A. and Tait, S. (2007) 'Prison officers and prison culture', in Y. Jewkes (ed.) *Handbook on Prisons*, Cullompton: Willan Publishing, 471–95.

Ashforth, B.E. and Kreiner, G.E. (1999) '"How can you do it?" Dirty work and the challenge of constructing a positive identity', *Academy of Management Journal*, 24, 3: 413–34.

Ashforth, B.E., Kreiner, G.E., Clark, M.A. and Fugate, M. (2007) 'Normalizing dirty work: managerial tactics for countering occupational taint', *Academy of Management Journal*, 50, 1: 149–74.

Audit Commission (1998) *A Fruitful Partnership – Effective Partnership Working*, London: Home Office.

Bailey, R. and Brake, M. (eds) (1975) *Radical Social Work*, London: Arnold.

Banton, M. (1964) *The Policeman in the Community*, London: Tavistock.

BBC News (13/7/2012) 'London probation contract won by private firm', available at www.bbc.co.uk/news/uk, accessed 13 July 2012.

Behan, B. (1958) *Borstal Boy*, London: Hutchinson.

Bennett, J. (2008) 'Reel life after prison: repression and reform in films about release from prison', *Probation Journal*, 55, 4: 353–68.

Berry, G., Briggs P., Erol, R. and van Staden, L. (2011) *The Effectiveness of Partnership Working in a Crime and Disorder Context: A Rapid Evidence Assessment*, London: Home Office Research Report 52.

Birkbeck, J. (1982) 'I believe in you', *Probation Journal*, 29, 3: 83–6.

Blauner, P. (1991) *Slow Motion Riot*, London: Penguin Books.

Bonnett, A. (2010) *Left in the Past: Radicalism and the Politics of Nostalgia*, London: Continuum.

Brake, M. and Bailey, R. (eds) (1980) *Radical Social Work and Practice*, London: Arnold.

Brogden, M. (1991) *On the Mersey Beat: Policing Liverpool between the Wars*, Oxford: Oxford University Press.

Bullock, K. (2011) 'The construction and interpretation of risk management technologies in contemporary probation practice', *British Journal of Criminology*, 51, 1: 120–35.

Burke, L. and Davies, K. (2011) 'Introducing the special edition on occupational culture and skills in probation practice', *European Journal of Probation*, 3, 3: 1–14.

Burnett, R. and Stevens, A. (2007) 'Not of much significance (yet): NOMS from the perspective of prison staff', *Prison Service Journal*, 172: 3–11.

Burnett, R., Baker, K. and Roberts, C. (2007) 'Assessment, supervision and intervention: fundamental practice in probation', in L. Gelsthorpe and R. Morgan (eds) *Handbook of Probation*, Cullompton: Willan Publishing, 210–47.

Button, M. (2007) *Security Officers and Policing: Powers, Culture and Control in the Governance of Private Space*, Aldershot: Ashgate.

Cain, M. (1973) *Society and the Policeman's Role*, London: Routledge.

Caless, B. (2011) *Policing at the Top: The Roles, Values and Attitudes of Chief Police Officers*, Bristol: Policy Press.

Canton, R. (2011) *Probation: Working with Offenders*, Abingdon: Routledge.

Carlen, P. (1975/2010) 'Magistrates' courts: a game theoretic analysis', *Sociological Review*, 23, 2: 347–79, reprinted in P. Carlen, *A Criminological Imagination,* Farnham, Ashgate, 11–44.

—— (2008) 'Imaginary penalities and risk-crazed governance' in P. Carlen (ed.) *Imaginary Penalities*, Cullompton: Willan Publishing, 1–25.

Carter, P. (2003) *Managing Offenders, Reducing Crime: A New Approach*, London: Home Office.

Cartmell, M. and Green, N. (2011) 'Under arrest: police budgets', *PRWeek*, 17 November 2011, available at www.prweek.com/uk/features/1104418/under-arrest-police-budgets/, accessed 8 August 2012.

Casey, L. (2008) *Engaging Communities in Fighting Crime*, London: Cabinet Office.

Chan, J. (1997) *Changing Police Culture: Policing in a Multicultural Society*, Cambridge: Cambridge University Press.

Cherry, S. and Cheston, L. (2006) 'Towards a model regime for approved premises', *Probation Journal*, 53, 3: 248–64.

Clarke, D.R. (2010) *The Parole Officer*, Mustang, OK: Tate Publishing.

Clarke, J., Cochrane, A. and McLaughlin, E. (eds) (1994) *Managing Social Policy*, Sage: London.

Clear, T.R. (2005) 'Places not cases? Re-thinking the probation focus', *Howard Journal of Criminal Justice*, 44, 2: 172–84.

Collins, S. (2008) 'Statutory social workers: stress, job satisfaction, coping, social support and individual differences', *British Journal of Social Work*, 38: 1173–93.

Collins, S., Coffey, M. and Cowe, F. (2009) 'Stress, support and well-being as perceived by probation trainees', *Probation Journal*, 56, 3: 238–56.

Corbett, R. (1998) 'Probation blue: the promise (and perils) of probation–police partnerships', *Correctional Management Quarterly*, 2: 31–9.

Corcoran, M. and Fox, C. (2012) 'A seamless partnership? Developing mixed economy interventions in a non-custodial project for women', *Criminology and Criminal Justice*.

Crawley, E. (2005) *Doing Prison Work*, Cullompton: Willan Publishing.

Crawley, E. and Crawley, P. (2008) 'Understanding prison officers: culture, cohesion and conflict', in J. Bennett, B. Crewe and A. Wahidin (eds) *Understanding Prison Staff*, Cullompton: Willan Publishing, 134–52.

Crewe, B., Liebling, A. and Hulley, S. (2010) 'Staff culture, use of authority and prisoner quality of life in public and private sector prisons', *Australian and New Zealand Journal of Criminology*, 44, 1: 94–115.

Csikszentmihályi, M. (1975) *Beyond Boredom and Anxiety: The Experience of Play in Work and Games*, London: Jossey-Bass Limited.

Dale, H. (2007) 'Lesbians and gay men in probation', in R. Canton and D. Hancock (eds) *Dictionary of Probation and Offender Management*, Cullompton: Willan Publishing, 154.

Davidson, S. (1976) 'Planning and coordination of social services in multi-organisational contexts', *Social Services Review*, 50: 117–37.

Davies, K. (2009) 'Time and the probation practitioner', *British Journal of Community Justice*, 17, 3: 46–60.

Davis, F. (1979) *Yearning for Yesterday: A Sociology of Nostalgia*, New York: Free Press.

Deering, J. (2010) 'Attitudes and beliefs of trainee probation officers: a new breed?', *Probation Journal*, 57, 1: 9–26.

—— (2011) *Probation Practice and the New Penology: Practitioner Reflections*, Aldershot: Ashgate.

Dews, V. and Watts, J. (1994) *Review of Probation Officer Recruitment and Qualifying Training*, London: Home Office.

Dolman, F. (2008) *Community Support Officers, their Occupational Culture and the Development of Reassurance Policing*, European Society of Criminology Conference paper. Edinburgh University.

Donzelot, J. (1979) *The Policing of Families*, London: Hutchinson.

Dugdall, R. (2010) *The Woman Before Me*, London: Legend Press Ltd.

—— (2011) *The Sacrificial Man*, London: Legend Press Ltd.

Dunkley, E. (2007) 'Approved premises', in R. Canton and D. Hancock (eds) *Dictionary of Probation and Offender Management*, Cullompton: Willan Publishing, 12–13.

Durnescu, I. (2012) 'What matters most in probation supervision: staff characteristics, staff skills or programme?', *Criminology and Criminal Justice*, 12, 2: 193–216.

Eadie, T. (2000) 'From befriending to punishing: changing boundaries in the probation service' in N. Malin (ed.) *Professionalism, Boundaries and the Workplace*, London: Routledge, 161–77.

Ely, R.J. and Meyerson, D.E. (2000) *Theories of Gender in Organizations: A New Approach to Organizational Analysis and Change*, Working Paper No. 8, Boston, MA: Center for Gender in Organizations.

Emery, F.E. and Trist, E.L. (1965) 'The causal texture of organizational environments', *Human Relations*, 18: 21–32.

Evetts, J. (2012) *Professionalism in Turbulent Times: Changes, Challenges and Opportunities*, Paper presented at Propel International Conference, Stirling, available at www.propel.stir.ac.uk/conference2012/speakers.php, accessed 6 July 2012.

Farrell, D. (1983) 'Exit, voice, loyalty, and neglect as responses to job dissatisfaction: a multidimensional scaling study', *Academy of Management Journal*, 26, 4: 596–607.

Fawcett, R. (2010) *Rock Athlete*, Sheffield: Vertebrate Publishing.

Ferguson, E. (2012) 'Rewind TV: *Public Enemies*', *Observer*, 8 January. http://www.guardian.co.uk/tv-and-radio/2012/jan/08/sherlock-public-enemies-tv-review, accessed 11 October 2012 .

Ferrell, J. (2005) 'The only possible adventure: edgework and anarchy', in S. Lyng (ed.) *Edgework: The Sociology of Risk-Taking*, London: Routledge, 75–88.

Ferrell, J., Milovanovic, D. and Lyng, S. (2001) 'Edgework, media practices, and the elongation of meaning', *Theoretical Criminology*, 5, 2: 177–202.

Fieldhouse, P. and Williams, T. (1986) 'Shared working in prison', *Probation Journal,* 33, 4: 143–47.

Filkin, E. (2011) *The Ethical Issues arising from the Relationship between Police and Media. Advice to the Commissioner of Police of the Metropolis and his Management Board*, London: MPS.

Fitzgibbon, W. (2011) *Probation and Social Work on Trial: Violent Offenders and Child Abusers*, Basingstoke: Palgrave Macmillan.

Fletcher, H. (2012) 'TV drama *Public Enemies* reflects the reality of probation officers', *Guardian*, 3 January 2012.

Forbes, D. (2010) 'Probation in transition: a study of the experiences of newly qualified probation officers', *Journal of Social Work Practice*, 24, 1: 75–88.

Foster, J. (2003) 'Police cultures', in T. Newburn (ed.) *Handbook of Policing*, Cullompton: Willan Publishing, 196–227.

Fournier, V. (2000) 'Boundary work and the (un)making of the professions', in N. Malin (ed.) *Professionalism, Boundaries and the Workplace*, London: Routledge, 67–86.

Freidson, E. (2001) *Professionalism: The Third Logic*, Cambridge: Polity Press.

Garland, J. and Bilby, C. (2011) '"What next, dwarves?" Images of police culture in *Life on Mars*', *Crime Media Culture*, 7, 2: 115–32.

Gelsthorpe, L. (2007) 'Probation values and human rights', in L. Gelsthorpe and R. Morgan (eds) *Handbook of Probation*, Cullompton: Willan Publishing, 485–517.

Gieryn, T. (2002) 'What buildings do', *Theory and Society*, 31, 1: 35–74.

Glanfield, P. (1985) 'Withdrawal from prisons policy', *Probation Journal* 32, 2: 66.

Goffman, E. (1963) *Stigma: Notes on the Management of Spoiled Identity*, Englewood Cliffs, NJ: Prentice-Hall.

—— (1969) *Where the Action Is*, London: Penguin Press.

Goodman, A.H. (2012) *Rehabilitating and Resettling Offenders in the Community*, London: John Wiley and Sons Ltd.

Gregory, M. (2010) 'Reflection and resistance: probation practice and the ethic of care', *British Journal of Social Work*, 40, 7: 2274–90.

Haines, K. and Morgan, R. (2007) 'Services before trial and sentence: achievement, decline and potential', in L. Gelsthorpe and R. Morgan (eds) *Handbook of Probation*, Cullompton: Willan Publishing, 182–209.

Hallsworth, S. (2005) 'The feminization of the corporation, the masculinization of the state', *Social Justice*, 32, 1: 32–40.

Hardie-Bick, J. (2011) 'Skydiving and the metaphorical edge', in D. Hobbs (ed.) *Ethnography in Context, Vol. 3*, London: Sage.

Harris, R. (1980) 'A changing service: the case for separating care and control in probation practice', *British Journal of Social Work*, 10, 2: 163–84.

Harvey, J. (1987) *Hard Cases*, London: Ravette.

Haxby, D. (1978) *Probation: A Changing Service*, London: Constable.

Hedderman, C. (2003) 'Enforcing supervision and encouraging compliance', in W.H.

Chui and M. Nellis (eds) *Moving Probation Forward: Evidence, Arguments and Practice*, Harlow: Pearson Longman, 181–94.

Hedderman, C. and Hough, M. (2004) 'Getting tough or being effective: what matters?', in G. Mair (ed.) *What Matters in Probation*, Cullompton: Willan Publishing, 146–69.

Heer, G. (2007) 'Asian employees in the probation service', *Probation Journal*, 54, 3: 281–85.

Heer, G. and Atherton, S. (2008) '(In)visible barriers: The experience of Asian employees in the probation service', *Howard Journal of Criminal Justice*, 47, 1: 1–17.

Heidensohn, F. (1992) *Women in Control? The Role of Women in Law Enforcement*, Oxford: Clarendon Press.

Hilder, S. (2007) 'Anti-discriminatory practice', in R. Canton and D. Hancock (eds) *Dictionary of Probation and Offender Management*, Cullompton: Willan Publishing, 10–11.

Hirschman, A.O. (1970) *Exit, Voice and Loyalty: Responses to Decline in Firms, Organizations and States*, Cambridge, MA: Harvard University Press.

HM Government (2010) *The Coalition: Our Programme for Government*, London: Cabinet Office.

HM Treasury (2010) *Spending Review 2010*, London: The Stationery Office.

HMIC (2011) *Without Fear or Favour: A Review of Police Relationships*, London: HMIC.

Hochschild, A. (1983) *The Managed Heart: Commercialization of Human Feelings*, Berkeley, CA: University of California Press.

Holdaway, S. (1983) *Inside the British Police*, Oxford: Basil Blackwell.

Home Office (1998) *Joining Forces to Protect the Public*, London: Home Office.

—— (2004a) *Reducing Crime, Changing Lives*, London: Home Office.

—— (2004b) *Reducing Crime, Changing Lives* (press release 5/2004), London: Home Office.

House of Commons Justice Committee (2011) *The Role of the Probation Service*, London: The Stationery Office.

Hucklesby, A. (2011) 'The working life of electronic monitoring officers', *Criminology and Criminal Justice*, 11, 1: 59–76.

Hughes, E.C. (1951) 'Work and the self', in J.H Rohrer and M. Sherif (eds) *Social Psychology at the Crossroads*, New York: Harper and Brothers, 313–23.

Hughes, J.A., Sharrock, W.W. and Martin, P.J. (2003) *Understanding Classical Sociology: Marx, Weber, Durkheim*, 2nd edn, London: Sage.

Innes, M. (2004) 'Signal crimes and signal disorders: notes on deviance as communicative action', *British Journal of Sociology*, 55: 335–55.

Jepson, N. and Elliott, K. (1985) *Shared Working Between Prison and Probation Officers*, London: Home Office.

Jewkes, Y. (2006) 'Creating a stir? Prisons, popular media and the power to reform', in P. Mason, (ed.) *Captured by the Media*, Cullompton: Willan, 137–53.

—— (2008) 'Offending media: the social construction of offenders, victims and the Probation Service', in S. Green, E. Lancaster and S. Feasey (eds) *Addressing Offender Behaviour: Context, Practice and Values*, Cullompton: Willan, 58–72.

—— (2010) *Media and Crime*, 2nd edn, London: Sage.

Johnson, P. and Ingram, B. (2007) 'Windows of opportunity for unpaid work?', *Probation Journal*, 54, 1: 62–9.

Johnson, S.D., Chye Koh, H. and Killough, L.N. (2009) 'Organizational and occupational culture and the perception of managerial accounting terms: an exploratory study using perceptual mapping techniques', *Contemporary Management Research*, 5, 4: 317–42.

Katz, J. (1988) *Seductions of Crime: The Moral and Sensual Attractions of Doing Evil*, New York: Basic Books.

Kay, S. (1993) 'Judgements of worth', *Probation Journal*, 40, 2: 60–5.

Kemshall, H. and Maguire, M. (2001) 'Public protection, partnership and risk penality: the multi-agency risk management of sexual and violent offenders', *Punishment and Society*, 3, 2: 237–64.

Kemshall, H. and Wood, J. (2007) 'High risk offenders and public protection', in L. Gelsthorpe and R. Morgan (eds) *Handbook of Probation*, Cullompton: Willan Publishing, 381–97.

Kerfoot, D. (2002) 'Managing the "professional" man', in M. Dent and S. Whitehead (eds) *Managing Professional Identities: Knowledge, Performativity and the 'new' Professional*, London: Routledge, 81–95.

Kirton, G. (2012) *Women in NAPO: Survey of Women Members*, London: Queen Mary University.

Knight, C. (2002) 'Training for a modern service', in D. Ward, J. Scott and M. Lacey (eds) *Probation: Working for justice*, 2nd edn, Oxford: Oxford University Press, 276–96.

Kreiner, G.E., Ashforth, B.E. and Sluss, D.M. (2006) 'Identity dynamics in occupational dirty work: integrating social identity and system justification perspectives', *Organization Science*, 17, 5: 619–36.

Lacey, M. and Read, G. (1985) 'Probation working in prison', *Probation Journal* 32, 2: 61–5.

Leech, M. (1991) 'Recommended for release', *Probation Journal*, 38, 1: 10–14.

Le Mesurier, L. (1935) *A Handbook of Probation*, London: NAPO.

Leishman, F. and Mason, P. (2003) *Policing and the Media: Facts Fictions and Factions*, Cullompton: Willan Publishing.

Leonard, E. (1992/2007) *Maximum Bob*, London: Phoenix.

Liebling, A., Price, D. and Shefer, G. (2011) *The Prison Officer*, 2nd edn, Cullompton: Willan Publishing.

Lindblom, C.E. and Woodhouse, E.J. (1993) *The Policy Making Process*, 3rd edn, Englewood Cliffs, NJ: Prentice Hall.

Lipsky, M. (1980) *Street-level Bureaucracy: Dilemmas of the Individual in Public Services*, New York: Russell Sage Foundation.

Loader, I. (1997) 'Policing and the social: questions of symbolic power', *British Journal of Sociology*, 48, 1: 1–18.

—— (2006) 'Fall of the platonic guardians: liberalism, criminology and political responses to crime in England and Wales', *British Journal of Criminology*, 46, 3: 561–86.

Loftus, B. (2009) *Police Culture in a Changing World*, Oxford: Oxford University Press.

—— (2010) 'Police occupational culture: classic themes, altered times', *Policing and Society*, 20, 1: 1–20.

Lois, J. (2001) 'Peaks and valleys: the gendered emotional culture of edgework', *Gender and Society*, 15, 3: 381–406.

—— (2005) 'Gender and emotion management in the stages of edgework', in S. Lyng (ed.) *Edgework: The Sociology of Risk-Taking*, London: Routledge, 117–52.

Lyng, S. (1990) 'Edgework: a social psychological analysis of voluntary risk taking', *The American Journal of Sociology*, 95, 4: 851–86.

—— (2005) 'Sociology at the edge: social theory and voluntary risk taking', in S. Lyng (ed.) *Edgework: The Sociology of Risk-Taking*, London: Routledge, 17–49.

—— (2009) 'Edgework, risk, and uncertainty', in J.O. Zinn (ed.) *Social Theories of Risk and Uncertainty: An Introduction*, Oxford: Blackwell Publishing Ltd, 106–37.

McFarlane, M. (1993) 'Women and promotion', *Probation Journal*, 40, 2. 66–7.

McGarry, R. and Walklate, S. (2011) 'The soldier as victim: peering through the looking glass', *British Journal of Criminology*, 51, 6: 900–17.

McLean Parks, J.M., Ma, L. and Gallagher, D.G. (2010) 'Elasticity in the "rules" of the game: exploring organizational expedience', *Human Relations*, 63, 5: 701–30.

McNeill, F. (2001) 'Developing effectiveness: frontline perspectives', *Social Work Education*, 20, 6: 671–87.

McWilliams, W. (1981) 'The probation officer at court: from friend to acquaintance', *The Howard Journal of Criminal Justice*, 20, 2: 97–116.

Maguire, M. (2007) 'The resettlement of ex-prisoners', in L. Gelsthorpe and R. Morgan (eds) *Handbook of Probation*, Cullompton: Willan Publishing, 398–424.

Mahood, L. (1995) *Policing Gender, Class and Family Britain 1850–1940*, London: UCL Press.

Mair, G. (2004) 'What works: a view from the chiefs', in G. Mair (ed.) *What Matters in Probation*, Cullompton: Willan Publishing, 255–77.

Mair, G. and Burke, L. (2012) *Redemption, Rehabilitation and Risk Management: A History of Probation*, Abingdon: Routledge.

Mair, G., Burke, L. and Taylor, S. (2006) ' "The worst tax form you've ever seen?" Probation officers' views about OASys', *Probation Journal*, 53, 1: 7–23.

Manning, P.K. (1997) *Police Work: The Social Organization of Policing*, 2nd edn, Prospect Heights, IL: Waveland Press.

Mason, J. (1988) 'As good as you could hope for', *Probation Journal*, 35, 1: 37.

Mason, P. (ed.) (2006) *Captured by the Media*, Cullompton: Willan.

Mathiesen, T. (1965) *Defences of the Weak: A Sociological Study of a Norwegian Correctional Institution*, London: International Library of Criminology.

Mawby, R.C. (2002) *Policing Images: Policing, Communication and Legitimacy*, Cullompton: Willan.

—— (2003) 'Completing the "half-formed picture"? Media images of policing', in P. Mason (ed.) *Criminal Visions*, Cullompton: Willan Publishing, 214–237.

—— (2007) *Police Service Corporate Communications: A Survey of forces in England, Wales and Scotland*, Birmingham: University of Central England.

—— (2008) 'Built-in, not bolted-on', *Public Service Review: Home Affairs*, 17: 149–50.

—— (2010a) 'Chibnall revisited: crime reporters, the police and "law-and-order news" ', *British Journal of Criminology*, 50, 6: 1060–76.

—— (2010b) 'Police corporate communications, crime reporting, and the shaping of policing news', *Policing and Society*, 20, 1: 124–39.

—— (2012) 'Crisis? What crisis? Some research-based reflections on police-press relations', *Policing: A Journal of Policy and Practice*, 6, 4: 272–80.

Mawby, R.C. and Worrall, A. (2004) 'Polibation revisited: policing, probation and prolific offender projects', *International Journal of Police Science and Management*, 6, 2: 63–73.

—— (2011) ' "They were very threatening about do-gooding bastards": probation's changing relationships with the police and prison services in England and Wales', *European Journal of Probation*, 3, 3: 78–94.

Mawby, R.C., Crawley, P. and Wright, A. (2007) 'Beyond polibation and towards prisi-polibation? Joint agency offender management in the context of the Street Crime Initiative', *International Journal of Police Science and Management*, 9, 2: 122–34.

May, T. (1994) 'Transformative power: a study in a human service organization', *The Sociological Review*, 618–38.

Mayo, M., Hoggett, P. and Miller, C. (2007) 'Navigating the contradictions of public service modernization: the case of community engagement professionals', *Policy and Politics*, 35, 4: 667–81.

Milovanovic, D. (2005) 'Edgework: a subjective and structural model of negotiating boundaries', in S. Lyng (ed.) *Edgework: The Sociology of Risk-Taking*, London: Routledge, 51–72.

Ministry of Justice (2011) *Statistics on Race and the Criminal Justice System 2010*, London: Ministry of Justice.

—— (2012) *Punishment and Reform: Effective Probation Services*, Consultation Paper CP7/2012, London: Ministry of Justice.

Morgan, G. (2006) *Images of Organization,* London: Sage.

Morgan, J. (1991) *Safer Communities: The Local Delivery of Crime Prevention through the Partnership Approach, Report of the Home Office Standing Conference on Crime Prevention*, London: Home Office.

Morran, D. (2008) 'Firing up and burning out: the personal and professional impact of working in domestic violence offender programmes', *Probation Journal*, 55, 2: 139–52.

Morris, A. (1987) *Women, Crime and Criminal Justice*, Oxford: Blackwell.

Mott, J.R. (1992) *Probation, Prison and Parole: A True Story of the Work of a Probation Officer*, Lewes: Temple House Books.

Mullins, L. (2010) *Management and Organisational Behaviour*, 9th edn, London: Prentice Hall.

Murphy, D. and Lutze, F. (2009) 'Police-probation partnerships: professional identity and the sharing of coercive power', *Journal of Criminal Justice*, 37: 65–76.

NAPO (2007) *Changing Lives: An Oral History of Probation*, London: NAPO.

—— (2008) *Ex-armed Forces Personnel and the Criminal Justice System*, briefing paper, available at www.napo.org.uk/publications/Briefings.cfm, accessed 6 June 2012.

—— (2009) *Armed Forces and the Criminal Justice System*, briefing paper, available at www.napo.org.uk/publications/Briefings.cfm, accessed 6 June 2012.

—— (2012) *Newsletter: Centenary Souvenir Issue*, May, London: NAPO.

Nash, M. (1999) 'Enter the "polibation officer"', *International Journal of Police Science and Management*, 1, 4: 360–8.

—— (2004) 'A reply to Mawby and Worrall', *International Journal of Police Science and Management*, 6, 2: 74–6.

—— (2008) 'Exit the polibation officer? Decoupling police and probation', *International Journal of the Sociology of Law*, 10, 3: 302–12.

Nash, M. and Walker, L. (2009) 'Mappa – is closer collaboration really the key to effectiveness?', *Policing: A Journal of Policy and Practice*, 3, 2: 172–80.

National Audit Office (2001) *Joining Up to Improve Public Services*, London: HMSO.

National Probation Service (2001) *A New Choreography: An Integrated Strategy for the National Probation Service for England and Wales – Strategic Framework 2001–2004*, London: Home Office.

—— (2003) *The Heart of the Dance*, London: Home Office.

Naus, F., van Iterson, A. and Roe, R. (2007) 'Organizational cynicism: extending the exit, voice, loyalty, and neglect model of employees' responses to adverse conditions in the workplace', *Human Relations*, 60, 5: 683–718.

Nellis, M. (2007) 'Humanising justice: the English probation service up to 1972', in L.

Gelsthorpe and R. Morgan (eds) *Handbook of Probation*, Cullompton: Willan Publishing, 25–58.

—— (2008) '*Hard Cases*: a probation TV drama series', in P. Senior (ed.) *Moments in Probation*, Crayford: Shaw and Sons, 213–14.

—— (2010) 'Images of British probation officers in film, television drama and novels', unpublished paper.

NOMS (2006) *The NOMS Offender Management Model*, London: NOMS.

Oakley, A. (2011) *A Critical Woman: Barbara Wotton, Social Science and Public Policy in the Twentieth Century*, London: Bloomsbury Academic.

Omand, D. (2010) *Independent Serious Further Offence Review: The Case of Jon Venables*, www.justice.gov.uk/downloads/publications/corporate-reports/MoJ/2010/omand-review-web.pdf, accessed 23 June 2012.

Othen, M.J. (1975) 'Prison welfare – time to think again?', *Probation Journal*, 22, 4: 98–103.

Parker, T. (1963) *The Unknown Citizen*, London: Hutchinson.

Parkinson, G. (1988) 'It's not bad!', *Probation Journal*, 35, 1: 36.

Parsloe, P. (1967) *The Work of the Probation and After-Care Officer*, London: Routledge and Kegan Paul.

Pearson, G. (1983) *Hooligan: A History of Respectable Fears*, London: Macmillan.

Pease, K. (1992) 'Preface', in R. Statham and P. Whitehead (eds) *Managing the Probation Service: Issues for the 1990s*, Harlow: Longman, x–xi.

Peelo, M. (2006) 'Framing homicide narratives in newspapers: mediated witness and the construction of virtual victimhood', *Crime Media Culture: An International Journal*, 2, 2: 159–75.

Petrillo, M. (2007) 'Power struggle: issues for female probation officers in the supervision of high risk offenders', *Probation Journal*, 54, 4: 394–406.

Phillips, C. (2005) 'Facing inwards and outwards? Institutional racism, race equality and the role of Black and Asian professional associations', *Criminal Justice*, 5, 4: 357–77.

Phillips, C. and Bowling, B. (2012) 'Ethnicities, racism, crime, and criminal justice', in M. Maguire, R. Morgan and R. Reiner (eds) *The Oxford Handbook of Criminology*, 5th edn, Oxford: Oxford University Press, 370–97.

Phillips, J. (2010) 'The social construction of probation in England and Wales and the United States of America: implications for the transferability of probation practice', *British Journal of Community Justice*, 18, 1: 5–18.

—— (2011) 'Target, audit and risk assessment cultures in the probation service', *European Journal of Probation*, 3, 3: 108–22.

Poxton, R. (2004) 'What makes effective partnerships between health and social care?', in Glasby, J. and Peck, E. (2004) *Care Trusts: partnership working in action*, Abingdon: Radcliffe Medical Press, 11–22.

Pratt, M. (1975) 'Stress and opportunity in the role of the prison welfare officer', *British Journal of Social Work* 5, 4: 379–96.

Priestley, P. (1972) 'The prison welfare officer: a case of role strain', *British Journal of Sociology*, 23, 2: 221–35.

Punch, M. (1979) *Policing the Inner City: A Study of Amsterdam's Warmoesstraat*, London: Macmillan.

Rajah, V. (2007) 'Resistance as edgework in violent intimate relationships of drug-involved women', *British Journal of Criminology*, 47, 2: 196–215.

Raynor, P. and Robinson, G. (2009) *Rehabilitation, Crime and Justice*, Basingstoke: Palgrave Macmillan.

Reeves, C. (2011) 'The changing role of probation hostels: voices from the inside', *British Journal of Community Justice*, 9, 3: 51–64.

Reiner, R. (1991) *Chief Constables: Bobbies, Bosses or Bureaucrats?*, Oxford: Oxford University Press.

—— (1994) 'The dialectics of Dixon: the changing image of the TV cop', in M. Stephens and S. Becker (eds) *Police Force Police Service*, London: Macmillan, 11–32.

—— (2010) *The Politics of the Police*, 4th edn, Oxford: Oxford University Press.

Robinson, A. (2011) *Foundations for Offender Management: Theory, Law and Policy for Contemporary Practice*, Bristol: The Policy Press.

Robinson, G. and Burnett, R. (2007) 'Experiencing modernization: frontline probation perspectives on the transition to a NOMS', *Probation Journal*, 54, 4: 318–37.

Ross-Smith, A. and Huppatz, K. (2010) 'Management, women and gender capital', *Gender, Work and Organization*, 17, 5: 547–66.

Rowe, M. (ed.) (2007) *Policing Beyond Macpherson: Issues in Policing, Race and Society*, Cullompton: Willan.

Rumgay, J. (2003) 'Partnerships in the probation service', in W.H. Chui and M. Nellis (eds) *Moving Probation Forward*, Harlow: Pearson Education, 195–213.

Rutherford, A. (1993) *Criminal Justice and the Pursuit of Decency*, Winchester: Waterside Press.

Saunders, D. and Vanstone, M. (2010) 'Rehabilitation as presented in British film: shining a light on desistance from crime', *The Howard Journal*, 49, 4: 375–93.

Savage, M. and Williams, K. (eds) (2008) *Remembering Elites*, Oxford: Blackwell.

Schein, E. (2010) *Organizational Culture and Leadership*, 4th edn, San Francisco, CA: Jossey-Bass.

Senior, P. (2008) *Moments in Probation*, Crayford: Shaw and Sons.

Silvestri, M. (2007) ' "Doing" police leadership: enter the "new smart macho" ', *Policing and Society*, 17, 1: 38–58.

Simon, J. (2005) 'Edgework and insurance in risk societies: some notes on Victorian lawyers and mountaineers', in S. Lyng (ed.) *Edgework: The Sociology of Risk-Taking*, London: Routledge, 203–26.

Simpson, R. and Lewis, P. (2007) *Voice, Visibility and the Gendering of Organizations*, Basingstoke: Palgrave Macmillan.

Simpson, R., Slutskaya, N., Lewis, P. and Hopfl, H. (eds) (2012) *Dirty Work: Concepts and Identities*, Basingstoke: Palgrave Macmillan.

Singh, G. (2007) 'National Association of Asian Probation Staff', in R. Canton and D. Hancock (eds) *Dictionary of Probation and Offender Management*, Cullompton: Willan Publishing, 173–75.

Skeggs, B. (1997) *Formations of Class and Gender: Becoming Respectable*, London: Sage.

Skolnick, J. (1966) *Justice Without Trial*, New York: Wiley.

—— (2008) 'Enduring issues of police culture and demographics', *Policing and Society*, 18, 1: 35–45.

Smith, P. (2012) '*Public Enemies*, BBC One, review', *The Telegraph*, 4 January. www.telegraph.co.uk/culture/tvandradio/8990454/Public-Enemies-BBC-One-review.html, accessed 11 October 2012.

Stanton, A. (1985) 'Why probation isn't working in prison', *Probation Journal*, 32, 3: 107–8.

Statham, D. (1978) *Radicals in Social Work*, London: Routledge.

Stone, N. (1986) 'In discussion with the POA', *Probation Journal*, 33, 3: 81–6.

Strangleman, T. (2012) 'Work identity in crisis? Rethinking the problem of attachment and loss at work', *Sociology*, 46, 3: 411–25.

Sykes, G. and Matza, D. (1957) 'Techniques of neutralization', *American Sociological Review*, 22: 664–70.

Tait, S. (2011) 'A typology of prison officer approaches to care', *European Journal of Criminology*, 8, 6: 440–54.

Thomas, T. (1994) *The Police and Social Workers*, 2nd edn, Aldershot: Ashgate.

Thompson, N. (2006) *Anti-Discriminatory Practice*, 4th edn, Houndsmill: Palgrave Macmillan.

Thurston, P. (2002) 'Just practice in probation hostels', in D. Ward, J. Scott and M. Lacey (eds) *Probation: Working for Justice*, Oxford: Oxford University Press, 207–19.

Todd, M. (1964) *Ever Such a Nice Lady*, London: Victor Gollancz Ltd.

Towl, G. and Crighton, D. (2008) 'Psychologists in prison', in J. Bennett, B. Crewe and A. Wahidin (eds) *Understanding Prison Staff*, Cullompton: Willan Publishing, 316–29.

Treadwell, J. (2006) 'Some personal reflections on probation training', *The Howard Journal*, 45, 1: 1–13.

—— (2010) 'More than casualties of war? Ex-military personnel in the criminal justice system', *The Howard Journal*, 49, 2: 73–7.

Turney, B. (2002) *I'm Still Standing*, Winchester: Waterside Press.

Van Dyne, L., Ang, S. and Botero, I.C. (2003) 'Concetualizing employee silence and employee voice as multidimensional constructs', *Journal of Management Studies*, 40, 6, 1359–92.

Vanstone, M. (2004) *Supervising Offenders in the Community: A History of Probation Theory and Practice*, Aldershot: Ashgate.

Waddington, P.A.J. (1999) 'Police (canteen) sub-culture: an appreciation', *British Journal of Criminology*, 39, 2: 287–309.

Waldron, V. (2009) 'Emotional tyranny at work: suppressing the moral emotions', in P. Lutgen-Sandvik and B.D. Sypher (eds) *Destructive Organizational Communication*, London: Routledge, 9–26.

Walmsley, R. (2012) *World Female Imprisonment List*, 2nd edn, London: International Centre for Prison Studies.

Walker, H. and Beaumont, B. (1981) *Probation Work: Critical Theory and Socialist Practice*, Oxford: Blackwell.

Watson, K. (2012) '*Public Enemies* had a promising start but ultimately lost its edge', *The Metro*, 4 December. http://www.metro.co.uk/tv/reviews/886299-public-enemies-had-a-promising-start-but-ultimately-lost-its-edge#ixzz1sxAU1yw8, accessed 11 October 2012.

Weatheritt, M. (1986) *Innovations in Policing*, London: Croom Helm.

Weinberger, B. (1995) *The Best Police in the World: An Oral History of English Policing from the 1930s to the 1960s*, Aldershot: Scholar Press.

White, I. (1984) 'Residential work: the Cinderella of the probation service?', *Probation Journal*, 31, 2: 59–60.

Whitehead, P. and Statham, R. (2006) *The History of Probation: Politics, Power and Cultural Change 1876–2005*, Crayford: Shaw and Sons.

Wigley, J. (1992) *Out of Bounds: Story of Malcolm Worsley, Prisoner to Probation Officer*, Godalming: Highland Books.

Williams, B. (1991) 'Probation contact with long term prisoners', *Probation Journal* 38, 1: 4–9.

—— (2008) 'The changing face of probation in prisons', in J. Bennett, B. Crewe and A. Wahidin (eds) *Understanding Prison Staff*, Cullompton: Willan Publishing, 279–97.

Williams, R. (1973) *The Country and the City*, Oxford: Oxford University Press.

Wilson, D. and O'Sullivan, S. (2004) *Images of Incarceration: Representations of Prison in Film and Television Drama*, Winchester: Waterside Press.

—— (2005) 'Re-theorizing the penal reform functions of the prison film', *Theoretical Criminology*, 9, 4: 471–91.

Wincup, E. (2002) *Residential Work with Offenders: Reflexive Accounts of Practice*, Aldershot: Ashgate.

Worrall, A. (1995) 'Equal opportunity or equal disillusion? The probation service and anti-discriminatory practice', in B. Williams (ed.) *Probation Values*, Birmingham: Venture Press, 29–46.

—— (1997) *Punishment in the Community: The Future of Criminal Justice*, Harlow: Addison Wesley Longman.

—— (2008a) 'The "seemingness" of the "seamless management" of offenders', in P. Carlen (ed.) *Imaginary Penalities*, Cullompton: Willan Publishing, 113–34.

—— (2008b) 'Gender and probation in the second world war: reflections on a changing occupational culture', *Criminology and Criminal Justice*, 8, 3: 317–33.

Worrall, A. and Canton, R. (2013) 'Community sentences and offender management', in C. Hale, K. Hayward, A. Wahidin and E. Wincup (eds) *Criminology*, 3rd edn, Oxford: Oxford University Press.

Worrall, A. and Gelsthorpe, L. (2009) 'What works with women offenders: the past 30 years', *Probation Journal*, 56, 4: 329–45.

Worrall, A. and Hoy, C. (2005) *Punishment in the Community: Managing Offenders, Making Choices*, Cullompton: Willan Publishing.

Worrall, A., Mawby, R.C., Heath, G. and Hope, T. (2003) *Intensive Supervision and Monitoring Projects*, Home Office Online Report 42/03, London: Home Office.

Wrzesniewski, A. and Dutton, J. (2001) 'Crafting a job: revisioning employees as active crafters of their work', *Academy of Management Review*, 26, 2: 179–201.

Young, M. (1991) *An Inside Job: Policing and Police Culture in Britain*, Oxford: Clarendon Press.

Index

Page numbers in *italics* denote tables.